Y0-ARX-159

WILLIAM JAMES
Philosopher and Man

Quotations and references in 652 books

compiled by

Charles H. Compton

Librarian Emeritus, St. Louis Public Library

With a foreword

by

Lucien Price

The Scarecrow Press, Inc.

New York 1957

L. C. Card No. 57-6633

To Louis J. Bailey

FOREWORD

This book is a Hall of Mirrors. In the center is a crystal chandelier brilliantly lighted; the chandelier is William James; the mirrors are the minds he has illumined, giving back their illumination. Light comes from all sides, including above and below, and as we move about, the prismatic colors of the chandelier keep changing. Since this light is clearer than most, the commonest objects stand out with startling distinctness, -- our conduct of life, habits of thought, national traits, -- while the more distinguished ones, -- momentos of our Western civilization, its unwritten laws, and landmarks of our slow march from primitive barbarism toward . . . whithersoever we may be bound, -- shine forth dazzingly.

Philosopher is a word bandied about as carelessly as the word friend. We have few of either. Philosopher, in common parlance, may mean anybody from Plato to a dryasdust academic lecturer. In William James we have in the highest sense a true philosopher, and, as this volume shows, one who continues with us on our march.

The very alphabet befriends this book. Early in it come Henry Adams and John Jay Chapman, and any reader who ventures as far as A and C is likely to keep going. The compiler has transformed his task into an art. He, too, is one of the mirrors, giving back as his share of the rays a distinction of mind and discriminating taste.

James's wit is here as well as his wisdom. He needed both. A mind as candid as his was sure to stir repercussions. Chapman, as he was likely to do to anybody, once wrote James a blistering letter. After having allowed a period for cooling off, James replied that he was reminded of the witness at the coroner's inquest, who, being asked how the corpse looked, said, "Why, pleasant like, and foaming at the mouth."

Those of us who knew William James, either as students or friends, retain vividly the glow of his personality, his genial warmth, his spontaneous gaiety, as well as his high seriousness with its profound insights. Something else, too, was nominated in the bond. As student I was and remain deeply grateful both to Santayana and to James. Two years out of college, being ship news reporter for a Boston newspaper, I met on two successive September mornings James and Santayana on the decks of returning transatlantic steamships. Santayana was embarrassed and distant; James greeted me like a long-lost brother. We chatted. In England he had met Gilbert Chesterton, liked him, and said, "He loves his fellow men."

If North America were to be engulfed beneath the ocean waves like the fabled Lost Atlantis, whom have we produced on this continent as creative thinkers who would survive in the memory of mankind? Among the four or five names which readily occur, one is William James. But meanwhile we have not sunk, and here living and working among us still is William James.

Lucien Price

INTRODUCTION

There have probably been more quotations from the writings of William James and more references to him and to his writings than to any other author of his generation. This holds true also since his death in 1910 and promises to continue indefinitely.

This book is divided into two parts.

Part one consists of quotations from 264 books by 146 authors. Part two consists of references to 652 books by 344 authors. The references include those books which are in Part one.

Part two does not include nearly all of the books which have references to William James. The books listed however represent the examination, often page by page, of thousands of books. Quotations in Part one are those considered by the compiler as being the most interesting and significant.

The men and women who quoted William James in these books illustrate the wide spread influence which he had and now has on thinkers in many fields.

The following are typical of public men: Justice Oliver Wendell Holmes and Justice Benjamin N. Cardozo of the Supreme Court, Judge Learned Hand and Judge Jerome Frank; Theodore Roosevelt and Adlai E. Stevenson.

Ministers of distinction include Harry Emerson Fosdick, Washington Gladden, William Ralph Inge, Rufus M. Jones, Samuel McChord Crothers, Ralph W. Sockman, Reinhold Niebuhr and Elton Trueblood.

Philosophers are naturally well represented, including Josiah Royce, George Santayana, Bertrand Russell, Ralph Barton Perry, John Dewey, Irwin Edman, William E. Hocking, Morris Cohen, John Grier Hibben, L. P. Jacks, Jacques Maritain and Alfred North Whitehead.

Writers on literary and political subjects and on social problems make up a long list. They include Irving Babbitt, Jacques Barzun, Crane Brinton, Randolph Bourne, Van Wyck Brooks, W. E. Burghardt Du Bois, Henry Seidel Canby, John Jay Chapman, Stuart Chase, Gilbert K. Chesterton, Harold Laski, Walter Lippmann, Everett Dean Martin, Mumford Jones, Paul Elmer More, Lewis Mumford, F. S. C. Northrop, Bonaro W. Overstreet and Harry A. Overstreet, Bliss Perry, T. V. Smith, Graham Wallas and H. G. Wells.

Others who should be mentioned are Henry Adams, Jane Addams, Helen Keller, John Burroughs, Charles Eliot Norton, Edwin Godkin and William Dean Howells.

Two quotations in this Introduction are typical of those found in the body of the book.

John Jay Chapman a friend of William James wrote in his "Memories and Milestones:"

> "None of us will ever see a man like William James again; there is no doubt about that. And yet it is hard to state what it was in him that gave him either his charm or his power, what it was that we lack and feel the need of, now that he has so unexpectedly and incredibly died. I always thought that William James would continue forever; and I relied upon his sanctity as if it were sunlight.
>
> I should not have been abashed at being discovered in some mean action by William James; because I should have felt that he would understand and make allowance. The abstract and sublime quality of his nature was always enough for two; and I confess to having always trespassed upon him and treated him with impertinence, without gloves, without reserve, without ordinary decent concern for the sentiments and weaknesses of human character. Knowing nothing about philosophy, and having the dimmest notions as to what James's books might contain, I used occasionally to write and speak to him about his specialties in a tone of fierce contempt; and never failed to elicit from him in reply the most spontaneous and celestial gayety. Certainly he was a wonderful man.
>
> He was a sage and a holy man; and everybody put off his shoes before him. And yet in spite of this, --in conjunction with this, he was a sportive, wayward, Gothic sort of spirit, who was apt, on meeting a friend, to burst into foolery, and whose wit was always three parts poetry. Indeed his humor was as penetrating as his seriousness.

Both of these sides of James's nature--the side that made a direct religious appeal--became rapidly intensified during his latter years; so that, had the process continued much longer, the mere sight of him must have moved beholders to amend their lives.

William James in a letter of June 7, 1899 to Mrs. Henry Whitmen said:

> "As for me, my bed is made: I am against bigness and greatness in all their forms, and with the invisible molecular moral forces that work from individual to individual, stealing in through the crannies of the world like so many soft rootlets, or like the capillary oozing of water, and yet rending the hardest monuments of man's pride, if you give them time. The bigger the unit you deal with, the hollower, the more brutal, the more mendacious is the life displayed. So I am against all big organizations as such, national ones first and foremost; against all big successes and big results; and in favor of the eternal forces of truth which always work in the individual and immediately unsuccessful way, underdogs always, till history comes, after they are long dead, and puts them on the top."

Surely the influence of William James is "like so many soft rootlets or like the capillary oozing of water and yet rending the hardest monuments of men's pride, if you give them time."

Table of Contents

Special Acknowledgements

An expression of appreciation is due William James Jr. as Literary Executor for granting permission to reprint quotations from the published letters of William James.

Acknowledgement to Henry Holt and Company for granting permission to reprint quotations in books issued by other publishers from "Principles of Psychology," "Psychology, Briefer Course" and "Talks to Teachers" by William James.

Acknowledgement to Longmans, Green and Company, Incorporated, of New York for granting permission to reprint quotations in books issued by other publishers from "Essays in Radical Empiricism," "Essays on Faith and Morals," "Meaning of Truth," "Memories and Studies," "A Pluralistic Universe," "Pragmatism," "Some Problems of Philosophy," "Varieties of Religious Experience," and "The Will to Believe" by William James.

Acknowledgements to Publishers

ABELARD-SCHUMAN, INCORPORATED: -- Harold Taylor, "On Education and Freedom," c. 1954 by author.

ABINGDON PRESS: -- Emile Cailliet, "Christian Approach to Culture," c. 1953 by Pierce and Washabaugh. -- Lynn Harold Hough, "Great Humanists," c. 1952 by Pierce and Smith.

ADDISON-WESLEY PUBLISHING COMPANY, INCORPORATED: -- Gordon W. Allport, "Nature of Prejudice," c. 1954.

GEORGE ALLEN AND UNWIN LIMITED: -- John Dewey, "Experience and Nature," 1929. -- L.P. Jacks, "The Confessions of an Octogenarian," 1942. -- Sarvepalli Radhakrishnan, "History of Philosophy, Eastern and Western," 1953. -- Bertrand Russell, "Principles of Social Reconstruction," 1916; -- "Unpopular Essays," 1950.

APPLETON-CENTURY-CROFTS, INCORPORATED: -- Randolph Bourne, "Education and Living," c. 1917. -- T. V. Smith, "Constructive Ethics. With Contemporary Readings," c. 1948; -- "The Philosophic Way of Life," c. 1929.

CENTRAL BOOK COMPANY: -- "Justice Oliver Wendell Holmes. His Book Notices and Uncollected Letters and Papers." Edited and Annotated by Harry C. Shriver, c. 1936.

COLUMBIA UNIVERSITY PRESS: -- Benjamin Nathan Cardozo, "Paradoxes of Legal Science," c. 1928. -- Reinhold Niebuhr, "The Contribution of Religion to Social Work," c. 1932.

CONSTABLE AND COMPANY LIMITED: -- Graham Wallas, "Human Nature in Politics," 1910.

COWARD-McCANN, INCORPORATED: -- Charles Edward Montague, "Disenchantment," 1922.

THOMAS Y. CROWELL COMPANY: -- Herman S. Schwartz, "The Art of Relaxation," c. 1954 by author.

THE DIAL PRESS, INCORPORATED: -- Sidney Hook, "Education for Modern Men," c. 1946 by author.

DODD, MEAD AND COMPANY: -- Hugo Münsterberg, "American Problems from the Point of View of a Psychologist," c. 1910.

DOUBLEDAY AND COMPANY, INCORPORATED: -- Helen Keller, "Midstream. My Later Life," c. 1929 by author. -- Ralph W. Sockman, "How to Believe," c. 1953 by author.

THE DRYDEN PRESS, INCORPORATED: -- Robert J. Kreyche, "Logic for Undergraduates," c. 1954.

E. P. DUTTON AND COMPANY, INCORPORATED: -- Van Wyck Brooks, "The Confident Years, 1885-1915," c. 1952 by author; -- "Emerson and Others," c. 1927; --"The Flowering of New England," c. 1936; -- "On Literature Today," c. 1941 by author; -- "Opinions of Oliver Allston," c. 1941; -- "Sketches in Criticism," c. 1932; -- "The World of Washington Irving," c. 1944 by author; -- "The Writer in America," c. 1953 by author; -- "The World of H. G. Wells," c. 1915. -- Albert A. Ostrow, "How to Enjoy Yourself,"

c. 1954 by author.

FABER AND FABER: -- Leslie Paul, "The English Philosopher," 1953.

THE FREE PRESS: -- Morris R. Cohen, "Reason and Nature. An Essay on the Meaning of Scientific Method," c. 1931.

GRUNE AND STRATTON, INCORPORATED: -- C. P. Obendorf, "History of Psychoanalysis in America," c. 1953.

HARCOURT, BRACE AND COMPANY: -- Heywood Broun, "Collected Edition," Compiled by Heywood Hale Broun, c. 1941 by compiler. -- John Burroughs "The Breath of Life," c. 1915 by author. -- M. R. Werner, "Bryan," c. 1929 by author. -- Eric Temple Bell, "The Search for Truth," c. 1934 by Williams, Wilkins Company. -- Morris R. Cohen, "Law and the Social Order," c. 1933 by author. -- W. E. Burghardt DuBois, "Dusk at Dawn. An Essay Toward an Autobiography of a Race Concept," c. 1940. -- Matthew Josephson, "Portrait of the Artist in America," c. 1930 by author. -- Lewis Mumford, "The Condust of Life," c. 1951 by author. -- Benjamin Nathan Cardozo, "Law and Literature," c. 1931. -- Graham Wallas, "Art of Thought," c. 1926.

HARPER AND BROTHERS: -- Van Meter Ames, "Proust and Santayana," c. 1937. -- Joseph Gerard Brennan, "The Meaning of Philosophy," c. 1953. -- D. W. Brogan, "American Themes," 1947. -- Stuart Chase, "The Proper Study of Mankind. An Inquiry into the Science of Human Relations," c. 1948 by author; -- "Roads to Agreement. Successful Methods in the Science of Human Relations," c. 1951 by author. -- Stewart G. Cole and Mildred Wiese Cole, "Minorities and the American Promise. The Conflict of Principle and Practice," c. 1954. -- Merle Curti and Others, "A History of American Civilization," c. 1953. -- Dorothy Day, "The Long Loneliness. Autobiography," c. 1952. -- L. Harold DeWolf, "Theology of the Living Church," c. 1953. -- Louis Finkelstein, "American Spiritual Autobiographies. Fifteen Self Portraits," c. 1948. -- Harry Emerson Fosdick, "Adventurous Religion and Other Essays," c. 1926; -- "As I See Religion," c. 1932 by author; -- "A Faith for Tough Times," c. 1952; -- "A Great Time to be Alive," c. 1944; -- "On Being Fit to Live With," c. 1946; -- "On Being a Real Person," c. 1943; -- "Secret of Victorious Living," c. 1934; --

"Successful Christian Living. Sermons on Christianity Today," c. 1937. -- L. P. Jacks, "The Inner Sentinel. Ourselves and Something More," c. 1930. -- Ludwig Lewisohn, "Expression in America," c. 1932. -- Robert E. Luccock, "If God Be for Us. Sermons on the Gifts of the Gospel," c. 1954. -- Everett Dean Martin, "The Behavior of Crowds. A Psychological Study," c. 1920; -- "The Mystery of Religion. A Study in Social Psychology," c. 1924. -- J. H. Oldham, "Life is Commitment," 1953. -- Bonaro W. Overstreet, "Brave Enough for Life," c. 1941; -- "Freedom's People. How We Qualify for a Democratic Society," c. 1945; -- "Understanding Fear in Ourselves and Others," c. 1951. -- Max Schoen and H. G. Shrikel and Van Meter Ames, "Understanding the World. An Introduction to Philosophy," c. 1947. -- George Eaton Simpson and J. Milton Yinger, "Racial and Cultural Minorities. An Analysis of Prejudice and Discrimination," c. 1953. -- Elton Trueblood, "Alternative to Futility," c. 1948; -- "Common Ventures of Life," c. 1949 by Southwestern University; -- "The Knowledge of God," c. 1939; -- "Life We Prize," c. 1951. -- H. G. Wells, "Anticipations of the Reaction of Mechanical and Scientific Progress upon Human Life and Thought," c. 1901 by North American Review Publishing Company.

HARVARD UNIVERSITY PRESS. COPYRIGHT BY THE PRESIDENT AND FELLOWS OF HARVARD COLLEGE: -- James Harry Cotton, "Royce on the Human Self," c. 1954. -- Justice Oliver Wendell Holmes and Harold J. Laski, "Holmes-Laski Letters. The Correspondence 1918-1935." Edited by Mark DeWolfe Howe. 2 volumes, c. 1953; -- "Holmes-Pollock Letters. The Correspondence of Mr. Justice Holmes and Sir Frederick Pollock." Edited by Mark DeWolfe Howe, c. 1941. -- Howard Mumford Jones, "The Pursuit of Happiness," c. 1953. -- Ralph Barton Perry, "Defense of Philosophy," c. 1931; -- "General Theory of Value," c. 1926; -- Thought and Character of William James," c. 1948. -- Theodore Roosevelt, "Letters, Selected and Edited by Elting E. Morison," c. 1951, 1952.

D. C. HEATH AND COMPANY: -- John Dewey, "How We Think," c. 1910.

WILLIAM HEINEMANN LIMITED: -- Reginald Pound, "Arnold Bennett. A Biography." 1952. -- W. Somerset Maugham, "The Vagrant Mood," c. 1952 by author.

HENRY HOLT AND COMPANY, INCORPORATED: -- Morris

R. Cohen, "The Faith of a Liberal," c. 1946; -- "Studies in Philosophy and Science," c. 1949. -- John Dewey, "Characters and Events. Popular Essays in Social and Political Philosophy." Edited by Joseph Ratner. 2 volumes, c. 1929; -- "Human Nature and Conduct," c. 1922; -- "The Influence of Darwin on Philosophy and Other Essays in Contemporary Thought," c. 1910, -- "The Public and its Problems," c. 1927. -- Irwin Edman, "Four Ways of Philosophy," c. 1937. -- Hunter Mead, "Types and Problems of Philosophy. An Introduction," Revised Edition, c. 1953. -- Otto Klineberg, "Social Psychology." Revised Edition, c. 1954.

HOUGHTON MIFFLIN COMPANY: -- Lyman Abbott, "Henry Ward Beecher," c. 1903 by author. -- Henry Adams, "Letters, 1892-1918," Edited by W. C. Ford, c. 1938 by editor, -- "The Education of Henry Adams," c. 1918 by Massachusetts Historical Society. -- Irving Babbitt, "Democracy and Leadership," c. 1924 by author, -- "Literature and the American College," c. 1908 by author; "The Masters of Modern French Criticism," c. 1912 by author; -- "Rousseau and Romanticism," c. 1919 by author; -- "Spanish Character and Other Essays," c. 1940 by Dora B. Babbitt. -- John Burroughs, "The Heart of Burroughs' Journals," Edited by Clara Barrus, c. 1928 by editor; -- "The Summit of the Years," c. 1913 by author; -- "Under the Apple Trees," c. 1916 by author; -- "Under the Maples," c. 1921. -- Henry Seidel Canby, "Turn West, Turn East. Mark Twain and Henry James," c. 1951 by author. -- M. A. DeWolfe Howe, "John Jay Chapman and his Letters," c. 1937 by author. -- Samuel McChord Crothers, "Among Friends," c. 1910 by author; -- "The Dame School of Experience, and Other Papers," c. 1920 by author; -- "Humanly Speaking," c. 1912 by author. -- Irwin Edman, "Human Traits and Their Social Significance," c. 1920 by author. -- Henry James, "Charles W. Eliot," 2 volumes, c. 1930 by author. -- Paul Elmer More, "A New England Group and Others," c. 1921 by author. -- Charles Eliot Norton, "Letters with Biographical Comment by His Daughter and M. A. DeWolfe Howe," 2 volumes, c. 1913 by Sara Norton. -- Bliss Perry, "And Gladly Teach," c. 1935 by author; -- "Praise of Folly and Other Essays," c. 1923.

INDIANA UNIVERSITY PRESS: -- Ralph Barton Perry, "The Citizen Decides. A Guide to Responsible Thinking in Time of Crisis," c. 1951.

JOURNAL OF THE HISTORY OF IDEAS: -- Felix Cohen,

Editor, "The Holmes-Cohen Correspondence," c. Jan. 1948.

ALFRED A. KNOPF, INCORPORATED: -- Donald Gallup, Editor, "The Flowers of Friendship. Letters Written to Gertrude Stein," c. 1953 by editor. -- Learned Hand, "The Spirit of Liberty. Papers and Addresses." Collected, and With an Introduction by Irving Dilliard, c. 1952. -- Abraham Myerson, "Speaking of Man," c. 1950. -- Bert R. Sappenfield, "Personality Dynamics. An Integrative Psychology of Adjustment," c. 1954 by author.

THE LIBERAL ARTS PRESS, INCORPORATED: -- John E. Smith, "Royce's Social Infinite," c. 1950.

J. B. LIPPINCOTT COMPANY: -- Walter Bromberg, "Man above Humanity. A History of Psychotherapy," c. 1954. -- Ray Stannard Baker, "The Spiritual Unrest," c. 1910. -- Everett Carter, "Howells and the Age of Realism," c. 1954 by author. -- Leon Edel, "Henry James. The Untried Years," c. 1953 by author.

LITTLE, BROWN AND COMPANY: -- Jacques Barzun, "Romanticism and the Modern Ego, c. 1943 by author. -- Barrows Dunham, "Giant in Chains," c. 1953 by author. -- James Norman Hall, "My Island Home. An Autobiography," c. by Estate of author. -- Walter Lippmann, "Essays in the Public Philosophy," c. 1955. -- Alfred North Whitehead, "Dialogues as recorded by Lucien Price," c. 1954 by Lucien Price.

LIVERIGHT PUBLISHING CORPORATION: -- Waldo Frank, "Our America," c. 1919.

LONGMANS, GREEN AND COMPANY, INCORPORATED, New York: -- William Ralph Inge, "The New Twilight of the Gods," 1932; -- "Outspoken Essays. First Series," 1927. -- Ralph Barton Perry, "Present Conflict of Ideals. A Study of the Philosophical Background of the World War," c. 1918; -- Present Philosophical Tendencies. A Critical Survey of Naturalism, Idealism, Pragmatism, and Realism together with a Synopsis of the Philosophy of William James," c. 1912.

LONGMANS, GREEN AND COMPANY LIMITED, LONDON: -- Bertrand Russell, "Philosophical Essays," 1910.

McGRAW HILL BOOK COMPANY, INCORPORATED: --

George S. Hellman, "Benjamin N. Cardozo, American Judge," c. 1940 by author.

THE MACMILLAN COMPANY: -- Jane Addams, "The Excellent Becomes the Permanent," c. 1932; -- "Twenty Years at Hull House," c. 1910. -- Henry Seidel Canby, "Education by Violence. Essays on the War and the Future," c. 1919. -- Edwin Lawrence Godkin, "Life and Letters." Edited by Rollo Ogden, c. 1907. -- Washington Gladden, "Live and Learn," c. 1914. -- William E. Hocking, "Preface to Philosophy," c. 1946. -- L. P. Jacks, "My American Friends," c. 1933. -- Rufus M. Jones, "The Eternal Gospel," c. 1938; -- "The Luminous Trail," c. 1947; -- "Pathways to the Reality of God," c. 1931. -- Walter Lippman, "American Inquisitors. A Commentary on Dayton and Chicago," c. 1928; -- "A Preface to Morals," c. 1929. -- Virginia Moore, "The Unicorn, William Butler Yeats' Search for Reality," c. 1954 by author. -- F. S. C. Northrop, "The Meeting of the East and West. An Inquiry Concerning World Understanding," c. 1946. -- Josiah Royce, "The Problems of Christianity." 2 volumes, c. 1913. -- Robert E. Spiller, and Others, "Literary History of the United States." Revised Edition, c. 1953. -- Alfred North Whitehead, "Aims of Education and Other Essays," c. 1919; -- "Science and the Modern World," c. 1925.

THE NEWMAN PRESS: -- Charles A. Fecher, "The Philosophy of Jacques Maritain," c. 1953.

W. W. NORTON AND COMPANY, INCORPORATED: -- Everett Dean Martin, "Psychology. What It Has to Teach Us," c. 1924 by Peoples' Institute Publishing Company. -- Lewis Mumford, "The Golden Day. A Study in American Experience and Culture," c. 1926. -- Harry A. Overstreet, "About Ourselves. Psychology for Normal People," c. 1947; -- "The Great Enterprise. Relating Ourselves to Other People," c. 1952. -- Bertrand Russell, "Mysticism and Logic and Other Essays," 1925; -- "Skeptical Essays," c. 1928.

PANTHEON BOOKS, INCORPORATED: -- "Eranos-Jahrbuch, Spirit and Nature Papers 1954," c. 1954 by Bollingen Foundation Inc. (Published in the Bollingen Series for the Bollingen Foundation.)

PHILOSOPHICAL LIBRARY, INCORPORATED: -- John Dewey, "Problems of Men," c. 1946. -- Corliss Lamont, "Illusion of Immortality," c. 1935 by author.

PRENTICE-HALL, INCORPORATED: -- Edgar S. Brightman, "A Philosophy of Religion," c. 1940. -- Crane Brinton, "Ideas and Men. The Story of Western Thought," c. 1950. -- John Hospers, "An Introduction to Philosophical Analysis," c. 1953.

PRINCETON UNIVERSITY PRESS: -- Paul Elmer More, "Hellenistic Philosophies," c. 1923. -- Bliss Perry, "Emerson Today," c. 1931.

PUBLIC AFFAIRS PRESS: -- Louis Feller, "Randolph Bourne," c. 1943.

PUTNAM AND COMPANY LIMITED, LONDON: -- William Ralph Inge, "Our Present Discontents," 1938; -- "A Pacifist in Trouble," 1939; -- "The End of an Age," 1948.

G. P. PUTNAM'S SONS, NEW YORK: -- John Dewey, "Art as Experience," c. 1934 by author. -- Hans V. Kaltenborn, "Fifty Fabulous Years," c. 1950 by author.

RANDOM HOUSE, INCORPORATED: -- Adlai E. Stevenson, "Major Campaign Speeches," c. 1953.

RINEHART AND COMPANY, INCORPORATED: -- Henry Seidel Canby, "Alma Mater. The Gothic Age of the American College," c. 1936 by author. -- T. V. Smith, "Democratic Tradition in America," c. 1941 by author. -- Jacob Zeitlin and Homer Woodbridge, "Life and Letters of Stuart P. Sherman," c. 1929.

THE RONALD PRESS COMPANY: -- Beulah C. Bosselman, "The Troubled Mind. A Psychiatric Study of Success and Failure in Human Adaptation," c. 1953. -- W. D. Commins and Barry Fagan, "Principles of Educational Psychology," Second Edition, c. 1954. -- C. J. Ducasse, "A Philosophical Scrutiny of Religion," c. 1953.

RUTGERS UNIVERSITY PRESS: -- David Elliott Weingast, "Walter Lippmann. A Study in Personal Journalism," c. 1949.

SAMPSON LOW, MARSTON AND COMPANY LIMITED: -- Albert D. Belden, "George Whitefield. The Awakener: A Modern Study of the Evangelical Revival," 1930.

CHARLES SCRIBNER'S SONS: -- Nicholas Murray Butler,

"The Meaning of Education. Contributions to a Philosophy of Education," c. 1953. -- John Grier Hibben, "A Defense of Prejudice and Other Essays," c. 1911; -- "The Problems of Philosophy," c. 1898. -- Paul B. Maves, Editor, "The Church and Mental Health," c. 1953. -- William E. Hocking, "Types of Philosophy," c. 1939. -- L. P. Jacks, "Life and Letters of Stopford Brooke," 1917. -- Allan Nevins, "John D. Rockefeller. Industrialist and Philanthropist," c. 1953. -- Reinhold Niebuhr, "The Nature and Destiny of Man. A Christian Interpretation," c. 1941. -- Alex F. Osborn, "Applied Imagination. Principles and Procedures of Creative Writing," c. 1953. -- Ralph Barton Perry, "Approach to Philosophy," c. 1905; -- "Moral Economy," c. 1909. -- David Riesman, "Thorstein Veblen. A Critical Interpretation," c. 1953. -- Theodore Roosevelt, "History as Literature and Other Essays," c. 1913. -- Josiah Royce, "The Sources of Religious Insight," c. 1912 by the Trustees of Lake Forest University. -- George Santayana, "Persons and Places," Volume 1, "The Background of My Life," c. 1944; -- "Persons and Places," Volume 2, "The Middle Span," c. 1945; -- "Soliloquies in England," 1922; -- "Winds of Doctrine. Studies in Contemporary Opinion," c. 1913.

SHEED AND WARD, INCORPORATED: -- Gilbert K. Chesterton, "The Common Man," c. 1950.

SILVER BURDETT COMPANY: -- Carl L. Becker, "Modern History," c. 1952 by author.

SIMON AND SCHUSTER, INCORPORATED: -- Bernard Berenson, "Rumor and Reflection," c. 1952 by author. -- Will Durant, "Story of Philosophy," c. 1926. -- Ernest Dimnet, "What We Live By," c. 1932. -- Max Lerner, "Actions and Passions. Notes on the Multiple Revolution of Our Time," c. 1949 by author. -- John Cowper Powys, "Enjoyment of Literature," c. 1936. -- Bertrand Russell, "History of Western Philosophy," c. 1945 by author.

WILLIAM SLOANE ASSOCIATES, INCORPORATED: -- J. C. Furnas, "Voyage to Windward. The Life of Robert Louis Stevenson," c. 1951 by author.

TUDOR PUBLISHING COMPANY: -- Alfred North Whitehead, "Philosophy of Alfred North Whitehead." Edited by Paul A. Schlipp, c. 1941 by "The Library of Living Authors."

THE UNIVERSITY OF CHICAGO PRESS: -- T. V. Smith,

"The American Philosophy of Equality," c. 1927. -- Ella Flagg Young, "Isolation in the School," (University of Chicago Contributions to Education No. 1) c. 1901.

THE UNIVERSITY OF NORTH CAROLINA PRESS: -- Robert Winston, "Horace Williams, The Gadfly of Chapel Hill," c. 1942.

UNIVERSITY OF PENNSYLVANIA PRESS: -- George W. Holgate, "George Santayana," c. 1938.

THE VANGUARD PRESS: -- Ralph Barton Perry, "On all Fronts," c. 1941; -- "Puritanism and Democracy," c. 1944 by author; -- "Shall Not Perish from the Earth," c. 1940.

THE VIKING PRESS, INCORPORATED: -- Randolph Bourne, "History of a Literary Radical," c. 1929. -- Alvin Johnson, "Pioneer's Progress. An Autobiography," c. 1952 by author. -- Harold Laski, "Reflections on the Constitution," c. 1951.

WILLIAMS AND NORGATE LIMITED: -- L. P. Jacks, "The Alchemy of Thought," 1910.

THE H. W. WILSON COMPANY: -- Charles H. Compton, "Who Reads What?" c. 1934.

YALE UNIVERSITY PRESS: -- William H. Jordy, "Henry Adams, Scientific Historian," c. 1952. -- Charles A. Bennett, "The Dilemma of Religious Knowledge," c. 1931. -- Henry Steele Commager, "The American Mind in the Making," c. 1950. -- William E. Hocking, "The Meaning of God in Human Experience. A Philosophic Study of Religion," c. 1912. -- Harold Laski, "Foundations of Sovereignty," c. 1921. -- Sidney Lovett, "A Boy's Recollections of William James," c. 1954 from Yale Review. -- William Pepperell Montague, "Belief Unbound. A Promethean Religion for a Modern World," c. 1930. -- Benjamin Nathan Cardozo, "Growth of the Law," c. 1921; -- "Nature of the Judicial Process," c. 1921. -- F. S. C. Northrop, "Ideological Difference and World Order. Studies in the Philosophy and Science of the World Cultures," c. 1949.

Acknowledgements to Copyright Holders Other Than Publishers

JEROME FRANK: -- "Law and the Modern Mind," c. 1930,

1933, 1949.

GIRARD TRUST CORN EXCHANGE BANK, TRUSTEE, RUFUS M. JONES ESTATE: -- Rufus M. Jones, "The Inner Life," c. 1916; -- "The New Quest," c. 1928; -- "Some Exponents of Mystical Religion," c. 1930 by author; -- "The Trail of Life in College," c. 1929; -- "The Trail of Life in the Middle Years," c. 1934.

PHILIP GOSSE: -- Edmund Gosse, "Aspects and Impressions," 1922.

SIDNEY HOOK: -- "The Hero in History," c. 1943 by author.

ESTHER LINN HULBERT: -- Jane Addams, "Long Road of Woman's Memory," c. 1916; -- "Newer Ideals of Peace," c. 1907.

W. SOMERSET MAUGHAM: -- "The Vagrant Mood. Six Essays," c. 1952.

REINHOLD NIEBUHR: -- "Does Civilization Need Religion?," c. 1927.

LESLIE PAUL: -- "The English Philosophers," 1953.

ARTHUR B. PERRY: -- Bliss Perry, "Life and Letters of Henry Lee Higginson," c. 1921 by author.

BERTRAND RUSSELL: -- "Philosophical Essays," 1910.

JOHN RUSSELL: -- Logan Pearsall Smith, "Unforgotten Years," c. 1939 by author.

T. V. SMITH: -- "Beyond Conscience," c. 1934 by author.

EXECUTORS OF THE LATE H. G. WELLS: -- H. G. Wells, "Experiment in Autobiography," c. 1934 by author; -- "The Rights of Man. Or What Are We Fighting For," 1940.

HELEN WORDEN ERSKINE: -- John Erskine, "Democracy and Ideals," c. 1920.

MAY WALLAS: -- Graham Wallas, "The Great Society," c. 1914.

VINCENT BROME: --"H. G. Wells. A Biography," 1951.

ROBERTA L. DEWEY: -- John Dewey, "The School and Society," c. 1900.

QUOTATIONS

ABBOTT, Lyman. Henry Ward Beecher. 1903.

Though he was not a theological preacher, if by that is meant a preacher whose aim it is to expound a certain philosophy of religion, a simple but consistent theology underlay all his ministry from its beginning to its end. Professor William James, in his volume on the 'Varieties of Religious Experience," declares that 'there is a certain uniform deliverance in which religions all appear to meet. It consists of two parts: 1. An uneasiness; 2. Its solution. -- 1. The uneasiness, reduced to its simplest terms, is a sense that there is something wrong about us as we naturally stand. 2. The solution is a sense that we are saved from the wrongness by making proper connection with the higher powers.'

In the message of universal religion as interpreted by Professor William James, Henry Ward Beecher was a devout and earnest believer. (p. 124)

ADAMS, Henry. The Education of Henry Adams. 1918.

The livliest and most agreeable of men--James Russell Lowell, Francis J. Child, Louis Agassiz, his son, Alexander, Gurney, John Fiske, William James and a dozen others, who would have made the joy of London or Paris --tried their best to break out and be like other men in Cambridge and Boston, but society called them professors, and professors they had to be. While all these brilliant men were greedy for companionship, all were famished for want of it. Society was a faculty-meeting without business. (p. 307)

ADAMS, Henry. Letters, 1892-1918. Edited by W. C. Ford. 1938.

James wrote to Adams in a characteristic letter dated December 7, 1907:

'Don't you think that after this dark abyss of time and separation you owe me the approximation of letting me have a copy of your autobiography? Approximation, and reparation! for seeing a copy last summer at Molly Warner's house, I hastily looked in the index for the word

'James'--did you ever perform a similar act of egotism? --and found myself accused (along with others) of having made of Cambridge a conversational desert, or words to that effect. Properly only blood could wipe out such an insult, but you are an old man (70, by the living jingo, and I who have during all these years still considered you as about 40!) so in consideration of the volume I will compound the injury.

I may add that autobiographies are my particular line of literature, the only books I let myself buy outside of metaphysical treatises, and that I have the most extraordinary longing to read yours in particular.

Pray indulge me in this appetite, and believe me, wishing I could see you sometimes, yours always faithfully.' (p. 485)

Adams answered in an equally characteristic letter dated December 9, 1907, quoted in part:

'Of course you have a right to the volume you want. In fact it was printed only for communication to you and a few others who were to help me--I fondly hoped--to file it into shape.

If I did not send it to you at once, as I did to Charles Eliot, it was because I feared your judgement more than his.

With this I send the volume, which, as personal to me, is all in the last chapter. I mean to bid good-bye with graceful and sympathetic courtesy. The devil take it!' (p. 485-6)

Adams wrote to James, on February 11, 1908, evidently after having received his comments on the 'Education,' quoted in part:

You are as kind as possible, to write me a long letter. I am grateful for I can find no man to play with. The American is a singularly unsocial animal. For social purposes,--as far as I have read the records of society--he is the most complete failure ever known; and I am the champion failer of all.

As for the volume (Education), it interests me chiefly as a literary experiment, hitherto, as far as I know, never tried or never successful.

So fully do I agree with you in having no use for time, that I expect soon to dispense with it altogether, and try the experiment of timeless space. (p. 490)

Adams writes again on February 17, 1908, quoted in part:

As a wit and humorist I have always said that you were far away the superior to your brother Henry, and that you could have cut him quite out, if you had turned your fun that way. Your letter is proof of it.

If you will read my Chartres,--the last chapter is the only thing I ever wrote that I almost think good,--you will see why I knew my Education to be rotten.

You do not reflect that I am seventy years old--yesterday,--and quite senile. It is time to be gone. I want to burn the Education first, but it does not press. Nobody cares. (p. 490-1)

Letter to James, February 21, 1908, quoted in part:

The Chartres (Mont-Saint-Michel) I sent to the College Library.

I forgot to say that when you have done with the volume--and have entered on the margin such damnatory comments as we lavish on our own works--I should be grateful for its return. (p. 491)

Letter to Margaret Chanler, September 9, 1909. One short quotation.

I best like Bergson's frank surrender to the superiority of Instinct over Intellect. You know how I have preached that principle, and how I have studied the facts of it. In fact I wrote once a whole volume--called my Education--which no one ever saw, and which you must some day look into--borrow William James' copy, in hopes that he may have marginally noted his contempt for me,--in order to recall how Education may be shown to consist in following the intuitions of instinct. (p. 524)

Letter to Elizabeth Cameron, May 12, 1910. "William James came up yesterday, and looked a schoolmaster of retired senescence. When I last saw him he was a delightful, sparkling boy." (p. 539)

Letter written from Paris to Charles Milnes Gaskell. August 2, 1910.

My poor dear old friend and fellow William James alone has put up some sort of fight. Society is ready for collectivism; it has no fight left in it; and our class is as defunct as the dodo. We are just jellyfish, and flabby all through. Of course, I am thinking of America; but it is worse here, except that the few relics do scream and yell. They have intelligence at least, which America has not, and they do see where they are. To be sure, the socialists take good care to keep them awake. They never get four-and-twenty hours without a kick. (p. 546)

Letter to Henry James, January 22, 1911.

I did not write to you about your brother William, because I fancied that letters were a burden to you. The other reason is that I felt the loss myself rather too closely to talk about it. We all began together, and our lives have made more or less of a unity, which is, as far as I can see, about the only unity that American society in our time had to show. Nearly all are gone. Richardson, and St. Gaudens, La Farge, Alex Agassiz, Clarence King, John Hay, and at the last, your brother William; and with each, a limb of our own lives cut off. Exactly why we should be expected to talk about it, I don't know. (p. 558)

JORDY, William H. Henry Adams: Scientific Historian. 1952.

Adams was something of a latter-day St. Thomas, turning upside down the spiritual universe of God and man. Material power and something less than man marked the twentieth-century universe, where all had degraded in ironic harmony with the universal application of the second law.

William James can make the obvious reply, already mentioned, for the historians to whom Adams addressed the Letter. James stated his conviction with a witty decisiveness which warrants extensive quotation, the more so as Adams frankly avowed the telling effect of the criticism.

'To tell the truth it doesn't impress me at all, save by its wit and erudition; and I ask you whether an old man soon about to meet his Maker can hope to save himself from the consequences of his life by pointing to the wit and learning he has shown in treating a tragic subject. No, sir, you can't do it, can't impress God in that way.'

James went on to discuss the question of the universality of the second law of thermodynamics.

'So far as our scientific conceptions go, it may be admitted that your Creator (and mine) started the universe with a certain amount of 'energy' latent in it, and decreed that everything that should happen thereafter should be a result of parts of that energy falling to lower levels; raising other parts higher, to be sure, in so doing, but never in equivalent amount, owing to the constant radiation of unrecoverable warmth incidental to the process. It is customary for gentlemen to pretend to believe one another, and until some one hits upon a newer revolutionary concept (which may be tomorrow) all physicists must play the game by holding religiously to the above doctrine. It involves of course the ultimate cessation of all perceptible happening, and the end of human history. With this general conception as surrounding everything you say in your 'letter,' no one can find any fault--in the present stage of scientific conventions and fashions.'

Then James turned to the principal argument of the historian.

'The amount of cosmic energy it costs to buy a certain distribution of fact which humanly we regard as precious, seems to me to be an altogether secondary matter as regards the question of history and progress. Certain arrangements of matter on the same energy-level are, from the point of view of man's appreciation, superior, while others are inferior.. Physically a dinosaur's brain may show as much intensity of energy-exchange as a man's but it can do infinitely fewer things, because as a force of detent it can only unlock the dinosaur's muscles, while the man's brain, by unlocking far feebler muscles, indirectly can by their means issue proclamations, write books, describe Chartres Cathedral, etc., and guide the energies of the shrinking sun into channels which never would have been entered otherwise--in short, make history. Therefore the man's brain and muscles are, from the point of view of the historian, the more important place of energy-exchange, small as this may be when measured in absolute physical units.

'The 'second law' is wholly irrelevant to 'history'--save that it sets a terminus--for history is the course of things before that terminus, and all that the second law says is that, whatever the history, it must invest itself between that initial maximum and that terminal minimum of difference in energy level.'

Following some further discussion on the possibility that history might rise while energy fell, James concluded his critique with the suggestion that even a millennium was not impossible to history immediately preceding the extinction of the universe. Energies might be so 'skillfully canalised that a maximum of happy and virtuous consciousness would be the only result... You don't believe this and I don't say I do. But I can find nothing in 'Energetik' to conflict with its possibility. You seem to me not to discriminate, but to treat quantity and distribution of energy as if they formed one question.' (p. 214-6)

He finally saw himself in the role of a modern St. Augustine or Aquinas. To William James he confessed, in deprecating the Education, that 'St. Augustine alone has an idea of literary form,--a notion of writing a story with an end and an object, not for the sake of the object, but for the form.' (p. 253)

ADDAMS, Jane. The Excellent Becomes the Permanent. 1932.

Ideals are 'true' in the definition of William James in that they have been 'assimilated, validated, corroborated, and verified in an experience,' that they are fruits for life. A fine reward awaits a transfigured few who live up to this conviction, when they find that the culmination of man's search for the highest values does not lead to a house of dreams, but that, having climbed above the fogs, they see before them actual mountains whose glistening summits reflect a light more beautiful than the incandescence of man's imagination with which they sternly refused to be content. (p. 6)

ADDAMS, Jane. Long Road of Woman's Memory. 1916.

While I may receive valuable suggestions from classic literature, when I really want to learn about life, I must depend upon my neighbors, for as William James insists, the most instructive human documents lie along the beaten pathway. (p. xi)

ADDAMS, Jane. Newer Ideals of Peace. 1915.

An American philosopher (William James) has lately reminded us of the need to 'discover in the social realm the moral equivalent for war--something heroic that will speak to men as universally as war has done, and yet will be as compatible with their spiritual natures as war has proved itself to be incompatible.' (p. 24)

ADDAMS, Jane. Twenty Years at Hull House. 1930.

When, therefore, I became identified with the peace movement, both in its International and National Conventions, I hoped that this internationalism engendered in the immigrant quarters of American cities might be recognized as an effective instrument in the cause of peace. I first set it forth with some misgiving before the Convention held in Boston in 1904 and it is always a pleasure to recall the hearty assent given to it by Professor William James. (p. 308)

ALLPORT, Gordon W. Nature of Prejudice. 1954.

William James makes the point in the following passage: 'The baiting of the Jews, the hunting of Albigenses and Waldenses, the stoning of Quakers and ducking of Methodists, the murdering of Mormons and the massacring of Armenians, express much rather that aboriginal human neophobia, that pugnacity of which we all share the vestiges, and that inborn hatred of the alien and of eccentric and nonconforming men as aliens, than they express the positive piety of the various perpetrators. Piety is the mask, the inner force is tribal instinct.' (Varieties of Religious Experience) (p. 447)

AMES, Van Meter. Proust and Santayana. 1937.
As for the philosophy department then: 'The combination was interesting, but we were all commonplace. When Muensterberg came he was commonplace too, but he brought something different, a new element. Then there was Palmer; he is still vegetating there. William James was a moody person. Well, perhaps not moody, because he wasn't gloomy. One day he'd say to Mrs. James: 'How serene Palmer is; what a calm, wise, active person!' The next day he'd exclaim to her: 'What a hypocrite Palmer is, what an intriguing old woman!' Mrs. James was a very steadying influence on him; she led him along slowly but surely. James had money. That is, he had something beyond his professor's salary--four thousand dollars was the usual sum in those days--so that he could have a comfortable home. Poor Royce didn't have a thing except his salary, and the contrast between the way he lived and the way James did was very marked.' (Quotation from Santayana) (p. 52)

BABBITT, Irving. Democracy and Leadership. 1924.
James, again, though he felt himself in intimate accord with the ideas of Bergson, is nearer to the older romantic psychology. Consider for example, his essay 'On a Certain Blindness in Human Beings.' Men are not most human, it would seem, in their moments of strenuous effort with reference to a human law that they possess in common; on the contrary, they are most themselves in the reveries of their idle and irresponsible moments: they should at least try to enter sympathetically into one another's romantic dreams. (p. 329)

BABBITT, Irving. Literature and the American College. 1908.
'Why may not the advancing front of experience' says Professor James, 'carrying its imminent satisfaction and dissatisfaction, cut against the black inane, as the luminous orb of the moon cuts against the black abyss?' But the sun and moon and stars have their preordained courses, and do not dare, as the old Pythagoreans said, to transgress their numbers. To make Professor James's

metaphor just, the moon would need to deny its allegiance to the central unity, and wander off by itself on an impressionistic journey of exploration through space. It is doubtless better to be a pragmatist than to devote one's self to embracing the cloud Junos of Hegelian metaphysics. But that persons who have developed such an extreme sense of the otherwiseness of things as Professor James and his school should be called humanists--this we may seriously doubt. There would seem to be nothing less humane--or humanistic--than pluralism pushed to this excess, unless it be monism pushed to a similar extremity. (p. 27)

BABBITT, Irving. The Masters of Modern French Criticism. 1912.

We must grant that M. Bergson--and James, as it seems to me, even more than M. Bergson--has rendered a substantial service to philosophy in thus turning its attention to what Plato would have called the problem of the One and the Many. Most people, James admits, do not lose much sleep over this problem, yet he is right in thinking that all other philosophical problems are insignificant in comparison. If philosophy once gets firmly planted on this ground, it may recover a reality that it has scarcely possessed since the debates of Socrates and the sophists. Instead of the intricate fence with blunted foils to which the intellectualists have too often reduced it, we may once more see the flash of the naked blade. (p. ix)

We may note in passing that James not only defends the romantic attitude directly, but strives to discredit the word classical by adopting Taine's misapprehension of it, and making it synonymous with the scholastic and dryly rational. As a matter of fact the intellectualism of Taine is much nearer to being classical as he and James misunderstand the word than is the intuitive good sense of a Horace, let us say, or a Boileau. (p. 353-4)

BABBITT, Irving. Rousseau and Romanticism. 1919.

He merely asks that this drunkenness 'be gentle, amiable, accompanied by moral sentiments.' Perhaps this side of the movement is best summed up in the following passage of William James: 'The sway of alcohol over mankind is unquestionably due to its power to stimulate the mystical faculties of human nature, usually crushed to earth by the cold facts and dry criticisms of the sober hour. Sobriety diminishes, discriminates and says no; drunkenness expands, unites, and says yes. It is, in fact, the great exciter of the Yes function in man. It brings its votary from the chill periphery of things to the radiant core. It makes him for the moment one with truth.' (Varieties of Religious Experience) (p. 183-4)

In a letter to C. E. Norton (June 30, 1904) James praises Ruskin's Letters and adds: 'Mere sanity is the most philistine and at bottom unessential of a man's attributes.' (p. 384)

BABBITT, Irving. Spanish Character and Other Essays. 1940.

According to William James, usually taken to be the representative American philosopher, the very idea of the gentleman has about it something slightly satanic. 'The Prince of darkness,' says James, 'may be a gentleman, as we are told he is, but, whatever the God of earth and heaven is, he can surely be no gentleman.' (p. 231)

BAKER, Ray Stannard. The Spiritual Unrest. 1910.

'Men the world over,' says Professor James, 'Possess amounts of resource which only very exceptional individuals push to their extremes of use.' (p. 205)

Long ago, as Professor James says, Spinoza wrote that anything that a man can avoid under the notion that it is bad, he may also avoid under the notion that something else is good. He who habitually acts under the negative notion, the notion of the bad, is called a slave by Spinoza. To him who acts habitually under the notion of good, he gives the name of freeman. (p. 206)

BARZUN, Jacques. Romanticism and the Modern Ego. 1943.

Perceiving this long before Hitler's time, William James wrote an essay called 'The Moral Equivalent of War' which puts the burden where it belongs by demanding that society establish some socially useful means of channeling the surplus energies of men. (p. 190)

When the substance of this chapter formed by opening lecture before the Lowell Institute, it was prefaced by a few words which as they acknowledged a debt, it is fitting that I should insert here: 'Ladies and Gentlemen:--Today being the eleventh of January, I should like to begin with a word in commemoration of William James, whose one hundred and first anniversary falls on this date. To mention James here and now is appropriate for two reasons. In the first place, he is a thinker to whose work I stand greatly indebted, as will appear in the course of my remarks, and it enhances my pleasure in being here to have the opportunity of acknowledging my obligations to one who lived and worked among you, and who on two occasions stood where I now stand to address you. In the second place, to speak of William James is to plunge at once into the heart of my subject.' (p. 231)

BECKER, Carl L. Modern History. 1952.

William James, the philosopher, once said that he was always up against the 'irreducible brute fact.' With the best will in the world, it was impossible to make the Fourteen Points square with the 'irreducible brute facts' of European life. (p. 728)

BELDEN, Albert D. George Whitefield--The Awakener: A Modern Study of the Evangelical Revival. 1930.

As Professor James has put it in that inimitable discussion of the matter that opens his famous Gifford Lectures, 'By their fruits ye shall know them, not by their roots,' and again, 'If the fruits for life of the state of conversion are good, we ought to idealize and venerate it, even though it be a piece of natural psychology; if not, we ought to make short work with it, no matter what supernatural being may have infused it.' (p. 268)

BELL, Eric Temple. The Search for Truth. 1934.

Bluebottle was brandishing an enormous stein of foaming bock. Between gulps he started the ball rolling.

'C'm on! What's the matter, you fellows: Why doesn't somebody ask Professor James a question? We may not have another chance like this in a hundred years. If nobody else asks anything, I've got one. What's the discussion about this evening, anyway?'

'Thought,' James informed him tersely. 'Thinking!'

'Sure,' Bluebottle apologized. 'That's what the lecture was about, wasn't it? My mistake, Professor. Well, isn't anybody going to ask him a question?'

To the surprise of everyone, including the questioner himself, somebody did. And this is the question that came from somewhere in the general direction of the refreshment table:

'Can thought think about thought?'

Bluebottle slowly lowered his stein and his jaw dropped. For probably the first time in his philosophic career he was astonished, nonplussed, and flabbergasted by a philosophical question. James, on the other hand, was instantly alert. His eyes lit up with glad recognition, as if he had come upon a lifelong friend of his own secret musings in some public and unexpected place.

'Ah!' he exclaimed, leaning forward to catch a glimpse of the modest questioner shrinking behind the bock barrel. 'That was a very sensible question.'

'Excuse me, Professor James,' Bluebottle interrupted, 'but that was not a very sensible question.' He paused to gather emphasis. 'It was a damned silly question.' (p. 61-2)

I saw James just after the shake. He was in his right mind, but he wasn't as fully clothed as he thought he was. He was walking along with his head down and his hands behind his back. His shirt tail was hanging down over his pants, and he had forgotten to pull his suspenders over his shoulders. 'Morning Professor,' I said. 'Your shirt tail's out.'

James looked up and saw who I was, but didn't answer. He seemed sort of dazed. This was the time to give him the third degree and get the truth out of him, so I did.

'Still think the same about philosophy as you did the other night?' I asked.

He took a long time before answering. Then he came out with it.

'Young man,' he said, 'it takes nature to put us in our proper places.'

'Yes,' I said, 'but what about philosophy?'

James came through. 'It is all just words, words, words,' he said. (p. 65-6)

BENNETT, Charles A. The Dilemma of Religious Knowledge. 1931.

Thus James writes of Tolstoy after the period of his conversion:

'His later works show him implacable to the whole system of official values: the ignobility of fashionable life; the infamies of empire; the spuriousness of the Church; the vain conceit of the professions; the meannesses and cruelties that go with great success; and every other pompous crime and lying institution of the world. To all patience with such things his experience has been a permanent ministry of death.' (Varieties of Religious Experiences) (p. 84)

BERENSON, Bernard. Rumor and Reflection. 1952.

To return to Placci, this swift and sure turnover form the extreme of leftism to the opposite extreme was made easy in his own eyes by a book just published that I had in all innocence lent him: William James' The Will to Believe. It gave him the pragmatic justification for choosing the principles which his whim of the moment and his tropism led him to prefer. Like the Scot who when politely told that he was eating asparagus from the wrong end retorted, 'I prefer-r-r it,' Placci would hand the lid on every discussion by rejoicing in iniquity, despising reason, and rejoicing in the right James had extended to him, to believe what he willed. (p. 19)

I recall bringing William James here--I mean to the towered farm. He hated walking between high walls because they shut out the view. I protested that one enjoyed it all the more for not having it constantly before one. He would not listen. It was churlish to deprive one of the view. It made him mad. (p. 126)

BOSSELMAN, Beulah C. The Troubled Mind. A Psychiatric Study of Success and Failure in Human Adaptation. 1953.

The baby, assailed by eyes, ears, nose, skin and entrails all at once, feels it all as one great, blooming, buzzing confusion. (Principles of Psychology) (p. 3)

BOURNE, Randolph. Education and Living. 1917.

There looms up as a crucial need that 'moral equivalent for war,' with which William James first roused our imaginations. (p. 66)

To more and more of us the clue has come through James's conception of a productive army of youth, warring against nature and not against men, finding in drudgery and toil and danger the values that war and preparation for war have given. (p. 68)

BOURNE, Randolph. History of a Literary Radical. 1920.

In the music of MacDowell, the poetry of Whitman, the philosophy of James, I recognize a national spirit, 'l'esprit americain,' as superbly clear and gripping as anything the culture of Europe has to offer us, and immensely more stimulating, because of the very body and soul of to-day's interests and aspirations. (p. 42)

BOURNE, Randolph. Untimely Papers. 1919.

Where are the seeds of American promise? Men cannot live by politics alone, and it is small cheer that our best intellects are caught in the political current and see only the hope that America will find her soul in the remaking of the world. If William James were alive would he be accepting the war-situation so easily and complacently? Would he be chiding the over-stimulated intelligence of peace-loving idealists, and excommunicating from the ranks of liberal progress the pitiful remnant of those who struggle 'above the battle?' I like to think that his gallant spirit would have called for a war to be gallantly played, with insistent care for democratic values at home, and unequivocal alliance with democratic elements abroad for a peace that should promise more than a mere union of benevolent imperialisms. (p. 114-5)

I should prefer some philosophy of War as the grim and terrible cleanser to this optimism-haunted mood that continues unweariedly to suggest that all can yet be made to work for good in a mad and half-destroyed world. I wonder if James, in the face of such disaster, would not have abandoned his 'moral equivalent of war' for an 'immoral equivalent' which, in swift and periodic saturnalia, would have acted as vaccination against the sure pestilence of war. (p. 119)

FILLER, Louis. Randolph Bourne. 1943.

As Bourne warmed to his work in education, he came to admire Dewey's 'discreet' style and power for public influence--although he had originally preferred William James' pragmatism. (p. 63)

The very thought of military regimentation aroused in Bourne the keenest agitation, and out of his desperate denial of the idea came one of his most brilliant essays: 'A Moral Equivalent for Universal Military Service.' The preparedness advocates, he recognized, were on the offensive.

'We suddenly realize that if we are to defeat that militaristic trend which we loathe we shall have to offer some kind of action more stirring and more creative...How can we all together serve America by really enhancing her life? To more and more of us, the clue has come through James's conception of a productive army of youth, warring against nature and not against men, finding in drudgery and toil and danger the values that war and preparation for war have given.' (Quotation from Bourne) (p. 101-2)

BRENNAN, Joseph Gerard. The Meaning of Philosophy. 1953.

All this philosophizing about God is quite repugnant to William James, who has himself had considerable influence on modern religious thinking. To James, natural theology is an abomination of desolations. For just about all such rationalistic speculations can show for their trouble is some kind of metaphysical deity whose dubious existence is of little interest to anybody besides theistically inclined metaphysicians. James' approach to the problem of God is quite different. It is fideistic rather than rationalistic. That is, for James, God is not primarily an object of knowledge. He is an object of faith: 'There is one element of our active nature which the Christian religion has emphatically recognized, but which philosophers as a rule have with great insincerity tried to huddle out of sight in their pretentions to found systems of absolute certainty. I mean the element of faith.' (The Will to Believe) (p. 298)

On pragmatic principles, says James, if the hypothesis of God works satisfactorily, in the widest sense of the word, it is true. Does it make a difference, he asks, whether God exists or not? James believes that it does. If the materialist is right, he says, then the things that matter most are at the mercy of the things that matter least. If, however, there is a being which is the deepest power in the universe, a power conceived under the form of mental personality and which works for good, then life becomes immeasurably richer and more meaningful; an incomparable vista of values opens out before us. Is not the second alternative worth believing in? Should we shrink from it because we may be in error? To James (as to Pascal) belief in God represents the choice of a live option, a momentous choice well worth a gambler's risk. (p. 300)

BRIGHTMAN, Edgar S. A Philosophy of Religion. 1940.

No scientist begins by being a scientist. He begins by being born as a baby. He goes through the 'blooming, buzzing confusion' which William James made famous; gradually he learns to identify objects and to use language. (p. 8)

In 1901-1902, William James also gave Gifford Lectures, which were published at once as The Varieties of Religious Experience. Although primarily psychological, this work contained many philosophical ideas and did much to increase the confidence of the scholarly public in the normality and validity of religious experience. (p. 27-8)

William James (1902) proved vividly that the 'healthy-minded' soul, as he called it, experiences religion without a conversion crisis, while the 'sick soul' is a divided self that needs a radical conversion crisis to achieve integration. (p. 68)

James's Gifford Lectures in 1901 and 1902 are largely devoted to a study of mysticism, which he called 'the vital chapter.' His list of the traits of mystical experience is so famous that it should be given. These traits are: (1) Ineffability (it cannot be imparted in words; in this, we may add, it is like sense qualities, such as yellow, sweet, loud); (2) Noetic quality (it is a state of knowledge, affirming insight or illumination); (3) Transiency (it can be sustained at most for an hour or two; resentment against this inevitable transiency is expressed in Mark 9:5-9); (4) Passivity (the mystic may prepare for the experience, but when it comes he feels as if grasped by a superior power; this contrasts the mystic state with religious belief and religious action.) James's description is accepted by most psychologists. (p. 69)

Individuals are too individual to fit neatly into any scheme of typology. Yet if the 'types' be not taken rigidly, they may often serve as guides to the understanding of religious experiences. James' healthy-minded and sick souls, and Pratt's objective and subjective worshipers are examples of this. (p. 72)

Those who regard practical results as being the test of truth are called pragmatists. Pragmatism is one of the few original contributions which American philosophy has made, and it has exerted a wide influence in all fields including philosophy of religion. The empirical method of the present work owes much to both James and Dewey. (p. 126)

William James speaks of God as the 'higher part of the universe.' (p. 136)

Of the traits of that experience, the most important for the knowledge of God is the one called by William James its noetic quality. The mystic believes that he knows God in an immediate and absolutely certain experience. (p. 168)

William James (1842-1910), in his famous little book of Lowell Lectures, Pragmatism (1907), rejecting all 'tender-minded' absolutisms, went the 'tough-minded' road of the finite. He turned from neutralism, optimism, and pessimism, and accepted meliorism. God, for him, is the chief, primus inter pares, of 'the shapers of the great world's fate.' At the same time, James's eloquence of style and realistic facing of facts are not supplemented by a clear definition of the relation of God to the limits of the 'great world.' James's view, like so many others, is an intuition rather than an explanation. (p. 296)

In his oft-quoted phrase, William James calls selves 'fighters for ends.' Persons are selves who may become fighters for ideal ends, pursuers of good, avoiders of evil. Some end is sought by all normal human consciousness.

Whatever else it may be, all personal living is purposing. (p. 371-2)

BRINTON, Crane. Ideas and Men. The Story of Western Thought. 1950.

The American philosopher William James once made a famous rough-and-ready separation of philosophers into the 'tender-minded' and the 'tough-minded.' (p. 42)

The pragmatism of James and Dewey--the most distinguished American contribution to formal philosophic thought --is also in revolt against the certainties and the static quality of systematic thought. James held thought to be an instrument of the will; good thinking was thinking that got you what you wanted. He was not, of course, cynical or anarchistic or logical enough to hold that all wanting was good wanting, at least from the point of view of the individual wanter. For James, the good was what a sensitive, tolerant, kindly but at bottom respectable New England intellectual of his day would find good. He liked the odd and the troubled, and he agreed with John Mill that the good, the useful, the profitably new may come from the most unlikely sources. For James variety, conflict multanimity really are practical; they work--or did in 1900. (p. 496)

BROGAN, D. W. American Themes. 1947.

Holmes disliked attempts at making the universe more emotionally tolerable such as he thought he detected at the basis of William James's preaching of the power of faith. He saw in James his Irish blood leading him into preposterous positions, and he greatly preferred, at any rate in reasonably small dozes, the unfaith of Santayana. (p. 171)

BROMBERG, Walter. Man Above Humanity. A History of Psychotherapy. 1954.

Regarding Freud's visit to America in 1909, James commented:

'I hope that Freud and his pupils will push their ideas to their utmost limits, so that we may learn what they are. They can't fail to throw light on human nature; but I confess that he made on me personally the impression of a man obsessed with fixed ideas...A newspaper report of the congress said that Freud had condemned the American religious therapy (which has such extensive results) as very 'dangerous' because so 'unscientific.' (Thought and Character of William James edited by R. B. Perry) (p. 141)

BROOKS, Van Wyck. The Confident Years, 1885-1915. 1952.

Thus began the strenuous life of the man who typified his time, the symbol of the nineties, in America, and the years that followed,--the confident years before the first world war,--the Eastern and the Northern man who was half Southern by descent while he also knew the West like any cowboy. His philosophy of 'toil and risk' suggested William James, the sage who paralleled Roosevelt as a type of the epoch, while, photographed as he often was with doubled-up fists, he shared Tom Sawyer's feeling for effect and costume. (p. 19-20)

Roosevelt, the tenderfoot, distrustful of his own prowess, he said, afraid of mean horses, gun-fighters and grizzlies at first, had followed a principle of William James and by acting as if he was not afraid had actually, and quickly enough, ceased to be so. (p. 86)

Hapgood, though not an important writer, was himself a type of the new intellectual who was soon to abound in Greenwich Village and a man whose curiosity was symptomatic of the time, as one saw in his 'Types from City Streets.' A favourite of William James at Harvard who had studied in Berlin as well, a loafer, in Whitman's sense, in the Bowery or in Paris, in India or on the beach at Waikiki, he was an unstable offshoot of an old-fashioned family who had his own reasons for preferring the society of outcasts. (p. 128)

Veblen became a sort of hero to many an artist and writer, the legendary scholar who was also the classical sage. For he seemed to them the unbribed soul that William James had spoken of when he praised the ideal of poverty in ancient times; and Veblen, with his 'mail-order' clothes and his watch fastened on with a casual pin, was the modern American image of the ancient cynic. His tub was a shack in the woods and sometimes a cellar. (p. 200)

There was far less in John Jay Chapman that could ever weather time, nothing perhaps but a handful of character-sketches, but these, unique in their kind of America, bore witness to the writer's wit and his gifts of intuition and the happy phrase. A 'badly mixed critter,' as William James said of himself, and 'the only reincarnation of Isaiah and Job,' as James said Chapman was in his early days. (p. 403-4)

Mrs. (Julia Ward) Howe had been scarcely aware of the Boston self-sufficiency that left her in a world of her own, --like William James, to whom Chapman attributed the 'Emersonian immunity of remaining triumphant even after he had been vanquished.' (p. 405-6)

For Gertrude and Leo (Stein),--pragmatists both, in this reflecting of William James,--one's own pleasure in a work of art was the sole test of its worth, for they were indifferent to established good taste unless it affected them pleasantly, their only reason for loving anything. (p. 443)

'Prof. Dr. William James,' when Mencken finished speaking of him, was virtually indistinguishable from Orison Swett Marden. (p. 469)

He (Randolph Bourne) spoke to the young student class to which William James had appealed before him,--like Emerson in the New England of an earlier time,--in the hope that they would establish links with the young in other countries who shared their vision of a new free cultural order. (p. 494)

Like Gertrude Stein and Hutchins Hapgood, a favourite pupil of William James, Du Bois had first seen the South as a student from New England, a stranger in the Black Belt, unaccustomed to the jim-crow car and the kind of religion that sprang from voodooism. (p. 547)

It was precisely in this faith that America came into existence, affirming the capacity of men to govern themselves, and the main body of American tradition, as literature expressed it, exhibited this faith to the beginning of the first world war. William James, with his suspicion of absolutes and dogmas, continued the line that had run through Emerson and Whitman from Benjamin Franklin and others a century before, believing that, since 'mortality, compassion and generosity,' as Jefferson said, are 'innate elements of the human constitution,' men could dispense with authority and be trusted with freedom. (p. 585)

Before the first world war, however, there undoubtedly existed in the general mind a conscious belief in some variety of progress, and it was not till the nineteen-twenties that Henry Adams's point of view prevailed for many writers, over William James's. (p. 587)

BROOKS, Van Wyck. Emerson and Others. 1927.

Here was Emerson's American Scholar (Randolph Bourne) at last, but radiating an infinitely warmer, profaner, more companionable influence than Emerson had ever dreamed of, an influence that savored of Whitman and William James. (p. 127)

'The notion that a people can run itself and its affairs anonymously is now well known to be the silliest of absurdities.' Thus William James, in defence of the aristocratic principle; and what he says is as applicable to literature as to every other department of social life. But he continues: 'Mankind does nothing save through initiatives on the part of inventors, great and small, and imitation by the rest of us--these are the sole factors alive in human progress. Individuals of genius show the way and set the pattern, which common people then adopt and follow.' (p. 244)

BROOKS, Van Wyck. The Flowering of New England. 1937.

Emerson was proclaiming in these speeches and essays the doctrine which, according to William James, has marked all the periods of revival, the early Christian age and Luther's age, Rousseau's, Kant's and Goethe's, namely, that the innermost nature of things is congenial to the powers that men possess. (p. 207)

BROOKS, Van Wyck. On Literature Today. 1941.

William James marked the distinction. 'The fatalistic argument,' he said, 'is really no argument for simple determinism. There runs through it the sense of a force which might make things otherwise from one moment to another, if it were only strong enough to breast the tide. A person who feels the impotence of free effort in this way has the acutest notion of what is meant by it, and of its possible independent power. How else could he be so conscious of its absence and of that of its effects. But genuine determinism occupies a totally different ground: not the impotence, but the unthinkability of free will is what it affirms.' (p. 26)

When Europe too had its chance, and Americans were hankering for Europe, William James wrote, 'Europe has been made what it is by men staying in their homes and fighting stubbornly, generation after generation, for all the beauty, comfort and order they have got. We must abide and do the same.' (p. 28)

BROOKS, Van Wyck. Opinions of Oliver Allston. 1941.

Allston had no love of pragmatism, but regarding William James he said, 'I am drawn to his personality as helplessly as a filing to a magnet.' He regretted that he had never heard any of James's lectures:

To think that I was such a puppy as to go through Harvard College without once hearing or seeing William James. And then, one day, in New York,--it must have been in 1909,--I met him face to face in Twenty-third Street. I can see the spot now, at the southeast corner of Madison

Square. His face rose out of the crowd, hurrying beside him, shining with goodness and wisdom, just as I had seen it in the pictures, with the pepper-and-salt Norfolk jacket and all. I have always believed in William James's face, knowing that he must have been right at bottom. (p. 95-6)

I believe in the classical doctrine of poverty for those who are able to follow it. For I agree with William James, 'We have lost the power even of imagining what the ancient idealization of poverty could have meant; the liberation from material attachments, the unbribed soul, the manlier indifference, the paying our way by what we are and do and not by what we have, the right to fling away our life at any moment irresponsibly,--the more athletic trim, in short, the moral fighting shape.' (p. 115-6)

Drama implies will, and, in a sense, at least, free will, the will that creates the patterns of living; and Allston agreed with William James's statement, 'The rivalry of the patterns is the history of the world.' (p. 149)

As for this modern idol of the literary trade, he quoted William James, who certainly knew it: 'Of all insufficient authorities as to the total nature of reality, give me the 'scientists,' from Münsterberg up, or down...Their only authority at large is for method.' (p. 153)

Whatever their conscious beliefs may be, Americans are instinctive free-willers. They may think they are determinists, but, when this is the case, they always turn out to be fatalists, and that is quite a different matter. William James's 'Psychology' made this clear: 'The fatilistic argument is really no argument for simple determinism. There runs through it the sense of a force which might make things otherwise from one moment to another, if it were only strong enough to breast the tide. A person who feels the impotence of free effort in this way has the acutest notion of what is meant by it, and of its possible independent power. How else could he be so conscious of its absence and of that of its effects? But genuine determinism occupies a totally different ground; not the impotence but the unthinkability of free will is what it affirms.' (p. 160)

BROOKS, Van Wyck. Sketches in Criticism. 1932.

The Influence of William James. From this interesting chapter (p. 37-45) one typical paragraph is quoted:

Evidently, then, our American philosophers are somehow at fault for the stagnancy of our life; and indeed, to explain the lapse, the defection, the fatuity of our own intellectuals one need go no further back than their acknowledged master, William James, that golden man and poet whose every personal trait, even to his 'Gothic earnestness,' as Mr. Santayana would perhaps call it, was lovable and magnetic. To trust a spontaneous self that had not been leavened either with great new values or with great old values, to turn whatever values one actually has, whether great or small, into moral 'cash,' to live the life not of thought but of will, such is the virtual fiat of the Jamesian pragmatism; and as thought is not too common in America, and our present values are as stale and musty as values can well be, this, for us, is to beg the whole question of philosophy. By giving a fresh cachet to the ordinary working creed of a pioneer civilization, James led his disciples back into the wilderness from which they might otherwise have emerged; and there he left them. And their impulses trickled away into the sand. (p. 39-40)

William James complained of the style in which our philosophers clothe their thought. 'Our American philosophic literature,' he says in one of his letters, 'is dreadful from a literary point of view. Pierre Janet told me he thought it was much worse than German stuff--and I begin to believe so: technical and semi-technical language, half-clear thought, fluency, and no composition!' And again: 'I am getting impatient with the awful abstract rigmarole in which our American philosophers obscure the truth. It will be fatal. It revives the palmy days of Hegelianism. It means utter relaxation of intellectual duty, and God will smite it. If there's anything He hates, it is that kind of oozy writing.' (p. 146-7)

'We have lost,' said William James, 'the power even of imagining what the ancient idealization of poverty could have meant: the liberation from material attachments, the unbribed soul, the manlier indifference, the paying our way by what we are and not by what we have, the right to fling away our life at any moment irresponsibly.' (p. 177)

BROOKS, Van Wyck. The World of H. G. Wells. 1915.

I do not propose to discuss this question of logic. It is quite plain at least, as Wells observes, in the spirit of Professor James, that 'all the great and important beliefs by which life is guided and determined are less of the nature of fact than of artistic expression.' (p. 94-5)

Two conceptions of life, two general types of character, two ethical standards are here set in opposition, and this opposition is maintained throughout the novels of Wells.

Thus on the title-page of 'The New Machiavelli' appears the following quotation from Professor James: 'It suffices for our immediate purpose that tender-minded and tough-minded people...do both exist.' (p. 112)

BROOKS, Van Wyck. The World of Washington Irving. 1944.

Reading Mayne Reid in his boyhood years, later William James became convinced that a 'closet-naturalist' must be the 'vilest kind of wretch.' (p. 181)

BROOKS, Van Wyck. The Writer in America. 1953.

Was there not something of the boy-philosopher in William James, moreover, the philosopher who was once asked to be 'serious for a moment?'--and is this not even one of James's charms? (p. 64)

When, speaking of William James, whom he did not consider a true philosopher, Santayana suggested that, in his youth, James had never seen a philosopher 'whom he would have cared to resemble,' this writer was rash perhaps on two accounts. For, in the first place, James was undoubtedly a true philosopher, and moreover he had seen Emerson, whom he admired immensely. But how right is this point of Santayana's in other connections. (p. 75)

Others found it natural to follow the prescription of William James on returning to America from Europe, to 'pitch one's whole sensibility first in a different key,' though the moment of change might be 'lonesome.' Then 'gradually,' as James said, 'the quantum of personal happiness of which one is susceptible fills the cup,' and certainly for many writers this quantum of personal happiness was more and more identified with affection for the country. (p. 95-6)

Although the literary rank and file always naturally take for granted the absoluteness and permanence of the modes of any given present, these modes are mutable, they are destined to change, while the constant need remains to rehumanize whatever is dehumanized in life or in art. If this need is obvious now, is it not obvious also that we must break the habits of the recent past, following the advice of William James who said that if one acts a part one presently develops the feelings that implement the action? (p. 184-5)

For 'what proof is there,' said William James, 'that dupery through hope is so much worse than dupery through fear?' (p. 188)

To refer to William James again, his 'Varieties of Religious Experience' surveys and describes the minds of many saints, concluding that 'there is an organic affinity between joyousness and tenderness:' the saints are not hard or sad,--they are 'joyous and tender.' (p. 191)

BROUN, Heywood. Collected Edition. Compiled by Heywood Hale Broun. 1941.

William James said that mankind must find a moral equivalent for war. Blow, bugles, blow, and let us put a ribbon with palms upon the breast of Travis Harvard Whitney. No soldier could have been more gallant than the man who crumpled at his desk in the Civil Works Administration. (p. 303)

WERNER, M. R. Bryan. 1929.

In this campaign Mr. Roosevelt began that lifelong practice of calling everybody who did not agree with him on foreign policy weaklings and criminals. One of those who did not agree with him was Professor William James, who wrote to his friend Major Henry Lee Higginson:

'Nauheim, Sept. 18, 1900.

'...I read your political observations with respect, and see how you are professionally bound to resist Bryan. But I pray for his victory none the less. There are worse things than financial troubles in a Nation's career. To puke up its ancient soul, and the only things that gave it eminence among other nations, in five minutes without a wink of squeamishness, is worse; and that is what the Republicans would commit us to in the Philippines. Our conduct there has been one protracted infamy towards the Islanders, and one protracted lie towards ourselves. If we can only regain our old seat in the American saddle, and get back into some sincere relations with our principles and professions, it seems to me it makes very little permanent difference what incidental disturbances may accompany the process, for this crisis is one which is sure to determine the whole moral development of our policy in a good or a bad way for an indefinite future time.' (p.133-4)

William James once lectured on the Chautauqua platform, and his letters to his wife give a valuable picture of the intellectual atmosphere: 'I've been meeting minds so earnest and helpless that it takes them half an hour to get from one idea to its immediately adjacent next neighbor, and that with infinite creaking and groaning. And when they've got to the next idea, they lie down on it with their whole weight and can get no farther, like a cow on a doormat, so that you can get neither in nor out with them. Still, glibness is not all. Weight is something, even cow-weight....

'There is hardly a pretty woman's face in the lot, and they seem to have little or no humor in their composition. No epicureanism of any sort!....

'I see no need of going to Europe when such wonders are close by. I breakfasted with a Methodist parson with 32 false teeth, at the X's table, and discoursed of demoniacal possession. The wife said she had my portrait in her bedroom with the words written under it, 'I want to bring a balm to human lives'!!!!! Supposed to be a quotation from me!!! After breakfast an extremely interesting lady who has suffered from half-possessional insanity gave me a long account of her case. Life is heroic indeed, as Harry wrote....

'The Chautauqua week, or rather six and a half days, has been a real success. I have learned a lot, but I'm glad to get into something less blameless but more admiration-worthy. The flash of a pistol, a dagger, or a devilish eye, anything to break the unlovely level of 10,000 good people--a crime, murder, rape, elopement, anything would do....

'You bet I rejoice at the outlook--I long to escape from tepidity. Even an Armenian massacre, whether to be killer or killed, would seem an agreeable change from the blamelessness of Chautauqua as she lies soaking year after year in her lakeside sun and showers. Man wants to be stretched to his utmost, if not in one way then in another!'

And James wrote his brief conclusion to Miss Rosina H. Emmett: 'I have seen more women and less beauty, heard more voices and less sweetness, perceived more earnestness and less triumph than I ever supposed possible. Most of the American nation (and probably all nations) is white-trash,--but Tolstoy has borne me up--and I say unto you: 'Smooth out your voices if you want to be saved'!!' (p. 219-20)

BURROUGHS, John. The Breath of Life. 1915.

William James said that one of the privileges of a philosopher was to contradict other philosophers. I may add in the same spirit that one of the fatalities of many philosophers is, sooner or later, to contradict themselves. I do not know that James ever contradicted himself, but I have little doubt that a critical examination of his works would show that he sometimes did so; I remember that he said he often had trouble to make both ends of his philosophy meet. (p. 254)

BURROUGHS, John. The Heart of Burrough's Journals. Edited by Clara Barrus. 1928.

Read with keen intellectual pleasure William James's essay on Herbert Spencer in July 'Atlantic.' The most satisfactory discussion I have ever read of Spencer's claims. (p. 240)

Cool, fair. Still at Slabsides. At night sit before the open fire with my dog and read James on Pragmatism, a stimulating and delightful philosophical argument--good literature, and good logic. (p. 250)

BURROUGHS, John. The Summit of the Years. 1913.

And we are not on any more permanent ground, according to Professor James, in the case of man himself: 'A string of raw facts; a little of gossip and wrangle about opinions; a little classification and generalization on a mere descriptive level; a strong prejudice that we have states of mind, and that our brains condition them; but not a single law, in the sense physics shows us laws, not a single proposition from which consequences can casually be deduced.' (p. 187)

BURROUGHS, John. Under the Apple-Trees. 1916.

It is doubtless this quality of Bergson's work that led William James to say of it that it was 'like a breath of the morning and the singing of birds.' (p. 204-5)

BURROUGHS, John. Under the Maples. 1921.

There seems to me to be false reasoning in the argument from analogy which William James uses in his lectures on 'Human Immortality.' The brain, he admits, is the organ of the mind, but may only sustain the relation to it, he says, which the wire sustains to the electric current which it transmits, or which the pipe sustains to the water which it conveys. (p. 22)

BUTLER, Nicholas Murray. The Meaning of Education. Contributions to a Philosophy of Education. 1915.

Mr. James is simply summing up what physiology and psychology both teach when he exclaims: 'No reception without reaction, no impression without correlative expression - this is the great maxim which the teacher ought never to forget. An impression which simply flows in at the pupil's eyes or ears, and in no way modifies his active life, is an impression gone to waste. It is physiologically incomplete. It leaves no fruits behind it in the way of capacity acquired. Even as mere impression, it fails to produce its proper effect upon the memory; for, to remain fully among the acquisitions of the latter faculty, it must be wrought into the whole cycle of our operations. Its motor consequences are what clinch it.' (Talks to Teachers) (p. 113-14)

CAILLIET, Emile. Christian Approach to Culture. 1953.
William James took cognizance of the import of this theory in the conclusions of his 1901-2 Gifford Lectures on natural religion. 'There is a notion in the air about us that religion is probably only an anachronism, a case of 'survival,' an atavistic relapse into a mode of thought which humanity in its most enlightened examples has outgrown; and this notion our religious anthropologists at present do little to counteract.' (Varieties of Religious Experience.) (p. 92)

CANBY, Henry Seidel. Alma Mater. The Gothic Age of the American College. 1936.
But the educated men in our day were not often attracted to religion. Religion was either too dogmatic for them or too emotional. Herbert Spencer had destroyed the prestige of theology, and they were well aware that William James had described conversion as a phenomenon of psychology. Hence many with a fire of enthusiasm for the good, the beautiful, and the true turned to art, to the wonders of nature, and most of all to literature. (p. 120-1)

CANBY, Henry Seidel. Education by Violence. Essays on the War and the Future. 1919.
William James wrote of a moral substitute for war, hoping by hard service to the state to secure for man the splendid discipline, the self-sacrifice, the fighting emotion of war without its unhappy reactions. (p. 140)

CANBY, Henry Seidel. Turn West, Turn East. Mark Twain and Henry James. 1951.
William James saw Twain only when in 1892 they lived near each other in Italy, but it was enough for that great psychologist to see that he did not belong among the tough-minded in his famous categories.
'A fine soft-fibered little fellow,' so he described him in a letter to Josiah Royce, 'with the perversest twang and drawl, but very human and good. I should think one might get very fond of him.' (p. 13)
Henry James' early environment was, as his older brother William James very justly said, the James family.

It was an isolated culture of chosen intellectuals, of whom two younger brothers were of an extrovertish quality and his sister a nervous invalid of great intellectual force. Henry was a born artist, and William and his father students and speculators in human welfare and God. (p. 42)

Pragmatism, as William worked it out (and Henry said he had been practising it all his life), is an American, not at all a New England phenomenon. (p. 52)

Mr. James the father was getting out a somewhat abstruse book called Substance and Shadow, or Morality and Religion in Their Relation to Life. W. J. amused himself and all the family by designing a small cut to be put on the title page, representing a man beating a dead horse. This will illustrate the joyous chaff that filled the James' house. There was no limit to it. (p. 58)

That first great world crisis of modern times was to expose the foundations of the successful and so complacent nineteenth century to thoughtful men and women all over the Western World, and especially in England, the leader in the Industrial Revolution. The first effect upon a pragmatist like James--and it was in pragmatism only that he was in complete agreement with his brother--was moral. (p. 290)

CARDOZO, Benjamin Nathan. Selected Writings. Including also the complete texts of: Nature of the Judicial Process. Growth of the Law. Paradoxes of Legal Science. Law and Literature. 1947.

We are reminded by William James in a telling page of his lectures on Pragmatism, that every one of us has in truth an underlying philosophy of life, even those of us to whom the names and the notions of philosophy are unknown or anathema. There is in each of us a stream of tendency, whether you choose to call it philosophy or not, which gives coherence and direction to thought and action. Judges cannot escape that current any more than other mortals. (p. 109)

In the opening pages of this book on pragmatism, William James quotes a remark of Chesterton's to the effect that the most important thing about a man is his philosophy. The more I reflect about a judge's work, the more I am impressed with the belief that this, if not true for everyone, is true at least for judges. (p. 212)

'When the conclusion is there,' says William James, 'We have always forgotten most of the steps preceding its attainment.' (Principles of Psychology) (p. 287)

I take as my text two utterances that have consoled and

inspired me in many a doubting hour. The one is that of William James; the other is that of Emerson... 'Let no youth,' says James, 'have any anxiety about the upshot of his education whatever the line of it may be. If he keep faithfully busy each hour of the working day, he may safely leave the final result to itself. He can with perfect certainty count on waking up some fine morning to find himself one of the competent ones of his generations, in whatever pursuit he may have singled out. Silently, between all the details of his business, the power of judging in all that class of matter will have built itself up with him as a possession that will never pass away. Young people should know this truth in advance. The ignorance of it has probably engendered more discouragement and faint-heartedness in youths embarking on arduous careers than all other causes put together. (p. 419-20)

HELLMAN, George S. Benjamin N. Cardozo, American Judge. 1940.

From fellow Americans, preeminently William James and John Dewey, he gained a clearer view into the philosophy of pragmatism which, mingling with his own idealism, was to bring forth so much of near and far value in Cardozo's pronouncements as a judge. With undeviating vision he pursued his quest, learning, to use his own words, 'that the quest is greater than what is sought.' (p. 122-3)

CARTER, Everett. Howells and the Age of Realism. 1954.

Above all, it was in temperament, the true mother of philosophies, according to William James, that the realists had been most clearly pragmatic. Theirs had been the middle ground between a crass naturalism which would see man as the hopeless sport of external forces and an idealism which would turn its gaze away from the changing world of fact to a world of eternal essence. We can study God only by studying His creation, was the essence of James' position. Howells had been studying His creation for a generation. The buoyance of William James let him feel that the world could be made a better place by the application of human reason to its problems; this was the same hopefulness which motivated the development of satiric realism. And this buoyance, for both literary realist and philosophical pragmatist, was no saccharine acquiescence in the world as it was. Instead it was a mediation between a pessimism that, in the words of James, thinks 'the salvation of the world impossible,' and an optimism which 'thinks the world's salvation inevitable.' James called this middle ground 'meliorism,' an attitude which 'treats salvation....as a possibility.' The realistic novelists were all meliorists, and a sense of the possibilities of a world which can be made better by the commitments of reasonable men informs their fictions from The Gilded Age to A Hazard of New Fortunes. (p. 155-6)

But whereas William James (and Howells) found the test of all ideas to lie in experience and in action, Henry James considered it to reside in the growth of sensitivity of an individual's consciousness; and herein lay the first significan difference between Howells and William James and the dominant American attitude they represented on the one hand, and Henry James on the other. For Howells and William James an idea had to be tested in an active social relationship, with the outcome to be measured in terms of the peace or happiness of those involved in the relationship. But for Henry James the test did not lie in action or in doing, but in contemplation, or being, in an increase of the total awareness, in a heightening of sensitivity. (p. 253)

CHAPMAN, John Jay. Memories and Milestones. 1915.

None of us will ever see a man like William James again; there is no doubt about that. And yet it is hard to state what it was in him that gave him either his charm or his power, what it was that penetrated and influenced us, what it is that we lack and feel the need of, now that he has so unexpectedly and incredibly died. I always thought that William James would continue forever; and I relied upon his sanctity as if it were sunlight.

I should not have been abashed at being discovered in some mean action by William James; because I should have felt that he would understand and make allowances. The abstract and sublime quality of his nature was always enough for two; and I confess to having always trespassed upon him and treated him with impertinence, without gloves, without reserve, without ordinary decent concern for the sentiments and weaknesses of human character. Knowing nothing about philosophy, and having the dimmest notions as to what James's books might contain, I used occasionally to write and speak to him about his specialties in a tone of fierce contempt; and never failed to elicit from him in reply the most spontaneous and celestial gayety. Certainly he was a wonderful man. (p. 19-20)

The great religious impulse at the back of all his work, and which pierces through at every point, never became expressed in conclusive literary form, or in dogmatic utterance. It never became formulated in his own mind into a stateable belief. And yet it controlled his whole life and mind, and accomplished a great work in the world. The spirit of a priest was in him,--in his books and his private conversation. He was a sage, and a holy man; and everybody put off his shoes before him. And yet in spite of this,--in conjunction with this, he was a sportive, wayward, Gothic sort of spirit, who was apt, on meeting a friend, to burst into foolery, and whose wit was always three parts poetry. Indeed his humor was as penetrating as his seriousness. Both of these two sides of James's nature--the side that made a direct religious appeal--became rapidly intensified during his latter years; so that, had the process continued much longer, the mere sight of him must have moved beholders to amend their lives. (p. 25)

Chapman has a most delightful chapter on William James who was an intimate friend. The two quotations above are typical of the chapter as a whole.

There has recently been an age of agnosticism: it is closing. An age of faith is in progress. The Desert of Agnosticism has been crossed; and some of those leaders who helped multitudes to pass across it, were destined not to enter the promised land themselves. Such men are ever among the greatest of their generation. I am thinking of William James, who was in himself more than he either saw or thought. At the time he was writing I saw in him only the ineffectual thinker, but later I came to see in him the saint. The fear with which his mind was tinctured was the very vice of which I should accuse the Ethical Society-a fear of the symbols of religion. His heart had been a little scared by early terror. The intellectual part of him was enfeebled by the agnosticism of 1870. And yet what difference did it make? Some sort of light shone out of his cloud as he took his way across the sands, and men followed him. I speak of him here, because his life is a type of mystery. He is there before us, but he can no more be grasped than a phantom. (p. 160)

HOWE, M. A. DeWolfe. John Jay Chapman and his Letters. 1937.

From a letter to Mrs. Henry Whitman.

'I say I wonder whether James or Royce or any of those fellows will understand a psychological critique on Emerson. I'll bet they won't. I lay odds they won't.

'I have hopes of James--I will not give up James.

James is the son of Henry James--who by the way was the only decent human man that ever lived in Massachusetts--and I must remember that James is his son. I will be patient with James.' (p. 120-1)

Chapman's article on 'The Will to Believe' was neither more nor less impudent than the letters we shall find him writing to William James. He had small patience with philosophers as such, and less with those who were beginning to be called psychologists. Some years later he wrote, apropos of Josiah Royce: 'There is no such thing as philosophy. But there are such things as philosophers. A philosopher is a man who believes there is such a thing as philosophy, and who devotes himself to proving it. He believes that behind the multifarious, contradictory, and often very unpleasant appearances of the world there is a unity which he can put into typewriting. Probably there is, but certainly he can't.' (p. 136)

From a letter to James.

My wife and I are spending three days with Mrs. Dorr and saw a handsome boy of yours last night at Mrs. Whitman's, but didn't get a chance to more than shake hands with him--most distinguished looking fellow. We have seen the whole astronomy here--and a joy to find how little everyone has changed--all the people old and young I ever knew --and each one more so than ever--Royce especially in good form. If he could only get rid of the notion that there is such a thing as philosophy what a fellow he would be. Poor babe--he claims the privilege of not worrying over politics on the ground that he has more important things to attend to, and must perforce rely on the opinion of his nearest lawyer friend as to how to vote--little dreaming that he is giving the same reason that the average American gives--and furnishing a key to all our political life. O learning, and devotion to learning, how little dost thou differ from any other pursuit! (p. 177-8)

From a letter to James.

I don't seem to hear very good reports of you. They say you are in Rome--why Rome? A place of no stimulating power, full of catacombs inhabited by dead Americans. I believe I could cure you of whatever it is you've got, if you would definitely give up ambition and come immediately back to this country. Ambition ruins any man--poets and philosophers above all others, for it contradicts --as a man who shuts his mouth can't sing, and the wheels and maelstroms going around over here--why, the centre of force is over here--and--everything has changed during the last six months--does every six months--and--every man I know is different from what he was a year ago. You'll be an old flintlock discharging antiquated shrapnel when you get back. (p. 183)

It will be seen that I have been digressing and retrogressing, not following dates but memories and visions; for all these recollections are parts of Harvard. The academic part was only the gateway. My friendship with William James and my acquaintance with Josiah Royce were a later period, though both of them were circulating in the heavens above when we were in college. A lecture on the sexes was given before each Freshman Class and James performed the function in my first year. He looked quite young then, and very severe. But after all, what can the poor wretch of a lecturer say upon such an occasion? He becomes coldly philosophical at his peril; he can't be humorous; he can't be religious; he can't be purely scientific and medical. James left on me a strong impression of stoicism--a thing at variance with his nature, as I afterwards knew it. (p. 189)

I once made an attempt to express to James the consciousness which a simple-minded person might have of the presence of God as the causa causans of his own anatomy. I forget where the interview took place; I think we were standing in the corridor of a Boston hotel. At any rate, the surroundings were dreary in the extreme. At the close of my fable I said, 'Can you not imagine that such a creature under such emotional condition should cry out, Abba, Father!' James started like--not a guilty--but angry thing surprised, and a trap door opened under the interview.

So also with regard to Free Will. In the shipwreck of the elder conventional philosophic system--Reason, Emotion, Will, etc., James had preserved the Will. He believed in Free Will, and said that without that we had a 'Solid Universe,' which he thought very undesirable and therefore untrue. My own feeling has always been that the more one's will dissolved in the Will of the Universe and the nearer one could come to the feeling of a personal relation to God, the better it was. But like a well-trained lawyer who comes to believe in the reality of legal principles, James had accepted bits of the old philosophic machinery--a lever here and a turntable there. The Will was to him a reality. (p. 200)

Since writing the above I have looked into James's Letters published by his son. I find that James wrote to James Henry Leuba in April, 1904: 'My personal position is simple. I have no living sense of commerce with

God. I envy those who have, for I know the addition of such a sense would help me immensely. The Divine, for my active life, is limited to abstract concepts, which, as ideals, interest and determine me, but do so but faintly, in comparison with what a feeling of God might effect, if I had one.' (p. 201)

I cannot think that anyone every met James without feeling that James was a better man than himself. His altruism and his regard for Dr. Eliot led me to make one mistake which I knew about by accident. James had fished up in Berlin a brilliant, philosophic adventurer called Münsterberg, and had planted him in Harvard. Thereupon the place began to heave and surge with Münsterberg. Münsterberg had a head shaped like a watermelon and about as large. He spoke and wrote teutonically like a zoological monster. I once said to James, 'Why do you stand for the self-advertising of that adventurer, Münsterburg?' or words to that effect. James said, 'He's useful. He's ready to go to San Francisco and deliver a lecture at twenty-four hours notice.' This view accorded with the general policy of Dr. Eliot. All the same, James came to dislike Münsterburg. James had caught a Tartar. (p. 202)

James's lecture was very good--I hardly know how much it was understood. I wrote him a note about it. It seemed to me to be a destruction of all authority in philosophy--and that it ought to be called 'A Defense of Poesy.' I cannot be sure that he so meant it or whether he sees the consequences. But I got more impression of dawn than I ever had before at one of his lectures. The form of the thing was very peculiar--a close and long discussion of Achilles and the tortoise--which paradox proves the futility of logic and philosophical reasoning. Because Achilles does, you know, in real life overtake the tortoise--all this treated very dryly and gingerly, with a tongs. Then a sudden plunge to the suggestion that we must treat the whole living character, heart, body, soul, and being together--as it lives--all dissection is misleading.

One step beyond this--i.e., treating of all of them--of everything together as it lies--would be mysticism and religion. I think James would resent the name of mystic and yet he is coming to be what I call a mystic. (p. 231)

From a letter to James.

The 'Pluralism' has come and I am reading it with real pleasure, at least the essay on Hegel, (I have temporarily dropped the book out of the carriage on a drive and am getting another copy). The trouble is, I lost it just as I was beginning to be convinced I had some good ideas.

'You said something about a concept. Now what is a concept? Where does it begin and where does it end? Are you sure that there is such a thing?' (p. 238)

Quotations from it (Memories and Milestones) would have already been made at several points in this book. Yet here must be one more, in which Chapman, writing of William James, says very much what James might have said about him--and rather as James would have said it: 'In general talk on life, literature, and politics James was always throwing off sparks that were cognate only in this, that they came from the same central fire in him. It was easy to differ from him; it was easy to go home thinking that James had talked the most arrant rubbish, and that no educated man had a right to be so ignorant of the first principles of thought and of the foundations of human society. Yet it was impossible not to be morally elevated by the smallest contact with William James. A refining, purgatorial influence came out of him.' (p. 292)

CHASE, Stuart and CHASE, Marian Tyler. The Proper Study of Mankind. An Inquiry into the Science of Human Relations. 1948.

'A social organism,' said William James, 'is what it is because each member proceeds to his own duty with a trust that the other members will simultaneously do theirs. A government, an army, a commercial system, a ship, a college, an athletic team, all exist on this condition without which not only is nothing achieved, but nothing is even attempted.' (p. 62)

CHASE, Stuart. Roads to Agreement. Successful Methods in the Science of Human Relations. 1951.

Apparently the only way to get war out of a culture is to build a new institution to replace it--a 'moral equivalent,' in the words of William James. A super-government to replace the absolute sovereignty of Nations, the United Nations, the Lilienthal-Acheson plan. Many of us hoped that the A-bomb, and later the H-bomb, would add power to that effort, but it now seems clear that the threat of atomic fission alone will not create One World. (p. 210)

CHASE, Stuart. The Tyranny of Words. 1938.

'The ensemble of the metaphysical attributes imagined

by the theologian is but a shuffling and matching of pedantic dictionary adjectives. One feels that in the theologian's hands they are only a set of titles obtained by a mechanical manipulation of synonyms; verbality has stepped into the place of vision.' so observes William James. (p. 214)

John Jay Chapman was a kind of American Dr. Johnson, fond of striking his foot against great stones. In 1897, he wrote the following letter to William James concerning Josiah Royce, then a towering figure in philosophy at Harvard:

'I am driven to write to you because I so narrowly missed seeing you and regretted it so much. Also because I am concerned about Royce. I never heard a man talk so much nonsense in one evening--and a man too who is such a splendid fellow, a unique nature and a very wonderful mind. The inroads of Harvard University upon his intelligence, however, have been terrible. He said he was writing a paper on originality and his conversation betrayed some of the things he is going to say in it. This was that everything was imitative-in art you 'imitate the ideal.' This ought to be stopped. He is misleading the youth. I see why they killed Socrates. I say it is pernicious emptiness he is teaching your boys out there.

'I know you would say that it's mere philosophy and not to be taken seriously; but these things do have some influence sometimes. That man--mind you, I love and revere him--but he's not as interesting a man as he was ten years ago. His mind has less of life in it. His constant strain and endeavor to evacuate his mind and have nothing in it but destruction is beginning to tell. I hear he is going abroad. I am awfully glad. Let him have no money. Let him come in grinding contact with life. Let him go to Greece and get into a revolution--somewhere where he can't think--I mean do this thing he does, which is not thinking. Let his mind get full of images and impressions, pains, hungers, contrasts--life, life, life. He's drawing on an empty well.' (p. 218-9)

CHESTERTON, Gilbert K. The Common Man. 1950.

I was recently reading one of the late Harvey Wickham's exceedingly clever studies of modern thought; including the study of William James. I think the critic was mainly just about the philosophy, but not quite just about the philosopher. I do not myself think that Pragmatism can ever stand up as a serious rival to the permanent philosophy of Truth and the Absolute. But I do think that

William James did really stand up as a rattling good fighter and cleaner-up of the particular sort of solemn nonsense most current in his time. He may have indirectly served the cause of belief in belief. But he did a lot to serve the cause of unbelief in unbelief; a very wholesome object. But that is not my main point. It seems to me that where William James failed was exactly where Henry James succeeded; in making a whole scheme out of fine shades and doubtful cases. Now that can be done with a novel; for it only claims to be exceptional. It cannot be done with philosophy; for it must claim to be universal. (p. 31-2)

COHEN, Felix. Editor. The Holmes-Cohen Correspondence. (in the Journal of the History of Ideas. Jan. 1948)

Holmes to Cohen.

As you know, I reserve a theoretic doubt as to the cosmic ultimateness of our can't helps--but I have no doubt that they are our can't helps and govern our world. I regard the will to believe as of a piece with the insistence on the discontinuity of the universe which Bill James shares with Cardinal Newman, and which I suspect as induced by the wish to leave room for the interstitial miracle. When we were in our 20s W. James said to me (in substance) that spiritualism was the last chance to spiritualize or idealize the world. I then and ever since have regarded that as a carnal and superficial view. (p. 44)

COHEN, Morris R. The Faith of a Liberal. 1946.

I think the hostility of so much of the world's thought to excessive preoccupation with material economy should make us pause. May there not be some reason for our leading philosopher, William James, to refer to success as our 'bitch goddess' and for others to refer to our preoccupation with pecuniary profits as a mania? (p. 95)

William James, who did inestimable good by insisting on thoroughgoing naturalism in psychology, seems to me to have produced untold harm by the unhistorical assumption that religion must necessarily rest on the belief in the supernatural. To insist that God must necessarily be a person who, if we pray to Him, will help us against our enemies and whom we in turn might help or please by believing in Him, seems to me to rest on an appeal to the unenlightened multitude against the judgement of all reflective thought; an appeal as unjustified as the parallel appeal to the multitude in questions of natural science. (p. 310)

When my revered friend and teacher William James wrote an essay on 'A Moral Equivalent for War,' I suggested to him that baseball already embodied all the moral value of war, so far as war had any moral value. He listened sympathetically and was amused, but he did not take me seriously enough. All great men have their limitations, and William James's were due to the fact that he lived in Cambridge, a city which, in spite of the fact that it has a population of 100,000 souls (including the professors), is not represented at any baseball league that can be detected without a microscope. (p. 335-6)

For similar reasons also I think we must reject the apology for religion advanced by my revered and beloved teacher William James.

Let us take up his famous essay on 'The Will to Believe,' Consider in the first place his argument that science (which is organized reason) is inapplicable in the realm of religion, because to compare values or worths 'we must consult not science but what Pascal calls our heart.' But if it were true that science and reason have no force in matters of religion, why argue at all? Why all these elaborate reasons in defense of religion? Is it not because the arguments of men like Voltaire and Huxley did have influence that men like De Maistre and James tried to answer them? Who, the latter ask, ever heard of anyone's changing his religion because of an argument? It is not necessary for me to give a list of instances from my own knowledge. (p. 358)

The momentous character of the choice in regard to religion may be dissolved by reflection which develops detachment or what James calls lightheartedness. What is the difference between believing in one religion or in another or in none? A realization of the endless variety of religious creeds, of the great diversity of beliefs that different people hold to be essential to our salvation, readily liberates us from the compulsion to believe in every Mullah that comes along or else fear enternal damnation. James draws a sharp distinction between a living and a nonliving issue. To him, I suppose, the question of whether to accept Judaism, Islam, or Buddhism was not a living one. But the question of whether to investigate so-called psychical phenomena as proofs of immortality was a living one. But surely reflection may change the situation, and a student of religion may come to feel that James's choice was arbitrary and untenable. (p. 360)

William James has almost persuaded our present generation that progress in philosophy depends on the easy device of avoiding Kant rather than on the difficult job of going through him. But this advice, flattering to our vanity if not to our indolence has not brought any noticeable gains to philosophy. (p. 369)

Less than thirty years ago William James and Josiah Royce, anxious that their students should have the opportunity of hearing Charles S. Peirce, their master in philosophy, sought to arrange such a meeting. President Eliot, widely known as a courageous champion of academic as well as of other kinds of freedom, refused to allow Peirce to enter any room of Harvard University, and James and Royce had to hire a private hall. Now Harvard University is, at considerable expense, publishing Peirce's Collected Papers in ten magnificent volumes. This contrast between the scorn for the living and the glorification of the dead is not only dramatic but significant. (p. 391-2)

At the beginning of this century this traditional American liberalism was pronounced dead by a great American philosopher, William James. In addressing the Anti-Imperialist League he said in effect: We had better disband. We have been fighting to preserve the peculiar traditional American liberalism, which is inconsistent with imperialism. That liberalism, based on isolation and a free land economy, is dead. We have, for good or evil, entered into the arena with other nations. We are producing goods for other nations. We are going to have investments abroad. We can no longer maintain our isolation. We might as well recognize this and join with our natural comrades in other nations in the fight which is raging all over between liberalism and its enemies. (p. 446)

COHEN, Morris R. Reason and Nature. An Essay on the Meaning of Scientific Method. 1931.

To argue as James and others have, that the constant rules of logic cannot be true of a world in flux is a confusion as gross as to argue that motion cannot have a constant velocity or a fixed direction, or that one standing still cannot catch a flying ball. (Pluralistic Universe) (p. 19)

This right to believe has been defended by William James on the ground that since we must take risks in life, we have a right to believe those things that we believe may help us to attain our vital interests. Assuredly, every one does risk his life on his fundamental beliefs. But this does not prove them true, or even dispose of the doubts raised by those who actually challenge the beliefs.

We cannot by the will to believe in a personal God make Him come into existence. We cannot by the believing it even add a cubit unto our own stature. Reason in the form of logical science is an effort to determine the weight of evidence. To tip the scales by the will to believe is childish foolishness, since the real weight of things is not thereby changed. (p. 21)

The difficulties of reducing actual psychic life to sensational elements alone, were realized by no one more keenly than by James as a psychologist. His radical empiricism is in harmony with the efforts of Schuppe (and at times of Avenarius himself) to show that logical relations are just as much a part of the natural world as the sensations related. How, then, does James come in the end to draw so strong an opposition between experience and logical or conceptual thought? How can experience include everything important and yet exclude conceptual thought? The point is worth examining, not only to clear up the specific confusion which the term 'experience' covers, but also because it illustrates how generally fertile in confusion is every monistic effort to reduce the world exclusively to any one of two polar categories. (p. 42)

It seems to me of some importance to realize that James' hostility to logic was not necessitated by any of his psychological observations. To see the motives which led him to espouse Bergson's extreme anti-intellectualism, we must reflect on the peculiar fascination and repulsion which the neo-Hegelian, and especially the Bradleyan argument for the absolute, had for him. (p. 43-4)

One of the noblest manifestations of the empiricist temper in the practical realm is James' picturesque individualism. The preference for the 'thick' particular fact, as against 'thin' abstractions, shows itself in an admirable insistence on the reality and supreme worth of the actual human being before us, as against all abstract labels and conventional rules. (p. 45)

COHEN, Morris R. Law and the Social Order. Essays in Legal Philosophy. 1933.

Metaphysics is a bogeyman only to infantile minds. It is, after all, as James said, but an obstinate effort to think clearly. (p. 222)

The rationalistic and empirical motives cannot be fully understood unless they are seen in their application to the whole life that we call civilization. Thus the fundamental motive of all radical empiricism comes out most clearly, I venture to think, in James's essay on the 'Moral Equivalent of War,' with its expressed preference for all the horrors of war rather than a world of clerks and teachers, of coeducation and zoophily, of consumers' leagues, and associated charities. (p. 266)

COHEN, Morris R. Studies in Philosophy and Science. 1949.

From this point of view recent discussions of religion initiated by William James's Varieties of Religious Experience, seem to me singularly provincial and unilluminating. They throw no light on the main streams of human experience expressed in the great historic religions, such as Brahmanism, Buddhism, Zoroastrianism, Confucianism, etc. James's remark that the religious experience of the great mass of people is secondary, and only that of the founders is important, is certainly superficial. (p. 30)

Pragmatism, it is true, has made a great stir in our popular magazines, but is it really the pragmatic theory, rather than Professor James's striking style? As for his younger apostles, many of us, I dare say, have found more brilliant than illuminating. Certainly flashes of genius cannot permanently take the place of the steady light of reason. (p. 39)

COLE, Stewart G. and COLE, Mildred Wiese. Minorities and the American Promise. The Conflict of Principle and Practice. 1954.

The social differences in the personality patterns of the citizens of this country are as pronounced as are the varieties of culture groups. William James' remark is appropriate here: 'There is very little difference between one man and another, but what little there is is very important.' (p. 102)

COMMAGER, Henry Steele. The American Mind. An Interpretation of American Thought and Character Since the 1880's. 1950.

As early as 1880 James was writing disparagingly of the 'Hegelian wave which seems to me only another desperate attempt to make a short cut to paradise.' His objection was as much emotional as rational: 'The trough-and-trough philosophy, as it actually exists...seems too buttoned-up and white-chokered and clean-shaven a thing to speak for the vast, slow-breathing unconscious Kosmos with its dread abysses and its unknown tides.' He was scarcely less impatient with Kant. 'Pray contribute no farther,' he advised one young disciple, 'to philosophy's prison discipline of dragging Kant around like a cannon-ball tied to its ankle.' His fundamental criticism of Hegel and Kant was not logical or even aesthetic but moral: he thought their acquiescence in absolutes, their tendency to see the world as good rather than to strive to make it good, paralysed the will. (p. 92)

Mark Twain once observed that he had never known a real seeker after truth: sooner or later everyone engaged in that search found what he was looking for and gave up the quest. It was a pity that he did not know William James. For James believed, passionately, that truth was not something that was found, once and for all, but was forever in the making, that it was not single and absolute but plural and contingent. It was not only that he was tolerant and hospitable to a degree heretofore unknown in modern philosophy but that tolerance and hospitality were an essential ingredient in his philosophical system. Philosophy had for him, as his colleague and critic, Santayana observed, 'a Polish constitution; so long as a single vote was cast against the majority, nothing could pass.... It would have depressed him,' he added, 'if he had had to confess that any important question was finally settled.' (p. 93)

For, almost from the beginning, James confronted all dogma with skepticism and made skepticism itself a dogma. He turned his countenance from all absolutes, causes, finalities, fixed principles, abstractions, and rigidities, and embraced instead pluralism, uncertainty, practicality, common sense, adventure, and flexibility. To the philosophy of first causes he opposed one of consequences; to the philosophy of ultimates he opposed one of expediency; to the philosophy of determinism he opposed one of free will. To the concept that truth could be found either by the exercise of pure reason or by the scientific observation of nature, he opposed the concept that truth was not in fact to be found but to be made, that it was not something that was inert and static but something that happened to an idea or a course of conduct:

'The truth of an idea is not a stagnant property inherent in it. Truth happens to an idea. It becomes true, is made true by events: its verity is in fact an event, a process: the process namely of its verifying itself, its verification. Its validity is the process of its valid-ation ....The true is the name of whatever proves itself to be good in the way of belief, and good, too, for definite assignable reasons.' (Pragmatism) (p. 94)

'Grant an idea or belief to be true, what concrete difference will its being true make in anyone's actual life? How will the truth be realized? What experience will be different from those which would obtain if the belief were false? What, in short, is the truth's cash value in experiential terms? The moment pragmatism asks this question, it sees the answer. True ideas are those that we can assimilate, validate, corroborate and verify. False ideas are those that we can not. That is the practical difference it makes to us to have true ideas; that, therefore, is the meaning of truth, for it is all that truth is known as.' (Pragmatism) (p. 94-5)

'Suppose that the world's author put the case to you before creation, saying: I am going to make a world not certain to be saved, a world the perfection of which shall be conditional merely, the condition being that each several agent does its own level best. I offer you the chance of taking part in such a world. Its safety, you see, is unwarranted. It is a real adventure, with real danger, yet it may win through. It is a social scheme of cooperative work genuinely to be done. Will you join the procession? Will you trust yourself and trust the other agents enough to face the risk?' (Pragmatism) (p. 96)

COMMINS, W. D. and FAGAN, Barry. Principles of Educational Psychology. Second Edition. 1954.

As James says:

'We all cease analysing the world at some point, and notice no more differences. The last units with which we stop are our objective elements of being. Those of a dog are different from those of a Humboldt; those of a practical man from those of a metaphysician. But the dog's and the practical man's thoughts feel continuous, though to the Humboldt or the metaphysician they would appear full of gaps and defects. And they are continuous, as thoughts. It is only as mirrors of things that the superior minds find them full of omissions. And when the omitted things are discovered and the unnoticed differences laid bare, it is not that the old thoughts split up, but that new thoughts supersede them, which make new judgements about the same objective world.' (Principles of Psychology) (p. 51-2)

This gives empirical substance to the statement made long ago by William James, who pointed out that 'associations' and 'hooks' are in reality systematic relations:

'In mental terms, the more other facts a fact is associated with in the mind, the better possession of it our memory retains. Each of its associates becomes a hook to which it hangs, a means to fish it up by when sunk beneath the surface.... But this forming of associations with a fact, what is it but thinking about the fact as much as possible: Briefly, then, of two men with the same outward experiences and the same amount of mere native tenacity, the one who thinks over his experience most, and weaves them into systematic relations with each other, will be the one with the best memory.' (Psychology Briefer Course) (p. 663)

Even children, said William James, 'can enjoy abstractions, provided they be of the proper order; and it is a poor compliment to their rational appetite to think that anecdotes about little Tommies and little Jennies are the only kind of things their minds can digest.' (Talks to Teachers) (p. 739)

COMPTON, Charles H. Who Reads William James? (In Who Reads What p. 91-100). 1934.

To me the most human of James's books and the most interesting outside of his 'Letters' is his 'Varieties of Religious Experience,' but strange as it may seem the range of its readers whose names were taken from the library records is limited to college students and one dealer in municipal bonds. This is probably largely a matter of chance, as this book had a large sale and was widely read. My letter of inquiry brought an answer from one of the students who had read a number of James' books, having become interested thru college courses in psychology and philosophy. It is interesting in its comments on 'Varieties of Religious Experience.' This young man from his name and from an idealism running thru his letter--an idealism so common to his race--I judge to be a Jew. He says:

'Varieties of Religious Experience' is perhaps one of the best single books ever written on any single phase of social psychology. This sage, partial to no sect yet deeply religious, with dazzling brilliancy turns the revealing light of psychology upon religion. There is no partial creed feeling, no gloomy pessimism, nor for that matter rosy optimism to mar the unsurpassed psychology of James. The empiricism of the scientist which is interested in a fact merely because it is a fact is, in James, tempered by the philosophic attitude which demands to know the import of facts.' (p. 95-6)

The young Jewish student from whose letter I have already quoted writes feelingly regarding James's Letters:

'To read the Letters of William James is to indulge in

a real pleasure; it is to read something more entertaining than the best fiction ever written; it is to introduce one's self to the greatest of personalities: kind, gentle and wholesouled, warm, genial and courteous, a dazzling intellect combined with unobtrusive modesty, one who is blessed with a delicate but keen sense of humor, an idealist but not a dreamer, a philosopher but not a dogmatist, a scientist but not a doctrinaire.

One cannot know psychology without knowing James; one cannot read James without knowing him; one cannot know him without being strongly attracted to him.' (p. 97)

A young man engaged in selling musical instruments writes:

'My reading of James has been the natural result of an interest in philosophy and psychology. Altho lacking a university-trained mind, I nevertheless in a humble way can appreciate the master in James. In his Human Immortality, his sympathetic understanding of the hope of mankind, combined with a rare scientific insight, gives the book its charm and convincing qualities. However, the book that brings these qualities out prominently is Varieties of Religious Experience.' (p. 97)

An employe in one of the city offices writes:

'After going thru his book on The Will to Believe, it left a profound impression on me. I found it inspiring, logical and nutritious. His book on Habit's re-education of the mind is good, also the energies of men. His book on religious experiences was uplifting and edifying. His article on the sick soul was really a description of himself. He like myself had only a small store of energy. His ideal of life was to keep the mind always filled with thoughts of the good, the beautiful and the true. His books as I turned from page to page revealed my own inner weaknesses. He showed how to strengthen the inner life, making calmness an ideal free from passion, anger, selfishness and hatred. He showed how the mind can carry you to the heights in self confidence if you have the will to believe.' (p. 97-8)

An artist writes:

'While I am not a student of this famous American philosopher's writings I have derived much pleasure and instruction from reading some of his lectures. It is his general tone of common sense, in addition to his masterly exposition of facts, his unbiased philosophical view of the nature of the universe, his broad gauge. I had no special reason for reading a 'Pluralistic Universe' except that I am an admirer of all sound writings. In the writings of William James I found much to clarify the mind and to clean out the cobwebs of fear, superstition, etc. and he assisted me to think logically and not theologically.' (p. 98)

The writer of the next letter characterizes himself as twenty-five years of age, white, single, something of an idealist, tho fairly practical, interested in ideas about people rather than people themselves.

'You ask how I happened to be interested in Problems of Philosophy. Merely because James wrote it. You see, I've somehow acquired the conception of James as one of the outstanding figures in contemporary thought. (Partly from the opinions of others, and partly from things of his I have read, I suppose.) I can't discuss very intelligently the book you ask about, for I had merely looked at it a few times before the library began sending me a series of vigorous notes, telling me it was past due.

'I had--and have--the intention of reading about all of James that I could; but business leaves one's ambition rather enervated. If I can get some kind of a hold on the important things that have been written by James and a few others--Havelock Ellis, for instance--it will be better than reading aimlessly here and yon, it seems to me.

'My admiration for James comes chiefly, I think, from his wonderful ability to write. Ellis, it is said, writes in a manner 'at once intimate and grand.' I wish I had thought of that to say of James. I believe it would have then been even truer.

'James's style fascinates me particularly because I hope to learn some day a little of his art. At present I am doing a very elementary sort of writing: reporting for trade publications. But, nevertheless, I know good work when I see it. It's like a fiddler in a cheap theatre listening to Kreisler.' (p. 98-9)

COTTON, James Harry. Royce on the Human Self. 1954.

The friendship between the two men was informal and marked by good-natured banter. Each man eagerly enjoyed the sharp conflicts of ideas between them. They were savage philosophical enemies and their friendship thrived on that enmity. The only recorded complaint of James against Royce was that for a time (in 1905) they were too busy even for controversy. 'The fact is that the classroom exhausts our powers of speech. Royce has never made a syllable of reference to all the stuff I wrote last year--to me, I mean. He may have spoken of it to others, if he has read it, which I doubt. So we live in parallel trenches and hardly show our heads.' (p. 191)

From Germany James wrote under date of September 26, 1900:

'Beloved Royce, --

Great was my, was our pleasure in receiving your long and delightful letter last night. Like the lioness in Aesop's fable, you give birth to one young one only in the year, but that one is a lion. I give birth mainly to guinea-pigs in the shape of postcards; but despite such diversities of epistolary expression, the heart of each of us is in the right place. I need not say, my dear old boy, how touched I am at your expressions of affection, or how it pleases me to hear that you have missed me. I too miss you profoundly....You are still the centre of my gaze, the pole of my mental magnet. When I write, 'tis with one eye on the page, and one on you. When I compose my Gifford lectures mentally, 'tis with the design exclusive of overthrowing your system, and ruining your peace.' (Perry. Thought and Character of William James.)

In 1907 after writing a criticism of Pragmatism to James, Royce added, 'Meanwhile, no criticism of mine is hostile. Life is a sad long road, sometimes. Every friendly touch and word must be preciously guarded. I prize everything that you say or do, whether I criticize or not.' (Perry. Thought and Character of William James)

James' most severe criticism of Royce was written in letters. When he accuses Royce of lightness, of reducing philosophy to a game, one is tempted to think that James did not even know Royce. Thus:

'Since teaching the 'Conception of God,' I have to perceive that I didn't trust myself to believe before, that looseness of thought is R.'s essential element. He wants it. There isn't a tight joint in his system; not one. And yet I thought that a mind that could talk me blind and black and numb on mathematics and logic, and whose favorite recreation is work on those subjects, must necessarily conceal closeness and exactitudes of ratiocination that I hadn't the wit to find out. But no! he is the Rubens of philosophy. Richness, abundance, boldness, color, but a sharp contour never, and never any perfection.' (Letters)

Again after the publication of the World and the Individual,

'The book consolidates an impression which I have never before got except by glimpses, that Royce's system is through and through to be classed as a light production.

It is a charming, romantic sketch; and it is only by handling it after the manner of a sketch, keeping it within sketch technique, that R. can make it very impressive. In the few places where he tries to grip and reason close, the effect is rather disastrous, to my mind. But I do think of Royce now in a more or less settled way as primarily a sketcher in philosophy. Of course the sketches of some masters are worth more than the finished pictures of others.' (Letters)

The tributes that each man paid to the other were genuine. James once said that two hundred years hence Harvard would be known as the place where Josiah Royce had taught. He said more than once that he had learned more from Peirce's writings than from those of any other man --except Royce.

In the preface of his Philosophy of Loyalty Royce paid special tribute to James. In that volume he was to be a severe critic of his friend's pragmatism, 'a polemic directed against certain opinions recently set forth by one of the dearest of my friends, and by one of the most loyal of men.' It would be out of place, Royce adds, to include such a polemic in a book on loyalty, were James and he not agreed that truth 'is the greater friend.' Then he adds this tribute:

'Had I not very early in my work as a student known Professor James, I doubt whether any poor book of mine would ever have been written, --least of all the present one. What I personally owe him, then, I most heartily and affectionately acknowledge. But if he and I do not see truth in the same light at present, we still do well, I think, as friends, each to speak his mind as we walk by the way, and then to wait until some other light shines for our eyes. I suppose that so to do is loyalty.'

To this James replied in a letter,

'I am quite overwhelmed by the oriental hyperbole of your page x to me-wards. That the world owes your books to me is too awfully gracious a saying! But I thank you for the beauty of spirit shown and for the honor. I am sorry you say we don't see truth in the same light, for the only thing we see differently is the Absolute, and surely such a trifle as that is not a thing for two gentlemen to be parted by. I believe that at the bottom of your heart we see things more alike than any pair of philosophers extant! I thank you anyhow from the bottom of mine. Affectionately yours, Wm. James.'

Royce's Phi Beta Kappa address at Harvard in June, 1911, was a memorial to James, who had died the preceding August. Royce said that there had been three American philosophers who had combined vigorous independence of thought with the insight to express the deep meaning of the American culture of their day. They were Jonathan Edwards, Emerson, and James. Less than a year after his death, Royce continued, James had a much wider influence abroad than Emerson ever had. James, who protested every form of classicism, had already become a classic.

'I am sure that James himself was very little conscious that he was indeed an especially representative American philosopher. He certainly had no ambition to vaunt himself as such....And he always very little knew how important he himself was, of what vast inarticulate social forces were finding in him their voice.' (p. 192-4)

Peirce could write in 1911, within a year after James' death,

'After studying William James on the intellectual side for half a century--for I was not acquainted with him as a boy--I must testify that I believe him to be, and always to have been during my acquaintance with him, about as perfect a lover of truth as it is possible for a man to be.. ..In speaking, then, of William James as I do, I am saying the most that I could of any man's intellectual morality; and with him this was but one of a whole diadem of virtues. Though it is entirely out of place in this connexion, and I must beg the reader's pardon for so wandering from the point under consideration, I really lack the self-command to repress my reflexions when I have once set down his name. Though his lectures were delightful, they not at all exhibited the man at his best. It was his unstudied common behaviour that did so by the perfection of his manners, in their perfect freedom from expressing flattery or anything else false or inappropriate to the occasion. He did not express himself very easily, because rhetoric was his antipathy and logic an inconvenience to him....

'His comprehension of men to the very core was most wonderful. Who, for example, could be of a nature so different from his as I? He so concrete, so living; I a mere table of contents, so abstract, a very snarl of twine. Yet in all my life I found scarce any soul that seemed to comprehend, naturally, (not) my concepts, but the mainspring of my life better than he did. He was even greater (in the) practice than in the theory of psychology.' (p. 204-5)

CROTHERS, Samuel Mc Chord. Among Friends. 1910.

'Do you know,' said James's 'Pragmatism,' 'That I sometimes think that we books take ourselves too seriously. Why should n't our readers slip away from us if they can? It shows their sense. Just because we are bound volumes and sport a table of contents, we think there must be something in us. Sometimes there is, but the relation between printed matter and mind is variable. There is a great deal of superstition in the assumption of our educational value. It is far from absolute. I shouldn't wonder if we were some day put out of business by the fifteen-cent magazines.'

Crothers puts these words into James' mouth. (p. 107)

CROTHERS, Samuel Mc Chord. The Dame School of Experience. and Other Papers. 1920.

Let me read you a bit from a recently published letter of William James to his colleague Palmer. They are the kind of men you want to understand, for you can't afford to do without them.

'The great event in my life recently has been reading Santayana's book. Although I absolutely reject the Platonism of it, I have literally squealed with delight at the imperturbable perfection with which the position is laid down page after page, and grunted with delight at such thickening of our Harvard atmosphere. If our students now could begin really to understand what Royce means with his voluntaristic-pluralistic monism; what Münsterberg means with his dualistic scientificism, and what Santayana means with his pessimistic Platonism, and what I mean by my crass pluralism, and what you mean by your ethical idealism, that there are so many religions, ways of fronting life, and worth fighting for, we should have a genuine philosophic universe at Harvard.' (p. 154-5)

CROTHERS, Samuel Mc Chord. Humanly Speaking. 1912.

But one need not go so far as Emerson to see the higher reaches of the American temperament. Perhaps in no one have they been revealed with more distinctness than in William James. There are those who consider it dispraise of a philosopher to suggest that his work has local color. However that may be, William James thought as an American as certainly as Plato thought as a Greek. His way of philosophizing was one that belonged to the land of his birth.

He was as distinctly American as was Daniel Boone. Daniel Boone was no renegade taking to the woods that he might relapse into savagery. He was a civilized man who preferred to be the maker of civilization rather than to be its victim. He preferred to blaze his own way through the forest. When he saw the smoke of a neighbor's chimney it was time for him to move on. So William James was led by instinct from the crowded highways to the dim border-lands of human experience. He preferred to dwell in the debatable lands. With a quizzical smile he listened to the dignitaries of philosophy. He found their completed systems too stuffy. He loved the wilderness of thought where shy wild things hide--half hopes, half realities. They are not quite true now,--but they may be by and by.

As other men are interested in the actual, so he was interested in the possible. The possibilities are not so highly finished as the facts that have been proved, but there are a great many more of them, and they are much more important. There are more things in the unexplored forest than in the clearing at its edge. Truth to him was not a field with metes and bounds. It was a continent awaiting settlement. First the bold pathfinders must adventure into it. Its vast spaces were infinitely inviting, its undeveloped resources were alluring. And not only did the path-finder interest him but the path-loser as well. But for his heedless audacity the work of exploration would languish. Was ever a philosopher so humorously tender to the intellectual vagabonds, the waifs and strays of the spiritual world!

Their reports of vague meanderings in the border-land were listened to without scorn. They might be ever so absent-minded and yet have stumbled upon something which wiser men had missed. No one was more keen to criticize the hard-and-fast dogmas of the wise and prudent or more willing to learn what might, by chance, have been revealed unto babes. The one thing he demanded was space. His universe must not be finished or inclosed. After a rational system had been formulated and declared to be the Whole, his first instinct was to get away from it. He was sure that there must be more outside than there was inside. 'The 'through-and-through' universe seems to suffocate me with its infallible, impeccable all-pervasiveness. Its necessity with no possibilities, its relations with no subjects, make me feel as if I had entered into a contract with no reserved rights.'

Formal philosophy seemed to him to be 'too buttoned-up and white-chokered and clean-shaven a thing to speak for the vast, slow-breathing, unconscious Kosmos with its dread abysses and its unknown tides. The freedom we want is not the freedom, with a string tied to its leg and warranted not to fly away, of that philosophy. Let it fly away, we say, from us. What then?'

To this American there must be a true democracy among the faculties of the mind. The logical understanding must not be allowed to put on priggish airs. The feelings have their rights also. 'They may be as prophetic and as anticipatory of truth as anything else we have.' There must be give and take; 'what hope is there of squaring and settling opinions unless Absolutism will hold parley on this common ground and admit that all philosophies are hypotheses, to which all our faculties, emotional as well as logical, help us, and the truest of which will in the final integration of things be found in possession of the men whose faculties on the whole had the best divining power?'

Do not those words give us a glimpse of the American mind in its natural working. Its genius is anticipatory. It is searching for a common ground on which all may meet. It puts its trust not in the thinker who can put his thoughts in the most neat form, but the man whose faculties have on the whole the best divining power.

To listen to William James was to experience an illogical elation--and to feel justified in it. He was an unsparing critic of things as they are, but his criticism left us in no mood of depression. Our interest is with things as they are going to be. The universe is growing. Let us grow with it. (p. 80-4)

CURTI, Merle and Others. A History of American Civilization. 1953.

As new generations accepted science, the cosmic problem became a less intense issue, and philosophers stressed social questions. Such intellectuals as William James and John Dewey felt it unnecessary to worry much about the problem of the universe. Man was a part of nature, and he should make the best of it. One should neither worship nor condemn science, but direct it toward social betterment--the goal of the eighteenth-century Enlightenment. In choosing social goals, humans did not need to deal in absolutes. Things were true, said William James, if they were pragmatic--that is, if they worked well. If an ideal proved illusory, or a process unfortunate, it was not really good or true; and something more practical must be found.

Both James and Dewey sought to apply their principles in socially useful ways, as in improving education. As a psychologist, James felt that an understanding of the learning process was basic to teaching procedures. This prepared the way for Dewey's emphasis on the child-centered school, in which subjects would be fitted to children's needs, rather than (as heretofore) the children to the subjects.

The pragmatism of James and Dewey was a logical outgrowth of New World experience. Americans had always been practical people. Practical they remained in the age of science. (p. 502-3)

DAY, Dorothy. The Long Loneliness. Autobiography. 1952.

One afternoon as I sat on the beach, I read a book of essays by William James and came on these lines:

'Poverty is indeed the strenuous life,--without brass bands or uniforms or hysteric popular applause or lies or circumlocutions; and when one sees the way in which wealth-getting enters as an ideal into the very bone and marrow of our generation, one wonders whether the revival of the belief that poverty is a worthy religious vocation may not be the transformation of military courage, and the spiritual reform which our time stands most in need of.

'Among us English-speaking peoples especially do the praises of poverty need once more to be boldly sung. We have grown literally afraid to be poor. We despise anyone who elects to be poor in order to simplify and save his inner life. If he does not join the general scramble, we deem him spiritless and lacking in ambition. We have lost the power even of imagining what the ancient realization of poverty could have meant; the liberation from material attachments, the unbribed soul, the manlier indifference, the paying our way by what we are and not by what we have, the right to fling away our life at any moment irresponsibly,--the more athletic trim, in short, the fighting shape.' (p. 118-9)

DEWEY, John. Art as Experience. 1934.

What William James wrote about religious experience might well have been written about the antecedents of acts of expression. 'A man's conscious wit and will are aiming at something only dimly and inaccurately imagined. Yet all the while the forces of mere organic ripening within him are going on to their own prefigured result, and his conscious strainings are letting loose subconscious allies behind the scenes which in their way work toward rearrangement, and the rearrangement toward which all these deeper forces tend is pretty surely definite, and definitely different from what he consciously conceives and determines. It may consequently be actually interfered with (jammed as it were) by his voluntary efforts slanting toward the true direction.' Hence, as he adds, 'When the new center of energy has been subconsciously incubated so long as to be just ready to burst into flower, 'hands off' is the only word for us; it must burst forth unaided.' (p. 72)

But instead of being esthetic, it will be of the kind described by William James: 'I remember seeing an English couple sit for more than an hour on a piercing February day in the Academy in Venice before the celebrated 'Assumption' by Titian; and when I, after being chased from room to room by the cold, concluded to get into the sunshine as fast as possible and let the pictures go, but before leaving drew reverently near to them to learn with what superior forms of susceptibility they might be endowed, all I overheard was the woman's voice murmuring: 'What a deprecatory expression her face wears! What self-abnegation! How unworthy she feels of the honor she is receiving.' (p. 91)

DEWEY, John. Characters and Events. Popular Essays in Social and Political Philosophy. - Edited by Joseph Ratner. Two volumes. 1929.

Chapter on William James as man and philosopher (p. 107-22 Volume I) from which the following selections are made.

In any case Mr. James has added a precious gift to American philosophic thought. However much or however little it may follow in the path that Mr. James struck out, his influence has made it more hospitable to fact, more sensitive to the complex difficulties of situations, less complacently content with merely schematic unities.

This brings me to what I should name as the second of Mr. James's gifts--his power of literary expression. This power strikes both the layman and the professional philosopher, and strikes them at first glance. I shall not be so stupid as to enlarge upon it, and, not being a literary critic, I shall not attempt to describe it. But it is pertinent to remark that in Mr. James's case not only was the style very much of the man, but it was also of the essence of his vision and of his thought. (p. 109)

Even this slight note of appreciation would be incomplete did I not speak of one of the most delightful traits of Mr. James's generous personality--his cordial attitude toward anything that struck him as genuine and individual in the efforts of any other writer, no matter how remote the thought from Mr. James's own. 'Philosophy,' Mr. James used to say, 'is a lonely bug;' and the solitary reflections of many comparatively unknown men in America have been relieved by a word of appreciative encouragement from Mr. James. (p. 110)

He was essentially the man of letters, but the man of letters who made literature the medium of communicating ideas for the sake of public instruction. Never didactic, he was always the teacher. Always brilliant in literary style, he never indulged in literature, for its own sake. If the common people read him gladly, it was not alone for a clearness and a picturesqueness that will long be the despair of other philosophers, but because of their instinctive recognition that here at least was a philosopher who believed in life and who believed in philosophy because of his belief in life. (p. 111-2)

I do not know whether there is any precedent for a man finding himself as a philosopher and presenting himself as a master after the age of sixty. Yet this is what happened in the case of Mr. James. It is characteristic of the man that one does not associate years with Mr. James, to say nothing of thinking of him as old. Even to say that he was sixty-eight is like mentioning some insignificant external fact, like his weight. His intellectual vitality, his openness of mind, his freedom from cant, his sympathetic insight into what other people were thinking of, his frank honesty, his spirit of adventure into the unknown, did more than keep him young; they made age an irrelevant matter. Whatever fate may have in store for Mr. James's pragmatism as a system, it is a great thing for university life and for higher culture in America that Mr. James united the wise maturity of rich experience with the ardor and enthusiasm of youth, and both with the gallantry of a free soul that was all his own.

America will justify herself as long as she breed those like William James; men who are thinkers and thinkers who are men. I love, indeed, to think that there is something profoundly American in his union of philosophy with life; in his honest acceptance of the facts of science joined to a hopeful outlook upon the future; in his courageous faith in our ability to shape the unknown future. When our country comes to itself in consciousness, when it transmutes into articulate ideas what are still obscure and blind strivings, two men, Emerson and William James, will, I think, stand out as the prophetic forerunners of the attained creed of values. (p. 116-7)

DEWEY, John. Experience and Nature. 1929.

Said William James, 'Many were the ideal prototypes of rational order: teleological and esthetic ties between things....as well as logical and mathematical relations. The most promising of these things at first were of course the richer ones, the more sentimental ones. The baldest and least promising were mathematical ones; but the history of the latter's application is a history of steadily advancing successes, while that of the sentimentally richer ones is one of relative sterility and failure. Take those aspects of phenomena which interest you as a human being most....and barren are all your results. Call the things of nature as much as you like by sentimental moral and esthetic names, no natural consequences follow from the naming....But when you give the things mathematical and mechanical names and call them so many solids in just such positions, describing just such paths with just such velocities, all is changed....Your 'things' realize the consequences of the names by which you classed them.' (Principles of Psychology) (p. 130-1)

DEWEY, John. How We Think. 1910.

In an often quoted passage, Mr. James has said: 'The baby, assailed by eyes, ears, nose, skin, and entrails at once, feels it all as one great blooming, buzzing confusion.' (Principles of Psychology) (p. 121)

DEWEY, John. Human Nature and Conduct. An Introduction to Social Psychology. 1922.

An immense debt is due William James for the mere title of his essay: The Moral Equivalents of War. It reveals with a flash of light the true psychology. (p. 112)

DEWEY, John. The Influence of Darwin on Philosophy and other Essays in Contemporary Thought. 1910.

Compare James, 'Continuous transition is one sort of conjunctive relation; and to be a radical empiricist means to hold fast to this conjunctive relation of all others, for this is the strategic point, the position through which, if a hole be made, all the corruptions of dialetics and all the metaphysical fictions pour into our philosophy.' (p. 222)

For, as Mr. James remarks, after disposing of the question of free-will by relegating it to the domain of the metaphysician:--'Metaphysics means only an unusually obstinate attempt to think clearly and consistently'--and clearness and consistency are not things to be put off beyond a certain point. (p. 246)

DEWEY, John. Problems of Men. 1946.

William James made a great contribution in the title of one of his essays, The Moral Equivalent of War. The very title conveys the point I am making. Certain basic needs and emotions are permanent. But they are capable of finding expression in ways that are radically different from the ways in which they now currently operate. (p. 188-9)

Dewey has a chapter (p. 379-95) entitled 'The Philosophy of William James' which gives intimate insight into James the man and James the philosopher. The following quotations are typical of the chapter as a whole.

The impression that I carry away from reading the record of the activities and connections of William James is that in respect to many-sidedness he is the most significant intellectual figure the United States has produced. There are those who surpass him in special points: Jefferson, for example, in depth and range of political thought, and Emerson in consistency and concentration of pure intellectual flame. But James seems all but unique in his variety of conjunctions with vital matters. (p. 379)

When James Ward complained, in a review, complimentary on the whole, of James' lack of systematic treatment of psychological topics, James replied admitting that he was too unsystematic, but added: 'In this case I permitted myself to remain so deliberately, on account of the strong aversion with which I am filled for the humbugging pretense of exactitude in the way of definition of terms and descriptions of states that has prevailed in psychological literature.' (p. 387)

A few years later, while still teaching physiology, he uttered golden words as to what philosophy and its teachings should be. 'Philosophic study means the habit of always seeing an alternative, of not taking the usual for granted, of making conventionalities fluid again, of imagining foreign states of mind...What doctrines students take from their teachers are of little consequence provided they catch from them the living philosophic attitude of mind, the independent, personal look at the data of life and the eagerness to harmonize them.' (p. 388)

I do not know any other modern thinker whose philosophy owes so little to dialectics and to tradition, to the second hand generally, and so much to predicaments that were vitally experienced; that in the large and proper sense of the word were moral in quality. In him the need for working out a viable philosophy was one with the need for finding a solution of matters that weighed heavily upon him as a living being. (p. 389)

Such allusions as he (William James) makes to churchly creeds and practices are, for him, unusually unsympathetic in tone. They are in the vein of the following:

'My training in natural science has completely disqualified me for sympathetic treatment of the ecclesiastic universe. It is impossible to believe that the same God established nature should also feel a special pride at being more immediately represented by clergymen than by laymen, or find a sweet sound in church-phraseology and intonation, or a sweet savour in the distinction between deacons, archdeacons and bishops. He is not of that prim temper.' (p. 390-1)

He asked in his diary, 'Can one with full knowledge and sincerely ever bring himself so to sympathize with the total process of the universe as heartily to assent to the evils that seem inherent in its details?...If so optimism is possible.' (p. 393-4)

The sincerely and depth of the personal experiences which gave to James the key to the genuine meaning of philosophical issues remained the ground-work of his teaching...They are to my mind the enduring source of what we still have to learn from even the more technical aspects of his thought. In his attempts at developed formulation he was subject to the limitations from which every independent thinker suffers. The more original the thought, the more it is betrayed by the fact that the only language in which original insight can be expressed is that formed by the very doctrines against which one is reacting. Hence it is doubly important that the students of the philosophy of James never lose hold upon its vital springs and source. (p. 395)

DEWEY, John. The School and Society. 1900.

Now we believe (to use the words of Mr. James) that the intellect, the sphere of sensations and ideas, is but a 'middle-department which we sometimes take to be final, failing to see, amidst the monstrous diversity of the length and complications of the cogitations which may fill it, that it can have but one essential function--the function of defining the direction which our activity, immediate or remote, shall take.' (p. 93)

DEWEY, John. The Public and its Problems. 1927.
The social consequences of habit have been stated once for all by James: 'Habit is the enormous fly-wheel of society, its most precious conservative influence. It alone is what keeps us within the bounds of ordinance, and saves the children of fortune from the uprisings of the poor. It alone prevents the hardest and most repulsive walks of life from being deserted by those brought up to tread therein. It keeps the fisherman and the deck-hand at sea through the winter; it holds the miner in his darkness, and nails the country-man to his log cabin and his lonely farm through all the months of snow; it protects us from invasion by the natives of the desert and the frozen zone. It dooms us all to fight out the battle of life upon the lines of our nurture or our early choice, and to make the best of a pursuit that disagrees, because there is no other for which we are fitted and it is too late to begin again. It keeps different social strata from mixing.' (p. 159-60)

DEWOLF, L. Harold. Theology of the Living Church. 1953.
As William James pointed out, the man of duty often 'speaks of conquering and overcoming his impulses and temptations. But the sluggard, the drunkard, the coward, never talk of their conduct in that way, or say they resist their energy, overcome their sobriety, conquer their courage, and so forth....And if a brief definition of ideal or moral action were required, none could be given which would better fit the appearances than this: It is action in the line of the greatest resistance.' (Psychology Briefer Course) (p. 190)
As William James pointed out in his famous Ingersoll Lecture, (Human Immortality) the functions of the body in relation to the human soul may be, as far as our evidence shows, transmissive rather than constructive. In other words, the scientific facts can all be accounted for on the supposition that the body serves as a means of communication, a mirror, imaging the soul to the outside world and the outside world to the soul. Determining the quality of the soul's communications, it affects profoundly the soul's own inner experience and the relevance of its responses to its environment so long as the soul remains within it. (p. 218)

DIMMET, Ernest. What We Live By. 1932.
William James says in his unique way: 'A deep and ineradicable instinct exists in each one of us preventing

him from regarding life as a mere joke or at best as an elegant comedy. No! life is an austere tragedy and what we relish the most in it is the bitterest it has to offer. On the scene of the world heroism, heroism alone, plays the great parts. In heroism, we realize it, lies hidden the mystery of life. A man is nothing if he is incapable of sacrifices. On the other hand, evident though the shortcomings of a man may be, if he is ready to give up his life for a cause, we forgive him everything. However inferior he may be to ourselves in other respects, if we cling to life while he throws it away like a flower, we bow to his superiority.'

Even the most debased individual, in his heart of hearts, knows that this is true. (p. 166)

DU BOIS, W. E. Burghardt. Dusk of Dawn. An Essay toward an Autobiography of a Race Concept. 1940.

So far my formal education had touched politics and religion, but on the whole had avoided economics. At Fisk a very definite attempt was made to see that we did not lose or question our Christian orthodoxy. At first the effort seemed to me entirely superfluous, since I had never questioned my religious upbringing. Its theory had presented no particular difficulties: God ruled the world, Christ loved it, and men did right, or tried to; otherwise they were rightly punished. But the book on 'Christian Evidences' which we were compelled to read, affronted my logic. It was to my mind, then and since, a cheap piece of special pleading. Our course in general philosophy under the serious and entirely lovable president was different. It opened vistas. It made me determine to go further in this probing for truth. Eventually it landed me squarely in the arms of William James of Harvard, for which God be praised. (p. 32-3)

The Harvard of 1888 was an extraordinary aggregation of great men. Not often since that day have so many distinguished teachers been together in one place and at one time in America. There were William James, the psychologist; Palmer in ethics; Royce and Santayana in philosophy; Shaler in geology and Hart in history. There were Francis Child, Charles Eliot Norton, Justin Winsor, and John Trowbridge; Goodwin, Taussig and Kittridge. The president was cold, precise but exceedingly just and efficient Charles William Eliot, while Oliver Wendell Holmes and James Russell Lowell were still alive and emeriti.

By good fortune, I was thrown into direct contact with many of these men. I was repeatedly a guest in the house of William James; he was my friend and guide to clear thinking; I was a member of the Philosophical Club and talked with Royce and Palmer; I sat in an upper room and read Kant's Critique with Santayana; Shaler invited a Southerner, who objected to sitting by me, out of his class; I became one of Hart's favorite pupils and was afterwards guided by him through my graduate course and started on my work in Germany. (p. 37-8)

At Harvard I started in with philosophy and then turned toward United States history and social problems. The turning was due to William James. He said to me, 'If you must study philosophy you will; but if you can turn aside into something else, do so. It is hard to earn a living with philosophy.' (p. 39)

In 1918 I had dinner in Boston with Glendower Evans, Margaret Deland and William James. It was small and intimate and thoroughly enjoyable. I would like to have known other and wider circles of America in this manner, but it was not easily possible. Only by something like accident and at long intervals did I emerge from my colored world. (p. 259-60)

DUCASSE, C. J. A Philosophical Scrutiny of Religion. 1953.

William James for instance, in describing his personal experience of the 1906 California earthquake--which occured after a friend expressed to him the hope that California would stage an earthquake during his visit there--speaks of 'certain peculiar ways in which my consciousness had taken in the phenomenon. These ways were quite spontaneous, and, so to speak, inevitable and irresistible.' First, he says, 'I personified the earthquake as a permanent individual entity...Animus and intent were never more present in any human action, nor did any human activity ever more definitely point back to a living agent as its source and origin. All whom I consulted on the point agreed as to this feature in their experience. 'It expressed intention,' 'It was vicious,' 'It was bent on destruction,' 'It wanted to show its power.' James adds that, although for science the earthquake is the disturbances themselves which occur in the earth's crust, nevertheless, for him at the time, the earthquake was 'the cause of the disturbances, and the perception of its living agent was irresistible. It had an overpowering dramatic convincingness.' And he remarks: 'I realize now better than ever how inevitable were men's earlier mythologic versions of such catastrophies.' (p. 320-1)

DUNHAM, Barrows. Giant in Chains. 1953.

The movement of thought which at first called itself 'pragmaticism,' and thereafter gracefully dropped the penultimate syllable, came into being as a revolt. 'Damn the Absolute!' cried William James to Josiah Royce as they sat on a stone fence, being photographed by James's daughter. The Hegelian armor, impenetrable by argument, could not even be scratched by mirthful profanity. But there was more than mirth in James's utterance, as Royce after years of friendly controversy, must have known very well. (p. 83-4)

William James is the only American philosopher--perhaps the only philosopher to whom one can apply the adjective 'adorable.' No thinker that I know of has contrived to be so genuinely and universally affectionate, so eager to find good in people, and so readily persuaded that he had found it. His latter years were filled with lame ducks and lost causes, and on behalf of both he risked his purse and his reputation.

James never allowed himself that exemption from social responsibility which is claimed by superior intellect when they are also inferior hearts. Once, when he was seeking help for a needy, seedy metaphysician, he wrote, 'Most men say of such a case, 'Is the man deserving?' Whereas the real point is, 'Does he need us?' One such philosopher will atone for a dozen Herbert Spencers. If pragmatism had been sustained by comparable spirits, its ethics would have been sublime.

Of all James's creations perhaps the most wonderful was that superb expository instrument, his prose style. Lithe and vivacious, it had that gift the lack of which Dr. Johnson lamented in the metaphysical poets: the gift of metaphors at once improbable and apt. No one but James, on seeing an enormous, fuzzy, and affectionate dog, could think of writing, 'He makes on me the impression of an angel hid in a cloud. He longs to do good.' No one but James would be likely to compare the Hegelian universe to a seaside hotel, where no one has any privacy. (p. 84-5)

For example, in July 1896, he delivered at the Chautauqua Assembly a series of lectures later published as Talks to Teachers. His impressions of Chautauqua are set down in letters to his wife; and anyone who is, as I am, old enough to remember the fearful solemnity of that institution will share James's feelings. Here are a few passages:

July 24. I've been meeting minds so earnest and helpless that it takes them half an hour to get from one idea to its immediately adjacent next neighbor and that with infinite creaking and groaning. And when they've got to the next idea, they lie down on it with their whole weight, like a cow on a doormat, so that you can get neither in nor out with them.

July 27. I took a lesson in roasting, in Delsarte, and I made with my own fair hands a beautiful loaf of graham bread with some rolls, long, flute-like, and delicious. I would have sent them to you by express, only it seemed unnecessary, since I can keep the family in bread easily after my return home.

August 2. I have seen more women and less beauty, heard more voices and less sweetness, perceived more earnestness and less triumph than I ever supposed possible. (p. 86)

In this spirit James sided with the Boers in their struggle against the British. He chanced, indeed, to be in England in 1900, when proposals were being made for a day of national humiliation and prayer. Arms having proved ineffectual, the God of Battles was to be invoked on behalf of empire. Says James:

'I wrote to the 'Times' to suggest, in my character of traveling American, that both sides to the controversy might be satisfied by a service arranged on principles suggested by the anecdote of the Montana settler who met a grizzly so formidable that he fell on his knees, saying, 'O Lord, I hain't never ask ye for help, and ain't agoin' to ask ye for none now. But for pity's sake, O Lord, don't help the bear.'

The Times ignored James's letter, and thus preserved the freedom of the press for Western civilization. (p. 88)

But, as we have seen, no inference from any one passage in James's writings will prove tenable for all the others. We owe it, then, to him (and to our own enlightenment) to quote one long paragraph, which shows how well he could understand the universe when it was a question of correcting someone else's mistakes. The paragraph describes Hegelian dialectic, not (in the Hegelian manner) as a relation of categories, but as a relation of events in a world of change; and it is the best such account that I know of.

'The impression that any naif person gets who plants himself innocently in the flux of things is that things are off their balance. Whatever equilibriums our finite experiences attain to are but provisional. Martinique volcanoes shatter our wordsworthian equilibrium with nature.

Accidents, either moral, mental, or physical, break up the slowly built-up equilibriums men reach in family life and in their civic and professional relations. Intellectual enigmas frustrate our scientific systems, and the ultimate cruelty of the universe upsets our religious attitudes and outlooks. Of no special system of good attained does the universe recognize the value as sacred. Down it tumbles, over it goes, to feed the ravenous appetite for destruction, of the larger system of history in which it stood for a moment as a landing-place and a stepping-stone. This dogging of everything by its negative, its fate, its undoing, this perpetual moving on to something future which shall supersede the present, this is the hegelian intuition of the essential provisionality, and consequent unreality, of everything empirical and finite. Take any concrete finite thing and try to hold it fast. You cannot, for so held, it proves not to be concrete at all, but an arbitrary extract or abstract which you have made from the remainder of empirical reality. The rest of things invades and over-flows both it and you together, and defeats your rash attempt. Any partial view whatever of the world tears the part out of its relations, leaves out some truth concerning it, is untrue of it, falsifies of it. The full truth about anything involves more than that thing. In the end nothing less than the whole of everything can be the truth of anything at all.' (Pluralistic Universe.) (p. 94-5)

DURANT, Will. Story of Philosophy. 1926.

In William James the voice and the speech and the very turn of phrase are American. He pounced eagerly upon such characteristic expressions as 'cash-value,' and 'results,' and 'profits,' in order to bring his thought within the ken of the 'man in the street;' he spoke not with the aristocratic reserve of a Santayana or a Henry James, but in a racy vernacular and with a force and directness, which made his philosophy of 'pragmatism' and 'reserve energy' the mental correlate of the 'practical' and 'strenuous' Roosevelt. And at the same time he phrased for the common man that 'tender-minded' trust in the essentials of the old theology which lives side by side, in the American soul, with the realistic spirit of commerce and finance, and with the tough persistent courage that turned a wilderness into the promised land. (p. 553-4)

'The true...is only the expedient in the way of our thinking, just as 'the right' is only the expedient in the way of our behaving. Expedient is almost any fashion; and expedient in the long run and on the whole, of course; for what meets expediently all the experiences in sight won't necessarily meet all further experiences equally satisfactorily....Truth is one species of good, and not, as is usually supposed, a category distinct from good, and co-ordinate with it. The true is the name of whatever proves itself to be good in the way of belief.' (Pragmatism) (p. 557-8)

'The history of philosophy is to a great extent that of a certain clash of human temperaments....Of whatever temperament a professional philosopher is, he tries, when philosophizing, to sink the fact of his temperament. Temperament is no conventionally recognized reason, so he urges impersonal reasons only for his conclusions. Yet his temperament really gives him a stronger bias than any of his more strictly objective premises.' (Pragmatism) (p. 559-60)

'If there be any life that it is really better that we should lead, and if there be any idea which, if believed in, would help us to lead that life, then it would be really better for us to believe in that idea, unless, indeed, belief in it incidentally clashed with other greater vital benefits.' (Pragmatism) (p. 562)

'I firmly disbelieve, myself, that our human experience is the highest form of experience extant in the universe. I believe rather that we stand in much the same relation to the whole of the universe as our canine and feline pets do to the whole of human life. They inhabit our drawing rooms and libraries. They take part in scenes of whose significance they have no inkling. They are merely tangent to curves of history, the beginnings and ends and forms of which pass wholly beyond their ken. So we are tangent to the wider life of things.' (Pragmatism) (p. 562)

EDEL, Leon. Henry James. The Untried Years. 1953.

Not all her letters had such a homely, gossipy air. She (William James' Mother) could smother Henry with maternal solicitude and denounce William, during his prolonged period of ill-health, as a too-articulate hypochondriac. 'The trouble with him is that he must express every fluctuation of feeling and especially every unfavorable sympton,' she wrote to Henry. 'He keeps his good looks, but whenever he speaks of himself, says he is no better. This I cannot believe to be the true state of the case, but his temperament is a morbidly hopeless one, and with this he has to contend all the time, as well as with his physical disability.' In a later letter she says: 'If, Dear Harry, you could only have imparted to him a few grains of your own blessed hopefulness, he would have been well long ago.' (p. 46)

William James many years later described Godkin as 'The towering influence in all thought concerning public affairs' and said that 'indirectly his influence has certainly been more pervasive than that of any other writer.' (p. 222)

Mary James, faced with two ailing sons, tended to exacerbate rather than ease the hidden tension in Quincy Street. She had for a long time openly showed her preference for Henry, the quiet one, and not a little hostility toward William, the active and effervescent. She might fuss over Henry's aches and pains to which the household was quite accustomed, but she considered Williams's sudden acquisition of analogous symptoms without indulgence and with a singular lack of sympathy. While showing maternal concern, she treated William as a self-centered hypochondriac. Her letters make quite free with his condition; he complains too much; he has a 'morbid sympathy' with every form of physical trouble; he worries excessively; 'he must express every fluctuation of feeling,' exclaims Mary James. (p. 244)

On December 5 William wrote to Henry, 'M. Temple was here for a week, a fortnight since. She was delightful in all respects, and although very thin, very cheerful.' He went on to describe her as 'a most honest little phenomenon' and to say that she was 'more devoid of 'meaness' of anything petty in her character, than anyone I know, perhaps, either male or female.' (p. 317)

EDMAN, Irwin. Four Ways of Philosophy. 1937.

'The philosopher and the lady-killer,' William James remarks somewhere in his Psychology, 'cannot keep house in the same tenement of clay.' (p. 288)

EDMAN, Irwin. Human Traits and Their Social Significance. 1920.

They are irresistible impulses to do just such-and-such particular things in such-and-such particular ways when confronted with just such-and-such particular situations. In the well-known words of James:

'The cat runs after the mouse, runs or shows fight before the dog, avoids falling from walls and trees, shuns fire and water, etc., not because he has any notion either of life or death, or of self-preservation. He has probably attained to no one of these conceptions in such a way as to react definitely upon it. He acts in each case separately, and simply because he cannot help it; being so framed that when that particular running thing called a mouse appears in his field of vision he must pursue; that when that particular barking and obstreperous thing called a dog appears there he must retire, if at a distince, and scratch if close by; that he must withdraw his feet from water, and his face from flame.' (Principles of Psychology) (p. 2)

In the famous words of James:

'The great thing, then, in all education, is to make our nervous system our ally instead of our enemy. It is to fund and capitalize our acquisitions, and live at ease upon the interest of the fund. For this we must make automatic and habitual, as early as possible, as many useful actions as we can, and guard against the growing into ways that are likely to be disadvantageous to us, as we would guard against the plague. The more of the details of our daily life we can hand over to the effortless custody of automatism, the more our higher powers of mind will be set free for their own proper work. There is no more miserable human being than one in whom nothing is habitual but indecision, and for whom the lighting of every cigar, the drinking of every cup, the time of rising and going to bed every day, and the beginning of every bit of work, are subjects of express volitional deliberation. Full half the time of such a man goes to the deciding, or regretting, of matters which ought to be so ingrained in him as practically not to exist for his consciousness at all. If there be such daily duties not yet engrained in any one of my readers, let him begin this very hour to set the matter right.' (Principles of Psychology) (p. 33-4)

'We all of us have a definite routine manner of performing certain daily offices connected with the toilet, with the opening and shutting of familiar cupboards, and the like. Our lower centers know the order of these movements, and show their knowledge by their 'surprise' if the objects are altered so as to oblige the movement to be made in a different way. But our higher thought centers know hardly anything about the matter. Few men can tell offhand which sock, shoe, or trousers-leg they put on first. They must first mentally rehearse the act; and even that is often insufficient--the act must be performed. So of the questions, Which valve of my double door opens first? Which way does my door swing? etc. I cannot tell the answer; yet my hand never makes a mistake. No one can describe the order in which he brushes his hair or teeth; yet it is likely that the order is a pretty fixed one in all of us.' (Principles of Psychology) (p. 34-5)

'The hell to be endured hereafter, of which theology tells, is no worse than the hell we make for ourselves in this world by habitually fashioning our characters in the wrong way. Could the young but realize how soon they will become mere walking bundles of habits, they would give more heed to their conduct while in the plastic state. We are spinning our own fates, good or evil, and never to be undone. Every smallest stroke of virtue or of vice leaves its never-so-little scar. The drunken Rip Van Winkle, in Jefferson's play, excuses himself for every fresh dereliction by saying, 'I won't count this time!' Well, he may not count it, and a kind Heaven may not count it, but it is being counted none the less. Down among his nerve cells and fibres, the molecules are counting it, registering and storing it up to be used against him when the next temptation comes. Nothing we ever do is, in strict scientific literalness, wiped out.' (Principles of Psychology) (p. 36-7)

'What kind of an emotion of fear would be left if the feeling neither of quickened heart-beats nor of shallow breathing, neither of trembling lips nor of weakened limbs, neither of goose-flesh nor of visceral stirrings, were present, it is impossible for me to think. Can anyone fancy the state of rage, and picture no ebullition in the chest, no flushing of the face, no dilation of the nostrils, no clenching of the teeth, no impulse to vigorous action, but in their stead limp muscles, calm breathing, and a placid face? The present writer, for one, certainly cannot. The rage is as completely evaporated as the sensations of its so-called manifestations, and the only thing that can possibly be supposed to take its place is some cold blooded and dispassionate judicial sentence, confined entirely to the intellectual realm, to the effect that a certain person or persons merit chastisement for their sins. In like manner of grief; what would it be without its tears, its sobs, its suffocation of the heart, its pang in the breastbone? A feelingless cognition that certain circumstances are deplorable, and nothing more.' (Principles of Psychology) (p. 41)

'Many Bostonians, crede experto (and inhabitants of other cities, too, I fear), would be happier men and women to-day if they could once for all abandon the notion of keeping up a Musical Self and without shame let people hear them call a symphony a nuisance.' (Principles of

Psychology) (p. 101)

William James in a famous essay recognizes clearly the enormous value of the fighting instinct in stimulating action to an intense effectiveness exhibited under no other circumstances, and proposes a 'moral equivalent for war' --an army devoted to constructive enterprises, reclaiming the waste places of the land, warring against poverty and disease and the like. (Memories and Studies) (p. 114-15)

'In the daily lives of most men and women, fear plays a greater part than hope. It is not so that life should be lived.' (Principles of Psychology) (p. 128)

But as James says suggestively:

'Love your enemies! Mark you not simply those who do not happen to be your friends, but your enemies, your positive and active enemies. Either this is a mere Oriental hyperbole, a bit of verbal extravagance, meaning only that we should, in so far as we can, abate our animosities, or else it is sincere and literal. Outside of certain cases of intimate individual relation, it seldom has been taken literally. Yet it makes one ask the question: Can there in general be a level of emotion so unifying, so obliterative of differences between man and man, that even enemity may come, to be an irrelevant circumstance and fail to inhibit the friendlier interests aroused. If positive well-wishing could attain so supreme a degree of excitement, those who were swayed by it might well seem superhuman beings. Their life would be morally discrete from the lives of other men, and there is no saying...what the effects might be: they might conceivably transform the world.' (Varieties of Religious Experience) (p. 136-7)

A man cannot be all things at once; 'the philosopher and the lady-killer,' as James merrily remarks, 'could not very well keep house in the same tenement of clay.' (p. 155)

'The emotions themselves of self-satisfaction and abasement are of a unique sort...each has its own peculiar physiognomical expression. In self-satisfaction the extensor muscles are innervated, the eye is strong and glorious, the gait rolling and elastic, the nostril dilated, and a peculiar smile plays upon the lips. This complex of symptoms is seen in an exquisite way in lunatic asylums, which always contain some patients who are literally mad with conceit, and whose fatuous expression and absurdly strutting or swaggering gait is in tragic contrast with their lack of any valuable personal quality. It is in these same castles of despair that we find the strongest examples of the opposite physiognomy, in good people who think they have committed 'the unpardonable sin' and are lost forever, who crouch and cringe and slink from notice, and are unable to speak aloud or look us in the eye.. We ourselves know how the barometer of our self-esteem and confidence rises and falls from one day to another through causes that seem to be visceral and organic rather than rational, and which certainly answer to no corresponding variations in the esteem in which we are held by our friends.' (Principles of Psychology) (p. 160)

'The magnanimity of these expansive natures is often touching indeed. Such persons can feel a sort of delicate rapture in thinking that, however sick, ill-favored, mean-conditioned, and generally forsaken they may be, they are yet integral parts of the whole of this brave world, have a fellow's share in the strength of the dairy horses, the happiness of the young people, the wisdom of the wise ones, and are not altogether without part or lot in the good fortune of the Vanderbilts and the Hohenzollerns themselves.' (Principles of Psychology) (p. 161)

'There is a whole race of beings-to-day whose passion is to keep their names in the newspapers, no matter under what heading, 'arrivals and departures,' 'personal paragraphs,' 'interviews'--gossip, even scandal will suit them if nothing better is to be had. Guiteau, Garfields' assassin, is an example of the extremity to which this craving for notoriety may go in a pathological case. The newspapers bounded his mental horizon; and in the poor wretch's prayer on the scaffold, one of the most heartfelt expressions was: 'The newspaper press of this land has a big bill to settle with thee, O Lord!' (Principles of Psychology) (p. 165)

'In one sense at least, the personal religion will prove itself more fundamental than either theology or ecclesiasticism. Churches when once established live at second hand upon tradition, but the founders of every Church owed their power originally to the fact of their direct personal communion with the divine. Not only the superhuman founders, the Christ, the Buddha, Mahomet, but all the originators of Christian sects have been in this case; so personal religion should still seem the primordial thing, even to those who esteem it incomplete.' (Varieties of Religious Experience) (p. 280)

'It is,' writes William James, 'an open question whether mystic states may not be superior points of view, windows through which the mind locks out on a more extensive and inclusive world.' (p. 289)

'The lugubrious picture of an utterly-meaningless world, blind, purposeless, and heartless, which materialistic science reveals, is sufficient to wreck the equanimity of a sensitive and thoughtful mind.

'That is the sting of it, that in the vast drifting of the cosmic weather, though many a jewelled shore appears, and many an enchanted cloudbank floats away, long lingering ere it be dissolved--even as our world now lingers for our joy--yet when these transient products are gone, nothing, absolutely nothing remains. Dead and gone are they, gone utterly from the very sphere and room of being. Without an echo, without a memory; without an influence on aught that may come after, to make it care for similar ideals. This utter wreck and tragedy is of the essence of scientific materialism, as at present understood.' (Pragmatism) (p. 291-2)

'A world with a God in it to say the last word may indeed burn up or freeze, but we then think of Him as still mindful of the old ideals, and sure to bring them elsewhere to fruition; so that where He is, tragedy is only provisional and partial, and shipwreck and dissolution not the absolutely final thing.' (Pragmatism) (p. 292)

'Whoever not only says but feels, 'God's will be done' is mailed against every weakness; and the whole historic array of martyrs, missionaries and religious reformers is there to prove the tranquil-mindedness, under naturally agitating or distressing circumstances, which self-surrender brings.' (Varieties of Religious Experience) (p. 293)

James quotes a reminiscence of Father Gratry, a Catholic philosopher:

...'All day long without respite I suffered an incurable and intolerable desolation, verging on despair. I thought myself, in fact, rejected by God, lost, damned! I felt something like suffering of hell. Before that I had never even thought of hell...Now and all at once, I suffered in a measure what is suffered there.' (Varieties of Religious Experience) (p. 302)

'Man is still moved by the same emotions, sensations, needs, and desires which have, from the dawn of history, provoked in him a sense of his relationships with the divine. There comes to nearly all individuals at some time, not without rapture, a sudden awareness of divinity.

'It is the terror and beauty of phenomena, the 'promise' of the dawn and of the rainbow, the 'voice' of the thunder, the 'gentleness' of the summer rain, the 'sublimity' of the stars, and not the physical laws which these things follow, by which the religious mind continues to be most impressed; and just as of yore, the devout man tells you that in the solitude of his room or of the fields he still feels the divine presence, that inflowing of help comes in reply to his prayers, and that sacrifices to this unseen reality fill him with security and peace.' (Varieties of Religious Experience) (p. 320-1)

JAMES, Henry. Charles W. Eliot. Two volumes. 1930.

A product of the old order once exclaimed to William James: 'I can't understand your philosophy. When I studied philosophy, I could understand it. We used to commit it to memory.' That was largely if not literally true of all teaching in the moral and political sciences in American colleges. (v. 1. p. 209)

There is a letter of William James's which describes the graduating exercises of the Class of '67 with Louis Agassiz on the platform. 'His look of mingled wonder, pain, and disgust at the flimsy badness of the dissertations,' says the letter, 'was amusing to observe.' The examination was formal but not formidable; in fact, rather like the mad tea-party in 'Alice in Wonderland.' (v. 1. p. 275)

William James wrote to his wife, after visiting the Continental universities in 1882: 'The total lesson of what I've done in the past month is to make me quieter with my home-lot and readier to believe that it is one of the chosen places of the Earth. Certainly the instruction and facilities at our university are on the whole superior to anything I have seen....We only lack abdominal depth of temperament and the power to sit for an hour over a single pot of beer without being able to tell at the end of it what we've been thinking about....The first thing to do is to establish in Cambridge a genuine German plebeian Kneipe club, to which all instructors and picked students shall be admitted. If that succeeds, we shall be perfect, especially if we talk therein with deeper voices.' (v. 2. p. 25)

Dear Dr. James, --You carry me back farther than anybody else--to 1861. I can see that I then had some of the same qualities and powers that I have now; but I had little range of observation, no breadth of experience, and small capacity for sympathetic imagination. You and I have, I think, the same fundamental reason for being moderately content with the years that are past:--We have a sense of growth and of increased capacity for useful service. We find our lives enriched and amplified from year to year. So long as that enlarging process goes on, we shall be content. If it stops suddenly we shall be content to that date. (v. 2. p. 86-7)

Your coming to the University and your career as a teacher and writer have been among my most solid grounds of satisfaction. So your words of cheer are of especial value to me. (To William James from Charles W. Eliot.) (v. 2. p. 87)

ERSKINE, John. Democracy and Ideals. 1920.

The tendency to set character above everything else, this sentimentality if I may call it so frankly, is not peculiar to any one race-strain in the total American complex; it characterizes all of us. Walt Whitman was truly American in his expression of diffuse and indiscriminate amiability. William James is truly American in putting an optimistic mood at the service of all his countrymen--an amiable project for a modern philosopher to devote himself to. (p. 61)

FINKELSTEIN, Louis. American Spiritual Autobiographies. Fifteen Self Portraits. 1948.

M. L. Wilson.

Not long after I had discussed with a friend this matter of my conflict between boyhood religious conceptions and science, my friend suggested I read William James' books. The first one I read was The Varieties of Religious Experience. This book, particularly the last chapter, made a very great impression on me. I read a number of James' other books in quick succession. At that time I had had no courses in philosophy, nor had I read in that field. Reading these books, therefore, was no introduction to philosophy and its problems. Out of this experience there came to be a reconciliation between what I called science and my childhood religious matrix. The idea of a pluralistic, open universe appealed to me. If I could not tie everything together in a consistent, unified whole, I need not have an inferiority complex when James couldn't do it either. Such ideas as a limited, struggling God--the reality of religious experiences--the justification of God as a warm cosmic companion, as God was to my mother, could and did meet a profound human need in some personalities. The possibilities of the science of religion--comparative religion--and the possibilities of deeper understanding of the psychological processes involved in religious experience, seemed to me very plausible. Yet I agreed with James that a science of religion would not be religion itself. I was greatly impressed with James' meliorism and his explanation of the 'problem of evil.' This reading of James' book at a time when my mind was in conflict, in what might be called religion versus science, and before I had read much in the field of philosophy or psychology, gave me almost what William James called the experience of 'conversion.' I could almost but not quite say that I was a convert to the religion of William James. (p. 13-4)

FOSDICK, Harry Emerson. Adventurous Religion and Other Essays. 1926.

As Professor William James put it, a man dealing with his own inward life at its best 'becomes conscious that this higher part is conterminous and continuous with a MORE of the same quality, which is operative in the universe outside of him, and which he can keep in working touch with, and in a fashion get on board of and save himself when all his lower being has gone to pieces in the wreck.' (p. 77)

FOSDICK, Harry Emerson. As I see Religion. 1932.

So William James, when asked once to define spirituality, hesitated and finally said that he was not sure that he could define the quality but he could point out a spiritual personality--Phillips Brooks. William James understood religion; he knew its native speech. It never wins the world by general propositions but by concrete embodiments of spiritual beauty. It knows that Jesus' religion is Jesus. (p. 148)

FOSDICK, Harry Emerson. A Faith for Tough Times. 1952.

As William James wrote: 'If this life be not a real fight, in which something is eternally gained for the universe by success, it is no better than a game of private theatricals from which one may withdraw at will. But it feels like a real fight.' (p. 34)

No wonder that William James, impatient with the worship of size, exclaimed: 'As for me, my bed is made. I am against bigness and greatness in all their forms, and with the invisible, molecular moral forces that work from individual to individual, stealing in through the crannies of the world like so many soft rootlets, or like the capillary oozing of water, and yet rending the hardest monuments of man's pride, if you give them time. (Letters) (p. 50-1)

FOSDICK, Harry Emerson. A Great Time to be Alive.

Sermons on Christianity in Wartime. 1944.

William James of Harvard said once: 'The difference between a good man and a bad one is the choice of the cause.' What do we belong to so loyally that though everything goes wrong, and the cross looms and the triumph of what we believe in and want seems indefinitely postponed, still we do not give in? In our democracies now we need that spirit--a powerful swing of emphasis to balance rights with duties, and never more so than after the war is won. Then we shall confront duties--immense, worldwide in their significance--upon whose recognition and discharge the future of humanity for centuries depend. (p. 224)

FOSDICK, Harry Emerson. On Being a Real Person. 1943.

The process by which real personality is thus attained is inward and spiritual. No environmental changes by themselves can so push a personality together as to bring this satisfying wholeness within. The achievement of integration carries one deep into the core of selfhood and suggests some such experience as William James described: 'The process, gradual or sudden, by which a self hitherto divided, and consciously wrong, inferior and unhappy, becomes unified and consciously right superior and happy, in consequence of its firmer hold upon religious realities.' (p. 47-8)

William James was writing as a good psychologist when he said: 'Love your enemies!' Mark you, not simply those who happen not to be your friends, but your enemies, your positive and active enemies. Either this is a mere Oriental hyperbole, a bit of verbal extravagance, meaning only that we should, as far as we can, abate our animosities, or else it is sincere and literal. Outside of certain cases of intimate individual relation, it seldom has been taken literally. Yet it makes one ask the question: Can there in general be a level of emotion so unifying, so obliterative of differences between man and man, that even enmity may come to be an irrelevant circumstance and fail to inhibit the friendlier interests aroused? If positive well-wishing could attain so supreme a degree of excitement, those who were swayed by it might well seem superhuman beings. Their life would be morally discrete from the life of other men, and there is no saying..what the effects might be: they might conceivably transform the world.' (p. 168)

As William James put it: 'We have in the fact that the conscious person is continuous with a wider self through which saving experiences come, a positive content of religious experience which, it seems to me, is literally and objectively true as far as it goes...God is the natural appellation, for us Christians at least, for the supreme reality, so I will call this higher part of the universe by the name of God. We and God have business with each other; and in opening ourselves to his influence our deepest destiny is fulfilled.' (p. 214)

As William James said, 'The philosopher and the lady-killer could not well keep house in the same tenement of clay.' (p. 226)

'Every sort of energy and endurance,' said William James, 'of courage and capacity for handling life's evils, is set free in those who have religious faith.' (p. 245)

FOSDICK, Harry Emerson. On Being Fit to Live With. 1946.

There must be something here that lasts, some strand of abiding unity upon which the changes are all strung; else, as William James said, this whole creation were no better than a silly moving picture film that might as well be run backward as forward, because it means nothing either way. We must not believe in a senseless universe like that if we can help it. Our Easter thought is serious business. We are pleading for the presence somewhere of something that abides. (p. 212)

FOSDICK, Harry Emerson. The Secret of Victorious Living. 1934.

I have been surprised before by biographies of men I thought I knew but never more so than when in letters of William James I ran on phrases like this, 'All last winter, for instance, when I was on the continual verge of suicide.' My word! That from William James! So, his radiance was a victory. He did not find life worth living; he made it worth living. When in his essay on 'Is Life Worth Living?' he says, 'My final appeal is to nothing more recondite than religious faith,' he meant that. That was William James, the man, rediscovering after nearly two thousand years what Paul found, that if all things are to work together for good in any man's life he must have within him a spiritual contribution of personal religion, of creative faith. (p. 5)

Another of this family is the idea that human life as a whole is a great adventure, with open doors ahead of it. In all our best hours it feels that way. As William James put it, life 'feels like a real fight,--as if there were something really wild in the universe which we, with all our idealities and faithfulnesses, are needed to redeem.' In the nature of the case that cannot be proved. How can we prove a victory before it is won? (p. 242)

FOSDICK, Harry Emerson. Successful Christian Living. Sermons on Christianity Today. 1937.

William James describes a man in a passion, the turbulence of cupidity or lust or temper noisy within him, in a fit mood to ruin himself withal, and fighting off all listening to the cool, calm voices of reasonable ideas. Concerning this familiar situation James says, 'Passion's cue accordingly is always and everywhere to prevent their still small voice from being heard at all,' to which he adds, 'The strong-willed man...is the man who hears the still small voice unflinchingly.' (p. 248)

FOSDICK, Harry Emerson. The Three Meanings, Prayer, Faith, Service. 1949.

The definition of man as a 'praying animal,' while not comprehensive, is certainly correct. The culture of prayer, therefore, is not importing an alien, but is training a native citizen of the soul. Professor William James of Harvard was thinking of this when he wrote: 'We hear in these days of scientific enlightenment a great deal of discussion about the efficacy of prayer; and many reasons are given us why we should not pray, whilst others are given us why we should. But in all this very little is said of the reason why we do pray...The reason why we do pray is simply that we cannot help praying.' Prayer. (p. 9)

A certain trustful openheartedness, a willingness to venture in personal relationship and in attempts at service is essential to a rich and fruitful life. And what is true of man's relationship with man is true of man's relationship with God. So Prof. William James, of Harvard, states the case: 'Just as a man who in a company of gentlemen made no advances, asked a warrant for every concession, and believed no one's word without proof, would cut himself off by such churlishness from all the social rewards that a more trusting spirit would earn--so here, one should shut himself up in snarling logicality and try to make the gods extort his recognition willy-nilly, or not get it at all, might cut himself off forever from his only opportunity of making the gods acquaintance.' Wherever in life great spiritual values await man's appropriation, only faith can appropriate them. Faith. (p. 9)

FRANK, Jerome. Law and the Modern Mind. 1930.

William James' career is suggestive. As a young man 'a sense of the insecurity of life,' a consciousness of a 'pit of insecurity beneath the surface of life,' so obsessed him that he was seized with that morbid melancholy 'Which takes the form of panic fear' and reached the point of suicidal mania. He might, he reports, have gone insane, if he had not clung to scripture-texts such as 'The Eternal God is my refuge.' Suddenly he was cured. And the cure consisted in a sudden shift to a positive delight in the hazardous, incalcuable character of life. Life's very insecurity became its most inviting aspect. He came to enjoy an attitude which 'involves an element of active tension, of holding my own, as it were, and trusting outward things to perform their part so as to make it a full harmony, but without any guaranty that they will. Make it a guaranty--and the attitude immediately becomes to my consciousness stagnant and stingless. Take away the guaranty, and I feel...a sort of deep enthusiastic bliss, of utter willingness to do and suffer anything'... This sudden shift from panic fear of insecurity to a deep enthusiastic bliss in the absence of security marked for James the advent of emotional adulthood. He then first began to play a man's part. (p. 17-8)

'You know,' wrote William James, 'how men have always hankered after magic and you know what a great part in magic words have always played. If you have his name or the formula or incantation that binds him, you can control the spirit, genie, afrite or whatever the power may be...So the universe has always appeared to the natural mind as a kind of enigma of which the key must be sought in the shape of some eliminating or power-bringing word or name. That word means the universe's principle, and to possess it is after a fashion to possess the universe itself. 'God,' 'Matter,' 'Reason,' 'Absolute,' 'Energy,' are so many solving names. You can rest when you have them. You are at the end of your metaphysical quest.' (p. 60)

William James relates that, when a young man, he was assisting a professor who was giving a popular lecture on the physiology of the heart for which purpose he was employing a turtle's heart supporting an index-straw which threw a moving shadow, greatly enlarged, upon the screen, while the heart pulsated. The lecturer said that, when certain nerves were stimulated, they would act in certain ways which he described. To James's horror the turtle's heart refused to function as the lecturer had predicted. 'There was no time for deliberation,' says James, 'so, with my forefinger under a part of the straw that cast no shadow, I found myself impulsively and automatically imitating the rythmical movements which my colleague had prophesied the heart would undergo. I kept the experiment from failing; and...established in the audience the true view of the subject. The heart's failure would have been misunderstood by the audience and given the lie to the lecturer.' (p. 135-6)

FRANK, Waldo. Our America. 1919.

Any life is better than the dead. So in the benign hands of William James, Pragmatism became a tool of liberation from the old stocks, choking our colleges, of theological and metaphysical doctrine. John Dewey turned it, by his genius, into a stupendous lever that pried open the stuffy arcana of Education, let in fresh air, let in the reality of an intense American world. (p. 27)

GLADDEN, Washington. Live and Learn. 1914.

The soul that habitually and forever seeks in all its career the lines of least resistance goes by that road to its doom. That is not the path in which manhood is won; it is the path in which it is always lost. 'If a brief definition of ideal or moral action were required,' says Professor James, 'none could be given which would better fit the appearances than this: It is action in the line of the greatest resistance.' (p. 129)

'When a dreadful object is presented,' says Professor James again, 'or when life as a whole turns up its dark abysses to our view, then the worthless ones among us lose their hold on the situation altogether, and either escape from its difficulties by averting their attention, or, if they cannot do that, collapse into yielding masses of plaintiveness and fear. The effort required in facing and consenting to such objects it is beyond their power to make. But the heroic mind does differently. To it, too, the objects are sinister and dreadful--unwelcome, incompatible with wished-for things. But it can face them, if necessary, without for that losing its hold upon the rest of life. The world thus finds in the heroic man its worthy match and mate; and the effort which he is able to put forth to hold himself erect and keep his heart unshaken is the direct measure of his worth and function in the game of human life. He can stand this Universe. He can meet it and keep up his faith in it in presence of those same features which lay his weaker brethren low....And hereby he makes himself one of the masters and the lords of life. He must be counted with henceforth; he forms a part of human destiny.' (p. 130-1)

GODKIN, Edwin Lawrence. Life and Letters. Edited by Rollo Ogden. Two Volumes. 1907.

'To my generation, his was certainly the towering influence in all thought concerning public affairs, and indirectly his influence has certainly been more pervasive than that of any other writer of the generation, for he influenced other writers who never quoted him, and determined the whole current of discussion.' This estimate of Mr. Godkin's work in the Nation, and afterwards in the Evening Post as well, is from the competent pen of Professor William James. (v. 1. p. 221)

GOSSE, Edmund. Aspects and Impressions. 1922.

Fortunately, in 1913, the desire to place some particulars of the career of his marvellous brother William in the setting of his 'immediate native and domestic air,' led Henry James to contemplate, with minuteness, the fading memories of his own childhood. Starting with a biographical study of William James, he found it impossible to treat the family development at all adequately without extending the survey to his own growth as well, and thus, at the age of seventy, Henry became for the first time, and almost unconsciously, an autobiographer. (p. 19)

HALL, James Norman. My Island Home. An Autobiography. 1952.

We moved on and halted, moved on again, stumbled into ditches to make way for outgoing traffic, and moved on once more. Because of the enforced halts we would lose touch with the troops ahead and have to march at the double in order to catch up. It was weary work, to say the least. During this night march I discovered the truth of a statement I had read while at college in a textbook by William James. He said in effect that men have layers of nervous energy which they are rarely called upon to use, but which are assets of great value in times of heavy strain. I proved the truth of this, not once but at various times later when I thought I had all but reached the end of my resources of strength. (p. 147)

HAND, Learned. The Spirit of Liberty. Collected, and with an Introduction and Notes, by Irving Dilliard. 1952.

Jefferson is dead; time has disproved his forecasts; the society which he strove to preserve is gone to chaos and black night, as much as the empire of Genghis Khan; what has succeeded he would disown as any get of his. Yet back of the form there is still the substance, the possibility of the individual expression of life on the terms of him who has to live it. The victory is not all Hamilton's, nor can it be unless we are all to be checked as anonymous members regulated by some bureaucratic machine, impersonal, inflexible, a Chronos to devour us, its children. We shall not succeed by any attempt to put the old wine in new bottles; liberty is an essence so volatile that it will escape any vial however corked. It rests in the hearts of men, in the belief that knowledge is hard to get, that man must break through again and again the thin crust on which he walks, that the certainties of today may become the superstitions of tomorrow, that we have no warrant of assurance save by everlasting readiness to test and test again. William James was its great American apostle in modern times; we shall do well to remember him. (p. 82)

At times I cannot help recalling a saying of William James about certain passages of Hegel: that they were no doubt written with a passion of rationality; but that one cannot help wondering whether to the reader they have any significance save that the words are strung together with syntactical correctness. (p. 213)

As William James says somewhere: if a frog jumps at a piece of red flannel on a hook, that is hard on that particular frog, but red patches do often announce the presence of edibles, and frogs who jump at red are more likely to be fed than to be hooked. Life is made up of constant calls to action, and we seldom have time for more than hastily contrived answers; to follow one's hunch is usually better than lying doggo, and rough generalizations that have worked well in the past easily take on the authority of universals. (p. 258)

HIBBEN, John Grier. A Defense of Prejudice and Other Essays. 1912.

Professor James, the most brilliant apostle of this creed of change, insists that 'we must be prepared to find false to-morrow what is true to-day.' This is a statement which in a restricted sense is true, and which admits of an exceedingly wide range of illustration. (p. 146)

HIBBEN, John Grier. The Problems of Philosophy. 1898.

As an illustration of this theory, the following experience of Professor James will no doubt prove of interest: 'It is difficult for me to detect in mental activity any purely spiritual element at all. Whenever my introspective glance succeeds in turning around quickly enough to catch one of these manifestations of spontaneity in the act, all it can ever feel distinctly is some bodily process, for the most part taking place within the head.' (p. 82-3)

HILTNER, Seward. The New Concern of Recent Years. 1953. (In Maves, Paul B. Editor. The Church and Mental Health.)

It is true that William James, in the late years of the last century and the early ones of this, performed an immensely important function not only for the psychological study of religion but for the sciences of man generally. His own contributions in a technical sense were immense. But even more important historically was the way in which he showed that scientific study of man would not destroy any basic meaning and significance which was inherent in what was being studied. No one else in our century has done half so much to help us see this truth as James. (p. 63)

HOCKING, William E. The Meaning of God in Human Experience: A Philosophic Study of Religion. 1922.

'I believe that the logical reason of man operates in this field of divinity exactly as it has always operated in love, or in patriotism, or in any other of the wider affairs of life in which our passions or our mystical intuitions fix our beliefs beforehand. It finds arguments for our convictions, for indeed it has to find them. It amplifies and defines our faith, and dignifies it, and lends it words and plausibility. It hardly ever engenders it; it cannot now secure it.' (Varieties of Religious Experience) (p. 38)

No better summary of the failure of the alleged Absolute to make connections with human needs can be given than these words of William James: 'The absolute is useless for deductive purposes. It gives us absolute safety if you will, but it is compatible with every relative danger. Whatever the details of experience may prove to be, after the fact of them the absolute will adopt them. It is an hypothesis which functions retrospectively only, not prospectively.' (Pluralistic Universe) (p. 184)

James notes 'the remarkable fact that sufferings and hardships do not as a rule abate the love of life; they seem on the contrary to give it a keener zest.' (p. 220)

The 'noetic' character of mystic experience is so general that James includes it in his definition of mysticism.

In spite of what James tells us, that the mystic's knowledge is not binding on any but himself, it is obvious that the mystic is under some radical necessity of propagating his truth: is he not the most vehement propagandist of history? (p. 362-3)

It is hardly necessary to recall the familiar description which William James has given to the class of experiences he proposes to call mystical: they are ineffable and noetic, usually also transient and passive (Varieties of Religious Experience). In the character of ineffability, the indescribable, quality of the experience becomes a point of psychological description; and both this ineffability and the transiency are to be explained, as I shall try to show, on psychological grounds. (p. 390)

Mystic insight has been compared by William James with our occasional experiences of realizing, more or less suddenly, the meaning of words, sayings, points of view, which may have been familiar and empty possessions for a long time. Such realizing as this, we may observe, is never simply the discovery of the meaning of a general proposition. It is a flowing together after some artificial separation, of universal and particular. (p. 428)

The language of subconsciousness need not misrepresent the facts of religious experience. With the descriptive skill of James or of Pratt it conveys much truth which could hardly otherwise be so effectively expressed. But it almost inevitably misleads. For it hardly fails to suggest, first, a division that does not exist; and second, a superhuman resource which is different from the resource of our simple waking selves. (p. 537)

HOCKING, William E. and others. Preface to Philosophy. 1946.

William James says that we are so dependent on the notice, and the favorable notice, of each other that no more fiendish punishment could be devised than that a man should be turned loose in society and that no one should ever notice him. 'If no one turned round when we entered, answered when we spoke, or minded what we did, but if every person we met 'cut us dead' and acted as if we were non-existing things, a kind of rage and impotent despair would ere long well up in us, from which the cruelest bodily tortures would be a relief.' (p. 193)

HOCKING, William E. Types of Philosophy. Revised Edition. 1939.

William James thought that the splitting-place of opposing world-views lies in the contrast of temperaments: the 'tender-minded' want an architecturally handsome, rationalistic and idealistic philosophy, while the 'tough-minded' prefer a loose-ended, empirical, realistic view. (Pragmatism) (p. 19)

There was a strand of pragmatism in Tolstoi's philosophy. Mussolini has recently acknowledged that he owes much to Nietzsche and William James for his method of reaching his political beliefs. They led him to discard 'pure reason' or 'a priori principles,' and to adopt those policies which work out best in practice: the true policies are the expedient policies: this is political pragmatism. (p. 144)

James's revolt is in part a temperamental reaction, oblivious of much that the absolutists, especially Royce, had already written in view of just such difficulties. But he did the work of the genial innovator; he lured out the latent discontent under the pall of absolutism; he released the pent-up stream of a renewed pluralism and finitism, encouraged a reassertion of freedom and of the reality of time (Bergson), and if not a parent at least aided in the delivery of the 'New Realism,' which will shortly engage us. (p. 377)

HOLMES, Justice Oliver Wendell. His Book Notices and Uncollected Letters and Papers. Edited and Annotated by Harry C. Shriver. 1936.

Letter to John C. H. Wu, Feb. 5, 1924.

Very likely I told you of William James once asking me why I did not join the society for psychical research. I replied why don't you study Mahometan religion. Millions of men think you will be damned if you don't join it, yet you don't bother. The answer is the same. We have to divine which is likely to be the highroad and which a cul de sac. We may be wrong but we have to take the risks. I put Bacon-Shakespeare and spiritualism into the same bag. (p. 173)

HOLMES, Justice Oliver Wendell and LASKI, Harold J. Holmes - Laski letters. The Correspondence 1916-1935. Edited by Mark DeWolfe Howe. Two Volumes. 1953.

Quotations from Holmes.

Why use the word pragmatist unless you adhere to W. J.'s philosophy on that matter. I never could make anything out of his or his friends' advocacy of his nostrum except either that in motives depending upon human conduct effort affects the result--which we have heard--or that by yearning you can modify the multiplication table, which I doubt. His whole attitude--on the will to believe &c presupposes something that we can't change as the basis for recommending the will. Otherwise he has no answer if I say, 'I don't want to.' But I think as little of his philosophy as I do much of his psychology. He seems to me typically Irish in his strength and his weakness. (p. 69-70)

William and Henry James were pretty near superlative in their respective days--Bill more especially I think. (p. 905)

The whole lot certainly were unusual men. I may have told you of Bill James coming back from meeting the three and saying it was like meeting the augurs behind the altar and none of them smiling. They seemed to stir him up as he also said, 'Powerful race, those Adamses, to remain plebeians after so many generations of culture.' (p. 1031)

Quotations from Laski.

I wish I'd seen Bill James--or rather I wish he had been alive so that I could have had him as a colleague at Harvard for he cared about the same reforms as I should have liked to introduce if I had a chance. He did at least see that teaching is not offering information but ideas--and--forgive the inference--this last is so much the most difficult thing that it takes a first-rate person to decide to take it. (p. 321)

Did I ever tell you of Wells's remark to me that Henry J. would have been a great man if William J. had been always at his elbow. Wells said he once saw them together and when Henry had lost his fear that Bill would make a faux pas (in the European sense) he became most human and showed all the qualities of psychological insight that distinguished Bill. But, said Wells, that was because Bill set himself to make Henry talk. (p. 402)

I have discovered Pascal. Have you ever read the Pensees deliberately and slowly, in the proper manner of eating caviar? All other psychology seems petty and mean before the almost feverish insight of that poor, tortured soul. I have been literally swept away by the power he had to know the things that move one. Granted that their ultimate purpose is all wrong (though I note how amazingly it anticipates the religious side of James's philosophy) still the verve and range are extraordinary. It's at once and everywhere the clearest proof of the highest genius. The hunger to believe is so extraordinary, the crushing down of reason because it dares to suggest doubts he cannot supress, like a man who will not believe, despite the evidence, an evil tale of his wife. (p. 707)

I also bought and read in bed again William James's Letters. They are really entirely delightful, and his sly digs at Henry do my heart good--but as you know, I am a heretic about the latter. (p. 936)

HOLMES- POLLOCK Letters. The Correspondence of Mr. Justice Holmes and Sir Frederick Pollock. Edited by Mark DeWolfe Howe and John G. Palfrey. Two Volumes. 1941.

Quotations from Holmes.

W. James's book The Will to Believe has interested but more for its admirable writing and revelation of the essential Irishness of the writer than for the philosophic worth of its contents. He has a vivid feeling for the incident--the manifold in life--and also I think looks to Spiritualism as the one possible way of breaking away from a to him necessitarian unification of the world. There are other influences also which I won't stop to enumerate. The result to my mind is chaotic, but useful as a check on the unifying tendency. I don't think he is as strong in dialectics as he is in vivid presentation and enumeration. So his books seem to me to beong on the side of art and belles lettres rather than to the opposite pole, philosophy. (v. 1. p. 78)

As to pragmatism an interview in the paper the other day gave me some light. W. J. suggested that instead of truth it would be better to say truthfulness. He postulated that a certain reality exists, but, 'we don't pry into the question of the nature or constitution of that reality.' The truthfulness of our ideas consists in the fact that they will work, etc. And I now see, as I have seen in his other books that I have read, that the aim and end of the whole business is religious. I spoke of his free will and his answer to prayer the other day; the wind up of this (incauda venemum) is that just as an automatic sweetheart wouldn't work (the illustration is his) an automatic universe won't--or not so well as one that has a warm God behind it, that loves and admires us. But for that conclusion I don't believe we ever should have heard from him on the subject, taking that as the significance of the whole business I make it my bow. W. J. speaks for his own temperament and nature, and as usual there are fundamental differences that make one man's truth another man's falsehood. I think the reasoning humbug so far as the conclusion goes--as to the rest I agree with you. (v. 1. p. 140)

Wm. James's death cuts a root for me that went far into the past, but of late, indeed for many years, we had seen little of each other and had little communication except as he occasionally sent me a book. Distance, other circumstances and latterly my little sympathy with his demi spiritualism and pragmatism, were sufficient cause. His reason made him sceptical and his wishes led him to turn down the lights so as to give miracle a chance. (v. 1. p. 167)

It may be that William James made a valuable contribution in pointing out that ideas were not necessarily faint pictures of original experience, but on the Will to Believe he seems to come to this, that the body of compulsory truth is admitted, subject to the profound remark that we test it by experience, and that the will comes in in those cases where the result depends on our effort, in which cases our belief may help to bring about the result, and that we are warranted in choosing what seems to us the most effective and helpful view in cases where we have no proof either way. The first half of which hardly startles and the last is fishy. The alliance of philosophy with religion and the dogmatic foothold that it gets from a morality from which to bully nous autres seems to me to weaken its significance for us hard-headed ones. But just as preachers like Robertson and half way lots like M. Arnold and Clough filled a want half a generation ago, W. J.'s softness to spiritualism and other isms fills one for many now. He was a human being and a temperament and so he charmed the world--with his Irish blood he really contributed to psychology--but I don't think he was strong in logic or in that kind of abstract thinking that needs it. (v. 1. p. 191-2)

Bill James' posthumous book did not impress me much except as literature. I don't know that it doesn't prove that I fail to appreciate a real difficulty, but his recurring treatment of Achilles and the tortoise, etc., etc., as real, serious problems always amazes me. The argument as I understand it is that five minutes is conceptually infinitely divisible, an infinite series cannot be run out short of eternity, therefore five minutes equal eternity. That strikes me as bosh. If infinite divisibility be conceded at all, and I think it well may be suspected to be an unreal conception, it must be divisibility and a series consistent with the postulate, five minutes and if you can't state it consistently with that, you can't state it. (v. 1. p. 180)

Bill James used to say that in one hundred years he would be the dark planet believed to be greater than all the shining ones, because of the many correspondences with the illustrious, all treating him with deference, and of his having had the wit to suppress his answers. Now I suppose they are out. I will speak of him no more, except to note that no doubt many or some were indebted to him for kindness, and for a contact with cultivation otherwise inaccessible to them. But Oh Lor--Did you ever hear of his beginning a lecture to one of his classes: 'Probably none of you ever has seen a gentleman?' (v. 1. p. 211)

Among other things the notion of discontinuity of the universe which had struck me first in Newman and later in W. James and which I had accounted for by their desire for the interstitial miracle, Catholic or spiritualistic, by their wish for a chasm from which might appear phenomenal antecedents, I was interested to see went back to Du Bois-Reymond. Or again, I have often thought of the superfluity of energy that makes it necessary for man to act, as it makes a kitten play with its tail, as carrying with it a destiny to idealize, i.e., to persist in affirming the worth of ends--since every act has an end. (v. 1. p. 261)

HOOK, Sidney. Education for Modern Man. 1946.

'To have spent one's youth at college,' writes William James, 'in contact with the choice and rare and precious, and yet still to be a blind prig or vulgarian, unable to scent out human excellence or to divine it amid its accidents, to know it only when ticketed and labelled and forced on us by others, this indeed should be accounted the very calamity and shipwreck of a higher education.' (p. 81)

HOOK, Sidney. The Hero in History. 1943.

What William James is saying is that no significant social change has ever come about which is not the work of great men, and that the 'receptivities' of today which make that work possible are the result of the acts or examples of the outstanding individuals of yesterday. (p. 16)

Writing in 1880, William James banteringly asked Herbert Spencer whether he believed that if William Shakespeare had not been born at Stratford-on-Avon on April 26, 1564, the convergence of social and economic forces would have produced him elsewhere; and whether, if Shakespeare had died in infancy, another mother in Stratford-on-Avon would have delivered 'a duplicate copy' of him? 'Or,' he teasingly continues, 'might the substitute arise at Stratford-atte-Bowe.' (p. 81-2)

HOSPERS, John. An Introduction to Philosophical Analysis. 1953.

William James records the following incident:

'Some years ago, being with a camping party in the mountains, I returned from a solitary ramble to find everyone engaged in a ferocious metaphysical dispute. The corpus of the dispute was a squirrel--a live squirrel supposed to be clinging to one side of a tree trunk; while over against the tree's opposite side a human being was imagined to stand. This human witness tries to get sight of the squirrel by moving rapidly round the tree, but no matter how fast he goes, the squirrel moves as fast in the opposite direction, and always keeps the tree between himself and the man, so that never a glimpse of him is caught. The resultant metaphysical problem now is this: Does the man go round the squirrel or not? He goes round the tree, sure enough, and the squirrel is on the tree; but does he go round the squirrel? In the unlimited leisure of the wilderness discussion had been worn threadbare. Everyone had taken sides and was obstinate; and the numbers on both sides were even. Each side, when I appeared, therefore appealed to me to make it a majority. Mindful of the scholastic adage that whenever you meet a contradiction you must make a distinction, I immediately sought and found one, as follows: 'Which party is right,' I said, 'depends on what you practically mean by 'going round' the squirrel. If you mean passing from the north of him to the east, then to the south, then to the west, and then to the north of him again, obviously the man does go round him, for he occupies these successive positions. But if on the contrary you mean being first in front of him, then on the right of him, then behind him, then on his left, and finally in front again, it is quite obvious that the man fails to go round him for by compensating movements the squirrel makes, he keeps his belly turned towards the man all the time, and his back turned away. Make the distinction, and there is no occasion for any further dispute. You are both right and both wrong, according as you conceive the verb 'to go round' in one practical fashion or the other.'

'Although one or two of the hotter disputants called my

speech a shuffling evasion, saying they wanted no quibbling or scholastic hair-splitting, but meant just plain English 'round,' the majority seemed to think that the distinction had assuaged the dispute.' (Pragmatism) (p. 32)

HOUGH, Lynn Harold. Great Humanists. 1953.

When it came to William James, More's own critical sagacity met a sterner test with complete success. A philosophy based on change never stands still long enough to give you an opportunity to judge it. More saw that playing brilliantly with the flux is not a means for finding definite and permanent meanings. Confronted by conventions which have lost all vitality and a stability which is really the stability of death, we turn with a sense of great refreshment to the nimble and quick intelligence of William James. But he never gave us a world on which we can depend. He never gave us a truth which has any security. You must have found elements of changelessness in order to deal happily with change. This William James never understood. And this Paul Elmer More understood quite well. It marks the difference between a mind which moved with a quality like quicksilver and possessed an evanescent intelligence and a mind which has found insights which give it a certain quality of permanence. (p. 181)

INGE, William Ralph. The End of an Age. 1948.

I have said little about asceticism except in connection with sex. In its traditional forms it is hardly a living question for us. But I am strongly in favour of a simpler mode of living, and of that constant though not severe self-discipline which even William James recommends. 'Do something every day for no other reason than because you don't want to do it.' (p. 77)

INGE, William Ralph. The New Twilight of the Gods. 1932.

William James says: 'Though the ultimate state of the universe may be its vital and physical extinction, there is nothing in physics to interfere with the hypothesis that the penultimate state might be the millennium. The last expiring pulsation of the universe's life might be: I am so happy and perfect that I can stand it no longer.' A thesis which can only be defended by such nonsense as this cannot be worthy of serious consideration. The penultimate state of a dying world has been vividly pictured in H. G. Wells' Time Machine. Of course, if James meant that value is independent of time, and that continuance in time beyond a certain point adds nothing to value, he would have been at least intelligible; but we know that James believed nothing of the sort. (p. 16)

INGE, William Ralph. Our Present Discontents. 1938.
William James, after a few days at a social settlement, tells us that he said: 'Pouf! How stifling! Where is the good old Devil?' (p. 325)

INGE, William Ralph. Outspoken Essays. First Series. 1927.
It is probably true, as William James says, that 'militarist writers without exception regard war as a biological or sociological necessity;' lawyers might say the same about litigation. But 'laws of nature' are not efficient causes, and it is open to any one to prove that they are not laws, if he can break them with impunity. It would be the height of pessimistic fatalism to hold that men must always go on doing that which they hate, and which brings them to misery and ruin. (p. 260)

INGE, William Ralph. A Pacifist in Trouble. 1939.
There is an amusing paragraph in which William James describes how he spent a few days in a sort of summer camp, exposed to the full force of moral and spiritual uplift. 'Ouf! What a relief!' he exclaimed when he escaped. He missed, he confesses, 'the dear old Devil.' A little girl once said, 'Mummy, if I am very good in Heaven, shall I sometimes be allowed to have a little devil up to play with?' She agreed with William James. (p. 221)

JACKS, L. P. The Alchemy of Thought. 1910.
For if Kant had never set us wrong, it is hard to see what 'difference would be made' by James setting us right; and whatever makes no difference is, according to Pragmatism, nothing. No tender mind, no tough: no Kant, no James. Pragmatism itself compels us to think that tender minds and tough are necessary correlates in an organic whole. They are like quarrel-some twins, each of whom finds if difficult to get on with the other, but impossible to get on without him. (p. 85)

JACKS, L. P. The Confessions of an Octogenarian. 1942.
As a philosopher Balfour had the advantage of not being a Professor of Philosophy. William James always disliked

being called 'Professor James' and once rated me soundly for inadvertently calling him so. (p. 195)

My feeling in the matter is identical with that of William James who, after he had been staying with me in Oxford, wrote to Charles Eliot Norton as follows:

'There is a great deal of flummery about Oxford, but if I were an Oxonian, in spite of my radicalism generally, I might vote against all change there. It is an absolutely unique fruit of human endeavour...Let other places of learning go in for all the improvements! The world can afford to keep her one Oxford unreformed.' (p. 239)

JACKS, L. P. The Inner Sentinel. A Study of Ourselves and Something More. 1930.

In our own time the two writers who have done most to stimulate vital thinking are probably William James and Henri Bergson. They at least are the two writers from whom I have myself learnt more about this matter than from anybody else. Of the two my debt is greater I think to Bergson than to James, though it is very great to him also. (p. 47)

The provision of a 'moral substitute for war' which provoked the earnest thought of William James, and has since furnished a topic for much windy eloquence in other quarters, is still an 'unsolved problem,' perhaps the gravest now confronting civilization. It is certain that a civilization which lives for objects not worth dying for is doomed to decay. (p. 175)

JACKS, L. P. Life and Letters of Stopford Brooke. 1917.

'Asked Jacks how William James was getting on. He is lecturing on Pragmatism (at Oxford), and the hall at Manchester College was so full that they have taken the Examination Hall for him. J. explained to me what Pragmatism was, and I listened like a three-year child.' (v. 2. p. 603)

JACKS, L. P. My American Friends. 1933.

It was Norton, I think, with his Dante readings and the subtle comments that flowed from them, and next to him William James, with his power of seeing through words and phrases to the realities they conceal (the essence of pragmatism) who first aroused me to open the eyes which mere book-learning had closed. (p. 14)

JOHNSON, Alvin. Pioneer's Progress. An Autobiography. 1952.

My new chief, W. G. Langworthy Taylor, head of the Department of Economics (University of Nebraska), was a man of a type which has since been discontinued. He was altogether a creature of will power. In his last year at Harvard he had had a devastating nervous breakdown, which he overrode by sheer force of will--acquired from his teacher William James. (p. 171)

At that time the Eastern colleges were ridden by a garden variety of psychology, degenerated from William James, which distinguished between the 'active' and the 'passive' in experience, as a substitute for the old distinction between virtue and vice. Listening to a lecture was passive; sitting in a room with thirty persons being quizzed by an instructor was 'active.' Psychologists of this school inveighed constantly against the 'lecture method,' oblivious of the fact that listening to a lecturer like William James was about as 'active' an experience as the nervous system will stand. (p. 210)

JONES, Howard Mumford. The Pursuit of Happiness. 1953.

William James delivered the address at the Emerson Centenary Celebration at Concord in 1903. It was an appropriate choice. The pragmatist owed much to the transcendentalist. 'The reading of the divine Emerson,' he wrote in a letter, 'has done me a lot of good, and, strange to say, has thrown a strong practical light on my path. The incorruptible way in which he followed his own vocation of seeing such truths as the Universal Soul vouchsafed him...and reporting them in the right literary form ...refusing to be entangled with irrelevancies...seems to me a moral lesson to all men who have any genius, however small, to foster.' (Letters) (p. 121)

Like Emerson, James had no patience with the block universe of either metaphysics or theology; like Emerson, he declared that 'the real thing to aim at is the liberation of the inner interests' of the soul; like Emerson, he experienced moments of mystical rapture, one of which he perfectly describes in a letter to his wife in 1898:

'I spent a good deal of (the night) in the woods, where the streaming moonlight lit up things in a magical checkered play, and it seemed as if the Gods of all the nature-mythologies were holding an indescribable meeting in my breast with the moral Gods of the inner life...The intense significance of some sort, of the whole scene, if one could only tell the significance; the intense inhuman remoteness of its inner life, and yet the intense appeal of it; its everlasting freshness and its immemorial antiquity and decay; its utter Americanism, and every sort of patriotic suggestiveness, and you, and my relation to you part and parcel of it all, and beaten up with it, so that memory and sensation all whirled inexplicably together; it was indeed worth coming for...one of the happiest lonesome nights of existence, and I understand now what a poet is.' (Letters) (p. 121-2)

Moreover, James's sardonic view of the theory that business success means happiness is as corrosive as Emerson's:

'Who that has travelled in Europe is not familiar with the type of the broken-down, American business-man, sent abroad to recruit his collapsed nervous system? With his haggard, hungry mien, unfitted by life-long habit for taking any pleasure in passive contemplation, and with too narrow a culture to be interested in the historical or aesthetic side of what meets his eye, he tries to cheat the tedium vitae by a feverish locomotion, and seems to draw a ghostly comfort from a foolish criticism of everything he meets--the tyranny of despots, the dinginess of the old paintings, and the mendacity of the natives, the absence of the ballot-box, the crookedness of the streets, the fearful waste of raw material in walls, harnesses, and conveyances, and the barbarousness of the window fastenings.' (p. 122-3)

James goes on:

'If we look on man's whole mental life as it exists, on the life of men that lies apart from their learning and science and that they inwardly and privately follow, we have to confess that the part of it of which rationalism can give an account is relatively superficial. It is the part that has the prestige undoubtedly, for it has the loquacity, it can challenge you for proofs and chop logic, and put you down with words. But it will fail to convince or convert you all the same, if your dumb intuitions are opposed to its conclusions. If you have intuitions at all, they come from a deeper level of your nature than the loquacious level which rationalism inhabits. Your whole subconscious life, your impulses, your faiths, your needs, your divinations, have prepared the premises, of which your consciousness now feels the weight of the result; and something in you absolutely knows that the result must be truer than any logic-chopping rationalistic talk, however clear, that may contradict it.' (Varieties of Religious Experience) (p. 124-5)

In a letter discussing the Varieties of Religious Experience, the book from which I have just quoted, he

(James) says that he has deliberately cut himself off in this study from theologies and scholasticisms, which have 'no proper intellectual deliverance of their own, but belong to a region deeper, and more vital and practical, than that which the intellect inhabits.' 'We cannot,' he says in the book itself, 'divide man sharply into an animal and a rational part. We cannot distinguish natural from supernatural effects.' And in the letter he continues:

'I attach the mystical or religious consciousness to the possession of an extended sublimal self, with a thin partition through which messages make irruption. We are thus made convincingly aware of the presence of a sphere of life larger and more powerful than our usual consciousness, with which the latter is nevertheless continuous. The impressions and impulsions and emotions and excitements which we thence receive help us to live, they found invincible assurance of a world beyond the sense, they melt our hearts and communicate significance and value to everything and make us happy.' (Letters) (p. 125)

'I can't possibly pray,' he (James) declared, 'I feel foolish and artificial;' and Conversion, which usually means the attainment of some form of religious happiness, seemed to him on the whole the subconscious incubation of some new center of psychological energy, which by and by bursts into flower, overflows, suffuses old pathways in both the subconscious and the conscious mind. Whatever we are is mysterious: 'our interests, our tendencies of attention, our motor impulses, the aesthetic, moral, and theoretic combinations we delight in, the extent of our power of apprehending schemes of relation...have all grown up in ways of which at present we can give no account; but whatever we are, we are unshakeably attached to our own nervous structures. Yet there are resources in us that naturalism with its literal and legal virtues never recks of, possibilities that take our breath away, of another kind of happiness and power, based on giving up our own will and letting something higher work for us, and these seem to show a world wider than either physics or philistine ethics can imagine...our natural experience, our strictly moralistic and prudential experience, may be only a fragment of real human experience.' (p. 126)

JONES, Rufus M. The Eternal Gospel. 1938.

William James in his little book, The Energies of Men, has given some striking illustrations of the way these hidden energies may suddenly become operative and change the line of march to victory for men who had thought they were defeated. James ends his important little book with the words: 'We need a topography of the limits of human power, similar to the chart which oculists use for the field of human vision. We need also a study of the various types of human being with reference to the different ways in which their energy-reserves may be appealed to and set loose.' (p. 167)

JONES, Rufus M. Fundamental Ends of Life. 1924.

William James in a letter to Henry W. Rankin in 1901 very well stated the substance of the affirmative testimony. 'Something, not our immediate self,' he says, 'does act on our life.' 'The mother-sea and fountain-head of all religions lie in the mystical experiences of the individual, taking the word mystical in a very wide sense. All theologies and all ecclesiasticisms are secondary growths superimposed.' 'We are thus,' i.e., through these mystical experiences, he continues, 'made convincingly aware of the presence of a sphere of life larger and more powerful than our usual consciousness, with which the latter is nevertheless continuous. The impressions and impulsions and emotions and excitements which we thence receive give us help to live by, they found invincible assurance of a world beyond the sense, they melt our hearts and communicate significance and value to everything and make us happy. They do this for the individual who has them, and other individuals follow him. Religion in this way is absolutely indestructible. Philosophy and theology give their conceptual interpretations of this experimental life.' (p. 104)

JONES, Rufus M. The Inner Life. 1916.

William James has given a very successful account of the way in which pleasure and pain as spiritual energies reinforce or damp the physical activities, so that the personal soul seems to take a unique part from within in determining the physical process. Here are his words:

'Tremendous as the part is which pleasure and pain play in our psychic life, we must confess that absolutely nothing is known of their cerebral conditions. It is hard to imagine them as having special centres; it is harder still to invent peculiar forms of processes in each and every centre, to which these feelings may be due. And let one try as one will to represent the cerebral activity in exclusively mechanical terms, I, for one, find it quite impossible to enumerate what seem to be the facts and yet to make no mention of the psychic side which they possess. However it be with other drainage currents and discharges, the drainage currents and discharges of the brain are not purely physical facts. They are psycho-physical facts, and the spiritual quality of them seems a codeterminant of their mechanical effectiveness. If the mechanical activities in a cell, as they increase, give pleasure, they seem to increase all the more rapidly for that fact; if they give displeasure, the displeasure seems to damp the activities. The psychic side of the phenomenon thus seems somewhat like the applause or hissing at a spectacle, to be an encouraging or adverse comment on what the machinery brings forth.' (Principles of Psychology) (p. 158-9)

Once more I quote William James, whom many of us of this generation revere both as teacher and friend:

'It often takes effort to keep the mind upon an object. We feel that we can make more or less of effort as we choose. If this feeling be not deceptive, if our effort be a spiritual force, and an indeterminate one, then of course it contributes coequally with the cerebral conditions to the result. Though it introduce no new idea, it will deepen and prolong the stay in consciousness of innumerable ideas which else would fade more quickly away. The delay thus gained might not be more than a second in duration--but that second may be critical; for in the constant rising and falling of considerations in the mind, where two associated systems of them are nearly in equilibrium it is often a matter of but a second more or less of attention at the outset, whether one system shall gain force to occupy the field and develop itself, and exclude the other, or be excluded itself by the other. When developed, it may make us act; and that act may seal our doom. The whole drama of the voluntary life hinges on the amount of attention, slightly more or slightly less, which rival motor ideas receive. But the whole feeling of reality, the whole sting and excitement of our voluntary life, depends on our sense that in it things are really being decided from one moment to another, and that it is not the dull rattling off of a chain that was forged innumerable ages ago. This appearance, which makes life and history tingle with such a tragic zest, may not be an illusion. Effort may be an original force and not a mere effect, and it may be indeterminate in amount.' (p. 159-61)

JONES, Rufus M. The Luminous Trail. 1947.

In my senior year in college I read the major part of Emerson's prose and poetry and he laid his mind on me. His essay on 'The Over-soul,' and many other haunting passages in his prose and poetry, sent me on a lifelong quest of the great mystics who have blessed the race. William James is another man who laid his mind on me and helped me to find my direction toward the goal-posts of life. These two men, though hardly any of us are their authentic disciples, have driven the goads of their wise words into the lives of hosts of persons across the world. (p. 136)

JONES, Rufus M. The New Quest. 1928.

William James in his Psychology, bears his positive testimony to the fact that man in his normal inner processes seeks and finds a 'Great Companion.' 'We hear,' he says 'in these days of scientific enlightenment, a great deal of discussion about the efficacy of prayer; and many reasons are given us why we should not pray, whilst others are given why we should. But in all this very little is said of the reason why we do pray, which is simply that we cannot help praying. The impulse to pray is a necessary consequence of the fact that whilst the innermost of the empirical selves of a man is a Self of the social sort, it can yet find its adequate Socius only in an ideal world.' 'We are haunted,' he goes on to say, 'by this sense of an ideal spectator.' (p. 141)

JONES, Rufus M. Pathways to the Reality of God. 1931.

James has stated his position in a telling way in what he used to call his 'faith-ladder,' with which he was accustomed to close his last college lecture each year:

On the first round of the ladder we say of a momentous view of life, or of the world, or of religion, that it is a possible view, it is not self-contradictory, it is not absurd; on the second round we say, it might well be true, so far as actual facts are concerned; on the third we say, it may be true now for all that anybody knows; on the fourth we add, it is fit to be true, it ought to be true, and in the sixth we affirm, it must be true. Well, then, we say at the top of the ladder, it shall be true, at any rate for me because I am going to adopt it as my truth and live by it henceforth. (p. 13)

William James writing to his wife in 1898 of a mystical experience which occured to him in the Adirondacks one night when he was working on his Gifford Lectures, which afterwards constituted Varieties of Religious Experience, calls it 'holding an indescribable meeting in my breast with the moral Gods of the inner life.' He speaks of 'its intense significance;' 'its everlasting freshness;' 'its intense appeal' and then he concludes: 'In point of fact, I can't find a single word for all that significance and don't know what it was significant of, so there it remains, a mere boulder of impression. (p. 37)

JONES, Rufus M. Some Exponents of Mystical Religion. 1930.

Next in importance, however, after Emerson and Whitman comes William James (1842-1910). He claimed not to have been a mystic himself--'my own constitution shuts me out from the enjoyment of mystical experiences'--but his Letters would indicate that there was a strong mystical tendency in him. In any case he was a sympathetic and penetrating interpreter of mysticism and of mystics. His Varieties of Religious Experience (1902), in spite of some striking defects, has stimulated hosts of readers and has given the world a very interesting interpretation of mysticism in terms of the subliminal life of man. (p. 219-20)

JONES, Rufus M. The Trail of Life in College. 1929.

I found in the library of Colby College, five miles away, all the books I needed for my studies in philosophy, and the librarian kindly gave me almost unlimited privileges. It was at this time that I came upon William James' Psychology in two great volumes. No man with my interests could ever forget an event like that. (p. 180)

JONES, Rufus M. The Trail of Life in the Middle Years. 1934.

William James, on the other hand, had the heartiest sympathy both with my interest in mysticism and with my devotion to Quaker ideals. I never had definite university work with him, but for many years I was strongly under his influence and guidance. I began to consult him even before I was a student at Harvard, and as soon as he discovered the main lines of my interest there was no limit to his readiness, in fact eagerness, to help me forward. It was a characteristic of James to see 'genius' in every young man who confided in him. He would always give up anything he might be doing to give aid and comfort to a chance visitor who was dreaming a great dream. He made one feel as though one's own ideas were Platonic in appearance. When you saw how enthusiastic this great man was over your half-born mental child, you were assured that it must be a superlative offspring. He gave a young person a new faith in himself. You quickly believed in his belief. Like Socrates, he was a midwife of the mind for the youth of his time, though he was not quite so discriminating as Socrates was in his judgment as to which offspring was worthy of nurture and likely to be 'a child of promise.'

William James was so fascinating and captivating that one was always in danger of being carried off his feet by that remarkable man's enthusiasms. I went too far in my early period toward the adoption of his theories of the religious significance of the subconscious, though I never did accept the central principles of his pragmatism as a sound theory of truth. But whether I agreed or disagreed with his views, I have never regretted any aspects of the part William James played in the formation of my intellectual life or my spiritual ideals. He helped me, among other ways, to discover the importance of simplicity, as I shall indicate at a later stage. (p. 7-8)

When William James died in 1910, I wrote my estimate of his work and my appreciation of his life. A short time afterwards, I received this surprising letter from Mrs. William James:

'My dear Mr. Jones:

I should like to thank you for the Editorial Letter in the American Friend on the death of William James. Many voices have been raised in affectionate memory of a man who truly loved his kind but no one has spoken more justly or with finer appreciation than yourself.

I should like to have read it to my dear husband who counted himself so lightly--and yet how he honored his work and loved it.

Thanking you for our children and myself I am,

Sincerely yours,

Alice H. James.'

(p. 8-9)

'Faith,' William James once said, 'is the sense of the exceedingness of the possible over the real,' and we worked on undefeated because we saw 'the exceedingness of the possible over the real.' (p. 52)

William James had written in his Varieties of Religious Experience: 'We and God have business with each other; and in opening ourselves to His influence our deepest destiny is fulfilled. The universe at those parts of it which our personal being constitutes takes a turn for the better or for the worse in proportion as each one of us fulfills or evades God's demands.' (p. 221)

JOSEPHSON, Matthew. Portrait of the Artist as American. 1930.

Even William James, whom we find at all moments so far apart from his brother, gives words upon at least one occasion to such a sadness of homecoming as other nationals would find hard to understand. 'Oh, the thin grass and ragged waysides,' he moans, 'the poverty-stricken land, and sad American sunlight over all--sad because so empty....The coming back makes one feel so strangely sad and hardens one in the resolution never to go away again unless one can go to end one's days....As England struck me newly and differently last time, so A-merican now-force and directness in the people, but a terrible grimness, more ugliness than I ever realized in things, and a greater weakness in nature's beauties, such as it is.

'One must pitch one's whole sensibility in a different key, --'he resumes with much good grace and wisdom, 'then gradually the quantum of personal happiness of which one is susceptible fills the cup--but the moment of change of key is lonesome....' (p. 101-2)

'All this dead civilization, crowding upon ones' consciousness,' he observes, 'forces the mind open again, and what my mind wants most is practical tasks.' (It was a presage of the William James who would become a veritable bull-in-the-china-shop for Hegelians!) 'My very enjoyment of what here belongs to the 'hoary eld,' has done more,' he ruminates, 'to reconcile me to the present hour, business, factories, etc, than anything I ever experienced.' He ended simply by describing himself as a barbarian mind having a 'plain Yankee stomach,' peculiarly immune to history and unable to endure either French or Roman ways of being and doing things, one who could never, in short, call Rome 'my country' or 'city of my soul,' like the too literary Henry. (p. 110)

Most pathetic of all, however, were the moments when men like William James acknowledged their deception or despair; when they sensed the dissociation of intelligence and force, of the doctrines of reason or moral judgment and those of preemption. The picture of William James and a few other professors holding a meeting of protest at the time of the Spanish-American War and debating what should be done lingers in the mind as minor American comedy, full of cruel overtones, which speak to us of the impotence of these intellectuals. The dissenters-for-an-hour would be forgotten, and they relapsed soon after to the unlovely level of a busy life filled with Chautauqua lectures and talks to ladies' clubs, while buoyed up by a sweet and uncritical faith in human nature, in free American institutions, and in the 'leaps and bounds of Progress.' (p. 282-3)

JUNG, C. G. The Spirit of Psychology (in Eranos-Jahrbuch, Spirit and Nature. Papers. p. 371-444). 1954.

I reproduce here what William James says about the importance of the discovery of the unconscious psyche (Varieties of Religious Experience, New York, 1902, p. 233): 'I cannot but think that the most important step forward that has occurred in psychology since I have been a student of that science is the discovery, first made in 1886, that....there is not only the consciousness of the ordinary field, with its usual center and margin, but an addition thereto in the shape of a set of memories, thoughts, and feelings, which are extra-marginal and out side of the primary consciousness altogether, but yet must be classed as conscious facts of some sort, able to reveal their presence by unmistakable signs. I call this the most important step forward because, unlike the other advances which psychology has made, this discovery has revealed to us an entirely unsuspected peculiarity in the constitution of human nature. No other step forward which psychology has made can proffer any such claim as this.' (p. 379)

Concerning the 'field of consciousness' James says (Varieties of Religious Experience, p. 232): 'The important fact which this 'field' formula commemorates is the indetermination of the margin. Inattentively realized as is the matter which the margin contains, it is nevertheless there, and helps both to guide our behavior and to determine the next movement of our attention. It lies around us like a 'magnetic field' inside of which our center of energy turns like a compass needle as the present phase of consciousness alters into its successor. Our whole past store of memories floats beyond this margin, ready at a touch to come in; and the entire mass of residual powers, impulses, and knowledges that constitute our empirical self stretches continuously beyond it. So vaguely drawn are the outlines between what is actual and what is only potential at any moment of our conscious life, that it is always hard to say of certain mental elements whether we are conscious of them or not.' (p. 396)

KALTENBORN, H. V. Fifty Fabulous Years. 1950.

Of all the Harvard professors of my time, William James seemed to me to combine the best features of the practical world and the academic world. He had a wonderfully catholic curious, and inquiring mind. He was probably the most genuinely open-minded person I have ever met. There was no aspect of human activity that did not interest him. He was always willing to explore any new avenue of belief, to experiment with it and to test it. He was always responsive to something that might open a new door to knowledge. He appealed to me as a romantic adventurer in the realm of ideas, eagerly hospitable to new thoughts. (p. 47-8)

I had the privilege of several visits at the home of William James while I was at Harvard and remember riding with him in an open trolley car from Boston to Cambridge. He always had the gift of striking expression. On this occasion, he told me that he thought we lived in a 'megaphonic era.' By this he meant that everything was exaggerated in sound, in importance, and in appearance. He pointed to the glaring headlines of the newspapers being read by our fellow travelers in the trolley. He called my attention to the exaggerated claims made by advertisers on the trolley car signs and on the giant billboards we passed. He called ours a megaphonic world even before the days of radio and loud speakers and a myriad other such mechanical devices through which we are accosted night and day by unseen sounds and voices coming from nowhere and everywhere so that silence has become one of man's most appreciated blessings.

When James retired from teaching, we devoted an entire issue of the Harvard Illustrated Magazine to him. The number was filled with appreciative essays contributed by his various colleagues. Bliss Perry wrote on 'James, the Master of English;' Josiah Royce wrote on 'James, the Philosopher;' and George Santayana wrote on 'James the Teacher.' This issue received attention not only in the United States but from readers in many countries outside the United States where James was known and loved. It became necessary to make several reprints of this particular James issue. He wrote me a very gracious letter of appreciation in which he used these memorable words: 'I have tried all my life to be good, but have only succeeded in becoming great.' (p. 49)

KELLER, Helen. Midstream. My Later Life. 1929.

An American who is somehow connected in my mind with Plato and Francis Bacon is Professor William James. When I was a little girl he came to see Miss Sullivan and me at the Perkins Institution for the Blind in South Boston. He brought me a beautiful ostrich feather. 'I thought,' he said, 'you would like the feather, it is soft and light and caressing.'

We talked about my sense perceptions and he wove a magic web into his discourse. He said then, and afterwards when I sent him a copy of The World I Live In, that in our problems and processes of thought we do not greatly differ from one another. He was not surprised to find my world so much like that of everyone else, though he said he was 'Quite disconcerted, professionally speaking,' by my account of myself before my 'consciousness' was awakened by instruction.'

His thought was clear like crystal. His body, like his mind, was quick and alert. In argument his tongue was like a rapier, but he was always ready to listen to the other side, and always made me ashamed of my cocksureness about many things.

He was not a mystic--his mind could not thrive on air as mine does--but I think he was something of a poet as well as a philosopher.

As a young woman I was extremely fortunate in having John Macy to counsel me with regard to books. He was a great reader and an enthusiastic admirer of all that is beautiful in poetry and prose. Whenever in his own reading he found anything particularly impressive he read the passage to me. He read long passages from William James's books as they came out, and many of Stevenson's letters. (p. 316-8)

KLINEBERG, Otto. Social Psychology. Revised edition. 1934.

William James also saw property in our society as an extension of the personality-as giving a sort of increase in psychic stature.

'It is clear that between what a man calls me and what he simply calls mine the line is difficult to draw....In the widest possible sense....a man's Self is the sum total of all that he can call his, not only his body, and his psychic powers, but his clothes and his house, his wife and children, his ancestors and friends, his reputation and works, his land and horses and yacht and bank account. All these things give him the same emotions. If they wax and prosper, he feels triumphant, if they dwindle and die away, he feels cast down-not necessarily in the same degree for each thing, but in much the same way for all.' (Principles of Psychology) (p. 107-8)

KREYCHE, Robert J. Logic for Undergraduates. 1954.

The only pitfall--if there is any--is one of impatience and discouragement. To guard against these, the student should be mindful of the following remarks of the well-known American psychologist William James:

...'A great mistake of my past life, which has been prejudicial to my education, is an impatience of results. Inexperience of life is the cause of it, and I imagine it is generally an American characteristic...Results should not be too voluntarily aimed at or too busily thought of. They are sure to float up of their own accord, from a long enough daily work at a given matter....' (Philosophy of William James edited by H. M. Kallen) (p. 15)

LAMONT, Corliss. Illusion of Immortality. Second edition. 1950.

As to the nature of the immortality promised by the Spiritualists, it was William James, long a most sympathetic student of psychic phenomena, who wrote: 'The spirit-hypothesis exhibits a vacancy, triviality, and incoherence of mind painful to think of as the state of the departed.' (p. 163)

William James evidently had something of the same feeling when he wrote to a lady who had just lost her husband: 'I can hardly express the sorrow I feel at your husband's being thus cut off almost before he had begun to show what was in him....The whole thing is one of those incomprehensible, seemingly wasteful acts of Providence, which, without seeing, we can only hope may some day be proved to spring from a rational ground.' (p. 172)

And perhaps William James, who laments with the futilitarian immortalists the transiency of earthly things, is more sensible than they when he writes: 'A world with a God in it to say the last word, may indeed burn up or freeze, but we then think of him as still mindful of the old ideals and sure to bring them elsewhere to fruition; so that where he is, tragedy is only provisional and partial, and shipwreck and dissolution and the absolutely final things.' (p. 202)

Probably the greater proportion of believers in the world today would agree with James that 'the surest warrant for immortality is the yearning of our bowels for our dear ones.' (p. 230-1)

LASKI, Harold. Foundations of Sovereignty. 1921.
'The pluralistic world,' said James, 'is...more like a federal republic than an empire or a kingdom. However much may be collected, however much may report itself as present at any effective center of consciousness or action, something else is self-governed and absent and unreduced to unity.' (Pluralistic Universe) (p. 169)

LASKI, Harold. Reflections on the Constitution. 1951.
The phenomenon has been brilliantly described by William James in the same remarkable essay from which I have already quoted.
'Everyone is familiar,' he wrote, 'with the phenomenon of feeling more or less alive on different days. Everyone knows that on any given day there are energies slumbering in him which the excitements of that day do not call forth, but which he might display if these were greater. Most of us feel as if a sort of cloud weighed upon us, keeping us below our highest notch of clearness in discernment, sureness in reasoning, or firmness in deciding. Compared with what we ought to be, we are only half awake. Our fires are damped, our draughts are checked. We are making use of only a small part of our possible mental and physical resources...to what do the better men own their escape? And, in the fluctuations which all men feel in their own degree of energizing, to what are the improvements due, when they occur? In general terms, the answer is plain: either some unusual stimulus fills them with emotional excitement, or some unusual idea of necessity includes them to make an extra effort of will. Excitements, ideas and efforts, in a word, are what carry us over the dam.' (p. 150-1)

LERNER, Max. Actions and Passions. Notes on the Multiple Revolution of Our Time. 1949.
While I was reading this book, (This is my Story) I found myself turning back to a book, published in 1902, dealing with the vagaries of the conscience and of conversion, with religious turns and returns--the great Gifford Lectures of William James, The Varieties of Relgious Experience. For me, the James of 1902 shed a good deal of light on the Budenz of 1947.
As James puts it, there is in all religious men an abiding sense of 'the More' and a persistent drive to a 'union' with it. Budenz happens to have come out of a

devout Catholic home in Indiana, and his sense of 'the More' takes, therefore and quite naturally, the symbolic figure of the Immaculate Virgin, to whom he dedicates his book. Had he been born in India or China, in a Chassidic village in Russia or in the Arabian desert, his hungering religious spirit would have taken quite different forms. (p. 53-4)

LEWISOHN, Ludwig. Expression in America. 1932.
Given his literary vividness and charm, I should discuss William James even though he had been a philosopher in a far stricter technical sense than in fact, he was or pretended to be. For the general validity of philosophical doctrine and vision is less in their 'truth' than in the breadth and reality of the human experience from which they seem authentically to speak. 'If art,' writes George Simmel, 'is an image of the world seen through a temperament, then philosophy may be called a temperament seen through its image of the world.' Now the image of the world which suited the mind of William James was not only described and propagated by him in a style at once warm and lively, correct and pungent, picturesque and eloquent, but it commended itself as a sympathetic and congenial image to so great a number of his countrymen and immediate contemporaries and seemed then as, through his disciples it seems still, to express the precise American sense of life so thoroughly and happily that no poet may be said ever to have spoken more directly for his age and people than did this philosophical essayest for the American business democracy of his time. He met with no opposition; surely criticism of him came from the academic and philosophical camp, not from the general reader or the average student or the pedagogue. (p. 331) (Quoted from pages 331-6 devoted to James)

LIPPMANN, Walter. American Inquisitors. A Commentary on Dayton and Chicago. 1928.
For us the words of William James are true: 'There is no complete generalization, no total point of view, no all-pervasive unity, but everywhere some residual resistance to verbalization, formulation and discursification, some genius of reality that escapes from the pressure of the logical finger, that says 'Hands off,' and claims its privacy, and means to be left to its own life...what the intellect, with its claim to reason out reality, thinks that it is in duty bound to resolve...remains; but it remains as something to be met and dealt with by faculties more

akin to our activities and heroisms and willingnesses, than to our logical powers.' (p. 117-8)

LIPPMANN, Walter. Essays in the Public Philosophy. 1955.

There is no final resting point, because 'in the flux of things,' as William James says, 'things are off their balance. Whatever equilibrium our finite experiences attain to are but provisional...everything is in...a surrounding world of other things.' And 'if you leave it to work there, it will inevitably meet with friction and opposition from its neighbors. Its rivals and enemies will destroy it unless it can buy them off by compromising some part of its original pretensions.' (A Pluralistic Universe) (p. 144)

LIPPMANN, Walter. A Preface to Morals. 1929.

Yet as William James once said, 'religion, in her fullest exercise of function, is not a mere illumination of facts already elsewhere given, not a mere passion, like love, which views things in a rosier light...It is something more, namely, a postulator of new facts as well.' James himself was strongly disposed toward what he so candidly described as 'overbeliefs;' he had sympathy with the beliefs of others which was as large and charitable as any man's can be. There was no trace of the intellectual snob in William James; he was in the other camp from those thin argumentative rationalists who find so much satisfaction in disproving what other men hold sacred. James loved cranks and naifs and sought them out for the wisdom they might have. But withal he was a modern man who lived toward the climax of the revolutionary period. He had the will to Believe, he argued eloquently for the Right to Believe. But he did not wholly believe. The utmost that he could honestly believe was something which he confessed would 'appear a sorry underbelief' to some of his readers. 'Who knows,' he said, 'whether the faithfulness of individuals here below to their own poor overbeliefs may not actually help God in turn to be more effectively faithful to his own greater tasks?' Who knows? And on that question mark he paused and could say no more. (p. 24-5)

WEINGAST, David Elliott. Walter Lippmann. A Study in Personal Journalism. 1949.

Perhaps the dominating intellectual influence of the Harvard years was William James. Although Walter was not a student in any of James's classes, the two met from time to time. In the philosopher's abiding wisdom the eager young scholar found lasting inspiration. (p. 6)

LOVETT, Sidney. A Boy's Recollections of William James. Yale Review. Volume 63: p. 524-33. 1954.

During my four years at Browne and Nichols School it was my good fortune to be a frequent luncheon guest at the James home, located at 95 Irving Street, Cambridge. The house with its exterior of brown shingles and dark green trim stood behind a hedge and close to the street, and near the residence of William James's friend and colleague, Josiah Royce. There was nothing unusual about the interior of the house and its appointments, save the fact that I had never seen so many books outside a public library as reposed in the professor's ample study. Arranged upon shelves, tier upon tier, they lined the four walls from floor to ceiling. A huge flat-topped desk, piled high with papers and periodicals, occupied the center of the room, and a very capacious couch faced a generous fireplace. There was no aura of privacy about this academic workshop. Alec and I would settle ourselves on the couch, before or after lunch, and denounce our teachers, criticize certain of our mates, and plan some new deviation from the rules and regulations of the school. I well remember, after a concerted outburst of disparagement, at the expense of our French teacher, a voice boomed out from behind the desk, 'Don't forget, boys, Christ died for him, too.' Now I had hitherto associated such a pious sentiment with Sunday School or church. This matter-of-fact reference to a sacred theme, this sudden intrusion of a holy admonition into the midst of one's daily conduct came as a shock to my unregenerate sensibilities. Could Alec's father be some kind of a preacher, as well as professor of a recondite subject called philosophy? But that particular ejaculation must have etched itself deep in the grain of my consciousness, for though I have never fulfilled its commandment, I have never forgotten it from that day to this, and its proper intention grows upon me with the years. (p. 527-8)

During the Christmas vacation of my freshman year, 1909, I went over to Cambridge to see William James, and to give him an account of my recent introduction and brief experience in New Haven. It was the last time I was to see him in the flesh. He presented the same animated concern with my welfare. His 'irascible blue eyes,' as a portrait painter called them, still flashed from beneath their heavy brows, with dome-shaped forehead above and the bushy beard below. His dress was informal, topped off as usual by the Norfolk jacket and a festive necktie. I think it was on that occasion that I told him of my desire in due course to enter the Christian ministry. Again his approval was immediate and reassuring. 'You must take some philosophy as soon as you can, with my pupil, Bakewell,' to whom he promised to write a word of introduction. In the course of our conversation, I spoke of my interest in the Yale Hope Mission and its ministry of reclamation to down-and-out men. From his absorption in my story you would never have dreamed he knew anything about the psychology of conversion.

Before I left he gave me a copy of a book, whose authorship he modestly professed, and which he thought might be of interest to me. It was the volume containing his famous Gifford Lectures of 1901-1902, 'The Varieties of Religious Experience.' Needless to say, I have treasured this book ever since, as a kind of final testament of William James's friendship for a young boy who had nothing to give in return, save a measure of devotion which has increased with the years, and to which these recollections bear true though inadequate witness. (p. 532-3)

LUCCOCK, Robert E. If God be for Us. Sermons on the Gifts of the Gospel. 1954.

When William James came to the end of his long career as a teacher at Harvard he spoke these sentences as a valedictory:

'These then are my last words to you: Be not afraid of life. Believe that life is worth living and your belief will help create the fact. The 'scientific' proof that you are right may not be clear before the day of judgment is reached. But the faithful fighters of this hour, or the beings that then and there will represent them, may turn to the faint-hearted who decline to go on, with words like those which Henry IV greeted tardy Crillon after a great battle had been gained: 'Hang yourself, brave Crillon! We fought at Arques, and you were not there.' (p. 133)

FECHER, Charles A. The Philosophy of Jacques Maritain. 1953.

For William James, the chief exponent of pragmatism, it consists surely enough in the quest for truth, but the true is simply that which has some recognizable and 'practical' value. 'The true...is only the expedient in the way of our thinking, just as the 'right' is only the expedient in the way of our behaving...expedient in the long run and on the whole, of course, for what meets expediently all the experiences in sight won't necessarily meet all further experiences equally satisfactorily...The true is the name of whatever proves itself to be good in the way of belief.' James did, of course, admit the existence of logically and morally useful truths, but nevertheless if such a system were to be carried to its extreme, one could say of the statement that the Great Nebula M-31 in Andromeda is 680,000 light-years from the earth that it cannot possibly be true because knowledge of the fact is perfectly useless. One can understand and sympathize with the Chinese scholar who told Somerset Maugham that pragmatism was the last refuge of those who want to believe the incredible. (Pragmatism) (p. 67)

MARTIN, Everett Dean. The Behavior of Crowds. A Psychological Study. 1920.

As William James said:

'The sense that anything we think is unreal can only come when that thing is contradicted by some other thing of which we think. Any object which remains uncontradicted is ipso facto believed and posited as 'absolute reality.' (p. 37)

As William James said:

'If the searching of our heart and reins be the purpose of this human drama, then what is sought seems to be what effort we can make. He who can make none is but a shadow; he who can make much is a hero. The huge world that girdles us about puts all sorts of questions to us, and tests us in all sorts of ways. Some of the tests we meet by actions that are easy, and some of the questions we answer in articulately formulated words. But the deepest question that is ever asked admits of no reply but the dumb turning of the will and tightening of our heartstrings as we say, 'Yes, I will even have it so!' When a dreadful object is presented, or when life as a whole turns up its dark abysses to our view, then the worthless ones among us lose their hold on the situation altogether, and either escape from its difficulties by averting their attention, or, if they cannot do that, collapse into yielding masses of plaintiveness and fear. The effort required for facing and consenting to such objects is beyond their power to make. But the heroic mind does differently. To it, too, the objects are sinister and dreadful, unwelcome, incompatible with wished-for things. But it can face them if necessary without losing its hold upon the rest of life. The world thus finds in the heroic man its worthy match and mate....He can stand this Universe.' (p. 127)

MARTIN, Everett Dean. The Mystery of Religion: A Study in Social Psychology. 1924.

Our thinking, as William James showed, depends upon the fact that we are interested, active spectators in the 'game.' Thinking is for the sake of doing. To think at all is to ignore some aspects of things, and to emphasize only those qualities and attributes which are relevant to our purposes. Hence thinking is essentially 'partial.' To a mind which was wholly impartial everything would be just as relevant and important as everything else. (p. 33)

James in 'The Varieties of Religious Experience,' spoke of religion as a total reaction to our world. The believer thus assumes an emotional attitude toward existence as a whole. He wishes to value it, assign to it a character, give it a meaning. (p. 89)

James was struck with the likeness between the 'conviction of sin' and the melancholia of the psychopathic patient. In 'The Varieties of Religious Experience' he says:

'In melancholics there is usually a similar change, only it is in the reverse direction. The world now looks remote, strange, sinister, uncanny. Its color is gone, its breath is cold. There is no speculation in the eyes it glares with. 'It is as if I lived in another century,' says one asylum patient. 'I see everything through a cloud,' says another; 'things are not as they were, and I am changed.' 'I see,' says a third, 'I touch, but the things do not come near me, a thick veil alters the hue and look of everything.' 'Persons move like shadows, and sounds seem to come from a distant world.' 'There is no longer any past for me; people appear so strange; it is as if I could not see any reality, as if I were in a theater; as if people were actors, and everything were scenery; I can no longer find myself; I walk, but why? Everything floats before my eyes, but leaves no impression.' 'I weep false tears, I have unreal hands: the things I see are not real things.' Such are expressions that naturally arise to the lips of melancholic subjects describing their changed state.

'Now there are some subjects whom all this leaves a prey to the profoundest astonishment. The strangeness is wrong. The unreality cannot be. A mystery is concealed, and a metaphysical solution must exist. If the natural world is so double-faced and unhomelike, what world, what thing is real? An urgent wondering and questioning is set up, a poring theoretic activity, and in the desperate effort to get into right relations with the matter, the sufferer is often led to what becomes for him a satisfying religious solution.' (p. 161-2)

The following passages which I quote from William James's 'Varieties of Religious Experience' will illustrate my point. James used these documents as examples of 'soul sickness,' or religious melancholy. His argument seems to be that the feeling of the great and imminent reality of evil in these cases is a more profound insight into the nature of life than is possessed by the more optimistic type of believer.

He says:

'The completest religions would therefore seem to be those in which the pessimistic elements are best developed. Buddhism, of course, and Christianity are the best known to us of these. They are essentially religions of deliverance; the man must die to an unreal life before he can be born into the real life...

'The normal process of life contains moments as bad as any of those which insane melancholy is filled with, moments in which radical evil gets its innings and takes its solid turn. The lunatic's visions of horror are all drawn from the material of daily fact. Our civilization is founded on the shambles, and every individual existence goes out in a lonely spasm of helpless agony. If you protest, my friend, wait till you arrive there yourself! To believe in the carnivorous reptiles of geologic times is hard for our imagination--they seem too much like mere museum specimens. Yet there is no tooth in any one of those museum-skulls that did not daily through long years of the foretime hold fast to the body struggling in despair of some fated living victim. Forms of horror just as dreadful to their victims, if on a smaller spatial scale, fill the world about us to-day. Here on our very hearths and in our gardens the infernal cat plays with the panting mouse, or holds the hot bird fluttering in her jaws. Crocodiles and rattlesnakes and pythons are at this moment vessels of life as real as we are; their loathsome existence fills every minute of every day that drags its length along; and whenever they or other wild beasts clutch their living prey, the deadly horror which an agitated melancholic feels is the literally right reaction on the situation...

'It may indeed be that no religious reconciliation with the absolute totality of things is possible. Some evils, indeed, are ministerial to higher forms of good; but it may be that there are forms of evil so extreme as to enter into no good system whatsoever, and that, in respect of such evil, dumb submission or neglect to notice is the only practical resource. But provisionally, and as a mere matter of program and method, since the evil facts are as genuine parts of nature as the good ones, the philosophic presumption should be that they have some rational significance, and that systematic healthy-mindedness, failing as it does to accord to sorrow, pain, and death any positive and active attention whatever, is formally less complete than systems that try at least to include these elements in their scope.'

This might lead us to the conclusion that melancholia and the feeling of sin are logical deductions from fact. Such however is not the case. James points out the fact that the problem of religious melancholy leads us to a consideration of cases which are clearly psychopathic. He says:

'In none of these cases was there any intellectual insanity or delusion about matters of fact; but were we disposed to open the chapter of really insane melancholia, with its hallucinations and delusions, it would be a worse story still--desperation absolute and complete, the whole universe coagulating about the sufferer into a material of overwhelming horror, surrounding him without opening or end. Not the conception or intellectual perception of evil, but the grisly, blood-freezing, heart-palsying sensation of it close upon one, and no other conception or sensation able to live for a moment in its presence. How irrelevantly remote seem all our usual refined optimisms and intellectual and moral consolations in presence of a need of help like this! Here is the real core of the religious problem: Help! Help!'

James cites numerous religious 'confessions' in order to show how closely this feeling of sin is related to psychopathic melancholia. (p. 169-73)

James in 'The Varieties of Religious Experience' says of confession as it occurs in religion:

'In regard to Confession I will also be most brief, saying my word about it psychologically, not historically. Not nearly as widespread as sacrifice, it corresponds to a more inward and moral stage of sentiment. It is part of the general system of purgation and cleansing which one feels one's self in need of, in order to be in right relations to one's deity. For him who confesses, shams are over and realities have begun; he has exteriorized his rottenness. If he has not actually got rid of it he at least no longer smears it over with a hypocritical show of virtue--he lives at least upon a basis of veracity. The complete decay of the practice of confession in Anglo-Saxon communities is a little hard to account for. Reaction against popery is of course the historic explanation, for in popery confession went with penances and absolution, and other inadmissible practices. But on the side of the sinner himself it seems as if the need ought to have been too great to accept so summary a refusal of its satisfaction. One would think that in more men the shell of secrecy would have had to open, the pent-in-abscess to burst and gain relief, even though the ear that heard the confession were unworthy. The Catholic church, for obvious utilitarian reasons, has substituted auricual confession to one priest for the more radical act of public confession. We English-speaking Protestants, in the general self-reliance and unsociability of our nature, seem to find it enough if we take God alone into our confidence.' (p. 251-3)

MARTIN, Everett Dean. Psychology What It Has to Teach You, Yourself and Your World. 1924.

The significance of William James' work in psychology is so great that it is impossible for any one to gain an insight into what psychology is about unless, he has for at least once in his life seen this subject from William James' point of view. Psychology was not an isolated thing to James. I mean to say that the student in sharing James' point of view not only gains a new insight into the subject matter psychology, but he gains something more valuable: a different point of view in his thinking about most of the problems of our life. There are some writers whom to know is to live through an experience which leaves one always thereafter different.

Many of the questions that James dealt with are still so controversial that we shall find ourselves referring to him again and again as we discuss the various problems of this science. In fact, James' work is still the classic text on the subject, and it is therefore highly important that we see just what it is that he did for our science.

In a sense, we shall have to take a very broad view of James. He was not only a psychologist but he was also a philosopher, and a great one. At one time he was more quoted and referred to than any other American thinker, and he is probably the most distinctively modern philosopher that America has produced. (p. 29)

Yet, William James says if we have to be conscious that we are conscious in order to be conscious, we might just as well say we have to dream that we dream in order to dream to dream or to swear that we swear in order to swear. (p. 61)

So important then is habit that many writers cannot resist preaching or moralizing about the subject to some degree. James, in the famous chapter on Habit in the 'Principles of Psychology,' was unable to resist this temptation to adorn his tale with a moral. This was excusable on James's part because he was a teacher of youth and was deeply concerned about developing among his students habits of study. (p. 76)

James also tells us that there are minds to whom the sunset means only supper time or calls up some superficial platitude. He says, 'If the habitual contiguities predominate, we have a prosaic mind; of rare contiguities or similarities have free play, we call the person fanciful, poetic or witty. But the thought as a rule is of matters of fact in their entirety.' (p. 118)

James says that the self of which we are conscious is just as truly an objective thing as are any of the things about us which we see and touch. (p. 135)

James says that along with the body the 'material me' includes also our possessions. There is no clear cut distinction between 'me' and 'mine.' (p. 139)

MAUGHAM, W. Somerset. The Vagrant Mood. Six Essays. 1953.

In 1910 I went to America for the first time and in due course paid a visit to Boston. Henry James, his brother having recently died, was staying at Cambridge, Massachusetts, with his sister-in-law, and Mrs. James asked me to dinner. There were but the three of us. I can remember nothing of the conversation, but I could not help noticing that Henry James was troubled in spirit, and after dinner, when the widow left us alone in the dining-room he told me that he had promised his brother to remain at Cambridge for, I think, six months after his death, so that if he found himself able to make a communication from beyond the grave there would be two sympathetic witnesses on the spot ready to receive it. I could not but reflect that Henry James was in so nervous a state that it would be difficult to place implicit confidence in any report he might make. His sensibility was so exacerbated that he was capable of imagining anything. But hitherto no message had come and the six months were drawing to their end. (p. 209-10)

MEAD, Hunter. Types and Problems of Philosophy. An Introduction. Revised Edition. 1953.

William James, in our own country and century, divided men into what he considered the basic classifications 'tough-minded' and 'tender-minded;' and this terminology has achieved wide acceptance.

James had the dual viewpoint of pschologist and philosopher. It is therefore significant that he suggested that the difference is probably one of temperament-and therefore as fundamental as any human differences that we know. Unfortunately, we know little more as to either the basis or the nature of 'temperament' than James did two generations ago. (p. 105)

James' philosophical enemy was the absolute idealism of the Hegelians, with its singularistic or 'block-view' of the universe. He felt that any system which achieved such singularistic unity could not possibly do justice to the richness and variety of human experience. James was, in short, appealing for support to our direct experience (common sense again, it should be noted) against the logical abstractionism of Hegel's Absolute. He believed that the degree of abstraction required to achieve this absolute synthesis, coupled with the number of intervening logical steps, could only result in a Real that was utterly empty-a 'night in which all cows are black.' For James, who loved life with all its multiplicity, complexity and challenging possibilities as few philosophers have loved it, any such singularistic outcome to the metaphysical quest seemed almost blasphemous. (p. 236)

There is no better spokesman for this melioristic view than William James. He believed there is a Power at the heart of things working toward order and goodness, but this Power is limited. It does not do more because It cannot. Great as God's power may be, the task of erecting a moral order within an indifferent universe is greater yet. Consequently God may fail unless He has our individual help-and this means the help of all of us. (p. 396)

Here again it is William James who probably expressed this attitude most clearly and most famously. His celebrated essay, 'The Will to Believe,' is a long pragmatic elaboration of this same question: since it is more satisfying to believe in God and immortality, and as this belief involves no risk but only great possible gain, why not believe? The French philosopher of the seventeenth century, Blaise Pascal, formulated what has come to be known as 'Pascal's wager,' and James admits he merely extends this. (p. 431)

James agrees with Pascal that reason cannot settle the question of God and immortality. But he is not satisfied to argue from our need for God to the existence of God, as Pascal had done before proposing his 'wager' as an additional argument for persons whose need for God was less urgent than his own. Instead James elaborates another idea made famous by Pascal: 'The heart has reasons which the head knows not.'

James defends the right of what he calls our 'passional nature' and its demands, which are roughly equivalent to what the contemporary psychologist calls our emotional needs. But James goes farther than merely asserting that all men require emotional satisfactions as well as those of the intellect. He argues that in the last analysis all vital decisions and judgments, even when they seem most rational and logically grounded, are actually emotional choices made by our 'passional nature.' (p. 432)

James thinks that the skeptic-agnostic is so afraid of being duped by hope that he flies to the other extreme and becomes duped by fear. To James this is absurd: if we are forced to choose between risks, he asks on what grounds should anyone select the risk offering no gain and all loss as against the one offering no loss and great possible gain. This brings us back to Pascal's wager; or, in James' characteristic language:

'Dupery for dupery, what proof is there that dupery through hope is so much worse than dupery through fear: I, for one, can see no proof; and I simply refuse to imitate the skeptic's option in a case where my own stake is important enough to give me the right to choose my own form of risk.' (p. 433)

MONTAGUE, Charles Edward. Disenchantment. 1922.

No doubt you know all about it from books, and you may prefer the wording of that tentative approach made by the most spiritually-minded of modern philosophers to a definition of God--'Something that is in and about me, in the consciousness of which I am free from fear and desire--something which would make it easy to do the most (otherwise) difficult thing without any other motive except that it was the one thing worth doing.' And William James has, of course, shown more skill in explaining what mystic ecstasy is and what is its place in religion, and what its relations to such mirages of itself as the mock inspirations of Anthony's lust and Burns' drunkenness. (p. 95)

MONTAGUE, William Pepperell. Belief Unbound. A Promethean Religion for a Modern World. 1930.

William James was right when he said that the higher

motives are not the stronger motives, and that it is necessary for us to throw the weight of our own free will into the scales if we would make higher win over lower. He was right also when he refused to let the determinist jockey him into the admission that the essence of freedom lay in choosing between this motive and that, as between being pulled to the left or being pulled to the right. (p. 53)

MOORE, Virginia. The Unicorn. William Butler Yeats' Search for Reality. 1954.

Needing an ally among close thinkers, he quoted William James on the sanity of visionaries: 'The great Spanish mystics....appear for the most part to have shown indomitable spirit and energy....St. Ignatius was a mystic, but his mysticism made him assuredly one of the most practical human figures that ever lived.' And again, in support of suprarationalism: 'If you have intuitions at all, they come from a deeper level of your nature than the loquacious level which rationalism inhabits.' (Varieties of Religious Experience) (p. 126-7)

MORE, Paul Elmer. Hellenistic Philosophies. 1923.

It is curious and illuminating to hear William James in our day applying the same dilemma, in still more vigorous terms, to a modern equivalent of the Stoic paradox:

'My trouble, you see, lies with monism. Determinism = monism; and a monism like this world can't be an object of pure optimistic contemplation. By pessimism I simply mean ultimate non-optimism. The Ideal is only a part of this world. Make the world a Pluralism, and you forthwith have an object to worship. Make it a Unit, on the other hand, and worship and abhorrence are equally one-sided and equally legitimate reactions. Indifferentism is the true condition of such a world, and turn the matter how you will, I don't see how any philosophy of the Absolute can ever escape from that capricious alternation of mysticism and satanism in the treatment of its great Idol, which history has always shown....Either close your eyes and adopt an optimism or a pessimism equally daft; or exclude moral categories altogether from a place in the world's definition, which leaves the world unheimlich, reptilian, and foreign to man; or else, sticking to it that the moral judgment is applicable, give up the hope of applying it to the world.' (Letters) (p. 157-8)

MORE, Paul Elmer. A New England Group and Others. 1921.

Charles Eliot Norton once had a sitting with Mrs. Piper in the home of William James, and this was the conclusion of his report: 'As to the origin of many of the phantasmagorias of her trance dreams, I formed a very distinct opinion, but many experiments would be required to test its correctness, and these I shall never make.' I hold Mr. Norton's taste to be a deeper wisdom than the unregulated 'open-mindedness' of his friend. When the last balance is made up, I even suspect that Mr. James will have been found among the disintegrating and deteriorating forces of the age.

For in its sum this movement, to which Mr. James lent the prestige of his great name, seems to me to lie in a backward direction towards disintegration. As it is not science, so it is not religion. (p. 159)

MUMFORD, Lewis. The Conduct of Life. 1951.

In taking this position I would recall certain illuminating perceptions of William James, which unfortunately he never sufficiently developed in his own philosophy. 'The spirit and principles of science,' he observed, 'are mere affairs of method; there is nothing in them that need hinder science from dealing successfully with a world in which personal forces are the starting-points of new effects. The only form of thing that we directly encounter, the only experience that we concretely have, is our personal life. The only complete category of our thinking, our professors of philosophy tell us, is the category of personality, every other category being one of the abstract elements of that. And this systematic denial on science's part of personality as a condition of events, this rigorous belief that in its own essential and innermost nature our world is a strictly impersonal world may, conceivably, as the whirligig of time goes round prove to be the very defect that our descendants will be most surprised at in our own boasted science, the omission that to their eyes will most tend to make it look perspectivenless and short.' (The Will to Believe) (p. 229)

MUMFORD, Lewis. The Golden Day. A Study in American Experience and Culture. 1926.

If one could reconstruct New England in Emerson, one could, I think, recover great tracts of pioneer and industrial America from the pragmatists, the pioneer especially in James, the industrialist in his great pupil, Dewey.

James's insistence upon the importance of novelty and freshness echoes on a philosophic plane the words of Mark Twain. 'What is it that confers the noblest delight?... Discovery! To know that you are walking where no others have walked, that you are beholding what human eye has not seen before; that you are breathing virgin atmosphere. To give birth to an idea--to discover a great thought--To find a new planet, to invent a new hinge, to find the way to make the lightning carry your message. To be the first--that is the idea.' James's opposition to a block universe, his notion that salvation had to be worked out, his feeling that there was no savor, no excitement, no interest 'in following the good path if we do not feel that evil is also possible and natural, nay, threatening and imminent'--what was all this, too, but the animus of the pioneer, translated into dialectic? (p. 186-7)

'For my part,' cried William James, 'I do not know what sweat and blood, what the tragedy of this life means except just this: if life is not a struggle in which by success, there is something gained on behalf of the universe, then it is no more than idle amusement.' (p. 189-90)

The carefully limited area he left to religious belief in The Will-to-Believe was transformed by ever-so-witty colleagues into the Will-to-make-believe. His conscious philosophy of pragmatism, which sought to ease one of the mighty, recurrent dilemmas of his personal life, was translated into a belief in the supremacy of cash-values and practical results; and the man who was perhaps one of the most cosmopolitan and cultivated minds of his generation was treated at times as if he were a provincial writer of newspaper platitudes, full of the gospel of smile. (p. 191)

William James had a style. Dreiser, Dewey, the commanding writers of the early Chicago school, were at one on this point: they had no style: they wrote in a language which, however concrete its objects, was as fuzzy and formless as lint. There is a homely elegance in James's writing, a beauty in the presentation of the thought, even if the concept of beauty was absent from his philosophy; in the earlier writing of Dewey, on the other hand, one looks in vain for either the concept or its literary equivalent. The comedown is serious. (p. 255)

MÜNSTERBURG, Hugo. American Problems from the Point of View of a Psychologist. 1910.

When the president of Harvard University gave up his administrative work, the old Harvard students and the whole country enthusiastically brought to him the highest thanks which he so fully deserved. But when, the year before, William James left Harvard, the most famous scholar who has worked in this Harvard generation, the event passed by like a routine matter. At the commencement festivities every speaker spoke of the departing administrative officer, but no one thought of the departing scholar. And that exactly expresses the general feeling. (p. 53)

MYERSON, Abraham. Speaking of Man. 1950.
Jung and William James had no more basis than Jurgen, the pawnbroker poet, when they posited a consciousness beyond ours, with which we were in communication, which flowed in and out of us, but which was eternal and gave everlasting values to life. (p. 36)

NIEBUHR, Reinhold. The Contribution of Religion to Social Work. 1932.
'When religion has become an orthodoxy,' declared William James, 'its day of inwardness is over; the spring is dry and the faithful live at second hand exclusively and stone the prophets in their turn.' (p. 59)

NIEBUHR, Reinhold. Does Civilization Need Religion? 1928.
The pluralism of William James, which has been criticized as scientifically inaccurate and metaphysically inconsistent, seems to have both scientific and metaphysical virtues. There is good reason to accept at least a qualified dualism not only because it is morally more potent than traditional monisms, but because it is metaphysically acceptable. (p. 213)

NIEBUHR, Reinhold. The Nature and Destiny of Man. A Christian Interpretation. Volume I. Human Nature. 1941.
Of those who follow Hume it may suffice to present one particularly illustrious example: William James. James denies both the unity of consciousness and the transcendent ego: 'If there were no passing states of consciousness, then indeed we might suppose an abiding principle, absolutely one with itself, to be the ceaseless thinker in each of us. But if the states of consciousness be accorded as realities no such 'substantial' identity in the thinker need be supposed. Yesterday's and today's states of consciousness have no substantial identity, for when one is here the other is irrevocably gone....The logical conclusion seems to be that the states of consciousness are all

that psychology needs to do her work with. Metaphysics or theology may prove the soul to exist; but for psychology the hypothesis of such a substantial principle of unity is superfluous.' (Psychology, Briefer Course) (p. 73)

NORTHROP, F. S. C. Ideological Differences and World Order. Studies in the Philosophy and Science of the World Cultures. 1949.

Without dogmatic ideology, save the presuppositions of democracy and Christianity, and minus a philosophy in the systematic sense, the New Deal embodied permanently only what is most typical of American two-party practice, with what has long been theoretically foregone. The New Deal serves to remind us that the profoundest philosophy of American life is that no philosophy is adequate to the free man's vocation. As William James, America's most typical professional in philosophy, says: 'There is no conclusion. What has concluded that we might conclude in regard to it?' (p. 221-2)

NORTHROP, F. S. C. The Meeting of the East and West. An Inquiry Concerning World Understanding. 1946.

William James, similarly identifying the self with this succession of associated sense data which he termed 'the flow of consciousness,' made the best makeshift for religion which is possible upon such positivistic premises, by the exceedingly treacherous recourse of grounding the Divine in an arbitrary decision to insist upon certain imaginatively given desires, very difficult to distinguish from wishful thinking, which he labeled very honestly, 'the will to believe.' (p. 116-7)

James, however, did make one unique and exceedingly important contribution. He noted that what we immediately apprehend is not limited, as Locke's theory of ideas requires and Hume tended consequently to maintain, to atomic sense data and their relations. Only in the center of the empirically given continuum of immediate experience are there sharply contoured atomic sensa. The remainder of the continuum, what James termed 'the periphery of consciousness,' is undifferentiated and indeterminate. (p. 117)

NORTON, Charles Eliot. Letters with Biographical Comment by his Daughter and M. A. DeWolfe Howe. Two volumes. 1913.

From May to September of 1904, Norton printed in the 'Atlantic' some of the letters from Ruskin which made up the two volumes of 'Letters of John Ruskin to Charles Eliot Norton,' published that autumn. On June 30, William James wrote: 'Dear Charles,--I have just read the July 'Atlantic' and am so moved by your Ruskin letters that I can't refrain from overflowing. They seem to me immortal documents--as the clouds clear away he will surely take his stable place as one of the noblest of the sons of men. Mere sanity is the most philistine and (at bottom) unessential of a man's attributes....Do you suppose that there are many other correspondents of Ruskin who will yield up their treasures in our time to the light? I wish that your modesty had not suppressed certain passages which evidently expressed too much regard for yourself. The point should have been his expression of that sort of thing--no matter to whom addressed!' (v. 2. p. 348)

From letter of Norton to Eliot Norton, June 11, 1907.

Mr. Howells was with us on Sunday, and seemed better than I had expected, considering how poorly he was during the greater part of the winter and spring. Pleasant as he always is, he never was pleasanter, and we had four or five hours of animated talk by which a vast deal of ground was covered. His humour was delightful as of old. One quick bit of wit is worth preserving. I was speaking to him of Dr. James's new book, and said that it was brilliant but not clear. 'Like his father,' said Mr. Howells, 'who wrote the Secret of Swedenborg and kept it.' (v. 2. p. 379)

From letter of Norton to Miss Gaskell, July 24, 1908.

James is an unusually delightful person, fresh, animated, with active and vigorous intelligence, often irrational, but all the more interesting for being so. He is the most independent and the most popular of metaphysicians and psychologists, and, as you know, is the great protagonist of the new doctrine of pragmatism which is worth to my mind just about as much as the systems of metaphysical speculation which have preceded it. James's spirit and temper do good to whoever comes within their range; and it is as much through their affections as through their intellects that his disciples are attracted to him. It shows how sweet his nature is, that he can get on with me who am absolutely a skeptic in regard to every metaphysical system and as to the value of every inquiry into the unknowable. (v. 2. p. 412)

OBERNDORF, C. P. History of Psychoanalysis in America. 1953.

Soon thereafter William James in one of his Lowell lectures on psychopathology in 1896 said: 'In the relief of certain hysterias, by handling the buried ideas, whether as in Freud or in Janet, we see a portent of the possible usefulness of these new discoveries. The awful becomes relatively trivial.' (Matthiessen, F. O. The James Family) (p. 41)

OLDHAM, J. H. Life is Commitment. 1953.

William James, writing from a standpoint outside the Christian faith, says: 'As for me, my bed is made: I am against bigness and greatness in all their forms, and with the invisible molecular moral forces that work from individual to individual, stealing in through the crannies of the world like so many soft rootlets, or like the capillary oozing of water, and yet rending the hardest monuments of man's pride, if you give them time.' (Letters) (p. 76)

William James, though he was not a professing Christian, understood this. 'Death,' he tells us, 'finally runs the robustest of us down. And whenever we feel this, such a sense of the vanity and provisionality of our voluntary career comes over us that all our well-doing appears the hollowest substitute for that well-being that our lives ought to be grounded in but alas! are not.' (Varieties of Religious Experience) (p. 77)

OSBORN, Alex F. Applied Imagination. Principles and Procedures of Creative Thinking. 1953.

As William James pointed out, 'In the dim background of our mind we know what we ought to be doing, but somehow we cannot start. Every moment we expect the spell to break, but it continues, pulse after pulse, and we float with it.' (p. 215)

OSTROW, Albert A. How to Enjoy Yourself. 1954.

Said James, 'Even if the day ever dawns in which it will not be needed for fighting the old, heavy battles against nature, it will still always be needed to furnish the background of sanity, serenity and cheerfulness to life, to give moral elasticity to our disposition, to round off the wiry edge of our fretfulness and make us good-humored and easy to approach.' (p. 52)

OVERSTREET, Bonaro W. Brave Enough for Life. 1941.

'All we contend for,' wrote James, 'is that we.... should now attack things as if there were no official answer preoccupying the field. At present we are bribed beforehand by our reverence or dislike for the official answer. We work with one eye on our problem, and with the other on the consequences to our enemy or to our lawgiver, as the case may be; the result in both cases is mediocrity.' (Philosophy and Philosophical Teaching in the United States) (p. 90)

As William James has pointed out, 'It is certain.... that the narrowest trade or professional training does something more for a man than make a skillful practical tool of him--it makes him also a judge of other men's skills. Whether his trade be pleading at the bar or surgery or plastering or plumbing, it develops a critical sense in him for that sort of occupation. He understands the difference between second-rate and first-rate work in his whole branch of industry; he gets to know a good job in his own line as soon as he sees it; and getting to know this in his own line, he gets a faint sense of what good work may mean anyhow....sound work, clean work, finished work: feeble work, slack work, sham work--these words express an identical contrast in many different departments of activity.' (Memories and Studies) (p. 119-20)

OVERSTREET, Bonaro W. Freedom's People. How we Qualify for a Democratic Society. 1945.

No one, perhaps, has more vividly presented the whole risky adventure of life than has William James:

'Suppose that the world's author put the case to you before creation, saying: 'I am going to make a world not certain to be saved, a world the perfection of which will be conditioned merely, the condition being that every single agent do its level best. I offer you the chance of taking part in such a world. It is a real adventure, with real danger; yet it may win through. Will you trust yourself and trust the other agents enough to take the risk?' (Pragmatism) (p. 51)

OVERSTREET, Bonaro W. Understanding Fear in Ourselves and Others. 1951.

'Peace' in military minds today is a synonym for 'war expected.' ....It may even reasonably be said that the intensely sharp competitive preparation for war is the real war, permanent, unceasing; and that the battles are only a sort of public verification of the mastery gained during the 'peace' interval.

Thus wrote William James in a Moral Equivalent For

War. (p. 124-5)

OVERSTREET, Harry A. About Ourselves. Psychology for Normal People. 1927.

William James tells the story of a Russian lady who sat weeping at the tragic fate of the hero in the opera while her coachman was freezing outside. One would have called her a lady of refined sensibilities; and had she lived long enough to lose her lands and be shouldered out by the revolution into a heartless world, one would have been angered by the injustice done to a sensitive soul. But William James knew better. Her sensitiveness was theatrical. It was a delight in feeling her own fictional sorrows. In short, she had ingrowing emotions. And so, with his robust humor, and with his eyes on this kind of emotional theatricality, James laid down the rule: 'When, through art, or music, or poetry, or drama, you are roused in your feelings, do something. Say a decent word to your mother-in-law; give an extra nickel to the waiter; buy your wife that long-needed bonnet. Otherwise the emotions, feeding only on themselves, turn into toxins. Sentimentalism is one of these toxins.' (p. 222)

OVERSTREET, Harry A. The Great Enterprise. Relating Ourselves to Our World. 1952.

Many years ago (September 21, 1876), in a letter printed in the Nation, William James wrote one of his characteristically William Jamesian sentences. Speaking of the need for educating young men in the colleges for a 'wider openness of mind and more flexible way of thinking,' he proposed this test of a healthy mind: 'Is there air and space in your mind, or must your companions gasp for breath when they talk with you?' (p. 117-8)

PAUL, Leslie. The English Philosophers. 1953.

Yet it is a somewhat casuistical argument that Perfection is Perfection just because it has so much imperfection about it. I think we can understand why, from the turn of the century, the Absolute was so much under fire. Much of the sniping came from pragmatists like the American, William James. He wrote (in Radical Empiricism) that the Absolute made him 'feel as if I had entered into a contract with no reserved rights, or rather as if I had to live in a large seaside boarding-house with no private bedroom in which I might take refuge from the society of the place....Certainly, to my personal knowledge all Hegelians are not prigs, but I somehow feel as if all prigs ought to end, if developed, by becoming Hegelians.' (Essays in Radical Empiricism) (p. 265-6)

PERRY, Bliss. And Gladly Teach. Reminiscences. 1935.

This mention of Chocorua reminds me, perhaps illogically, of a predicament of William James, not in the woods, but a place far more terrifying to a man of his temperament, a Banquet of the Universal Peace Congress in Boston. We were assigned seats together, as each of us had promised to make an after-dinner speech. 'There's Booker Washington!' exclaimed James as we took our places: 'let's get him over here with us.' But alas, Booker Washington was already placed at the high table with the foreign delegates. I have seen many men nervous at the prospect of making a speech, and I have been scared myself, but never so badly as William James on that occasion. 'What shall I do?' he whispered to me. 'I cannot remember one word of my address, and yet yesterday in Chocorua I recited it eleven times to my wife without a mistake!' 'Have you the manuscript?' I asked; and he pulled out of his pocket the sheets of yellow scribbling paper on which he had written every word in long hand. His fingers shook so that all the sheets dropped upon the floor. I picked them up, arranged them, and commanded him to read them when his turn came: the audience would be interested in his ideas, not in his capacity as a memorizer. Finally he pulled himself together and read beautifully the little address which was later printed in the Atlantic and in his Memories and Studies.

I never heard William James talk so brilliantly, however, as he did late one night when we had come out to Cambridge together, after a dinner of The Club. He had sat in one of his silent moods all through the dinner, and had scarcely spoken in the trolley-car. But as I was bidding him goodnight in front of the Harvard 'Coop,' something turned on the current in that powerhouse of his brain. He began to characterize two of his colleagues, Münsterberg and Santayana. I do not know how long he talked, but he had all the time there was, and he painted such full-length portraits of those two philosophers as will never be painted again. (p. 290-1)

PERRY, Bliss. Emerson Today. 1931.

The Centenary celebration at Concord can best be described from a letter by William James, who was one of many distinguished speakers: 'The weather, the beauty of the village, the charming old meeting-house, the descendants of the grand old man in such profusion, the mixture of Concord and Boston heads, so many of them of our own circle, the allusions to great thought and things, and the old-time New England rusticity and rurality, the silver polls and ancient voices of the vieille garde who did the orating (including this 'yer child) all made a matchless combination, took one back to one's childhood, and made the rarely realized marriage of reality with ideality, that usually only occurs in fiction or poetry. I let Ralph Waldo Emerson speak for himself....Reading the whole of him over again continuously has made me feel his real greatness as I never did before.' (Letters) (p. 7)

I am tempted, at this point, to remind the reader of the testimony of William James, already quoted. 'Reading the whole of him (Emerson) over again continuously has made me feel his real greatness as I never did before.' But perhaps William James--all unsuspected by his friends--lacked a 'steadily growing character!' (p. 103)

PERRY, Bliss. Life and Letters of Henry Lee Higginson. 1921.

From letter of James to Higginson.

The best thing about this university is the chance these fellows get of meeting one man after another in Sever Hall who stands for something in the world outside, and who gives them a glimpse of an example and makes one of those personal impressions that abide. I'm sure you hit the mark last night, and I'm sure the field will do all the good, and more than all the good, you can possibly hope from it. (p. 334)

From letter of James to Higginson.

'Think of the virtues of Roosevelt, either as permanent sovereign of this great country, or as President of H. U. I've been having a discussion with X____ about him, which has resulted in making me his faithful henchman for life, X____ was so violent. Think of the mighty good-will of him, of his enjoyment of his post, of his power as a preacher, of the number of things to which he gives attention, of the safety of his second thoughts, of the increased courage he is showing, and above all, of the fact that he is an open, instead of an underground leader.... Bless him--and d____ all his detractors like you and and X____....' (p. 360)

From letter of James to Higginson.

'You remember one day,' he wrote to Henry Higginson

in 1909, 'when I tried to convert you to the notion of Roosevelt as a Harvard President. He ceased to be my candidate after his speech to the men in the Harvard Union, in which, altho' he praised scientific research, there wasn't otherwise a single note of elevation or distinction in anything he said. Just the ordinary street-level talk of fairness and courage, and down with molly-coddles, meaning by them all the men with courage enough to oppose him. I gave him up! At the same time I believe his influence on our public life and on our people's feelings about public life has been of enormous value.' (p. 361-2)

'I was struck by Henry Higginson's high level of mental tension, so to call it, which made him talk incessantly and passionately about one subject after another, never running dry, and reminding me more of myself when I was twenty years old. It isn't so much a man's eminence of elementary faculties that pulls him through. They may be rare, and he do nothing. It is the steam-pressure to the square inch behind that moves the machine. The amount of that is what makes the great difference between us. Henry has it high.' (Letters) (p. 385)

It was the banker who suggested James as the orator for the dedication of the Shaw Memorial in Boston in 1897; but James, characteristically enough, rated Higginson's address on Shaw in Sanders Theatre more highly than his own. 'As for our speeches, yours was infinitely the more impressive, being the work of an honest man, and not that of a professional phrase-monger and paid rhetorician. Those are the bad devils!' (p. 414)

From letter of James to Higginson, September 18, 1900.

I read your political observations with respect, and see how you are professionally bound to resist Bryan. But I pray for his victory none the less. There are worse things than financial troubles in a Nation's career. To puke up its ancient soul, and the only things that gave it eminence among other nations, in five minutes without a wink of squeamishness, is worse; and that is what the Republicans would commit us to in the Philippines. Our conduct there has been one protracted infamy towards the Islanders, and one protracted lie towards ourselves. If we can only regain our old seat in the American saddle, and get back into some sincere relations with our principles and professions, it seems to me it makes very little permanent difference what incidental disturbances may accompany the process, for this crisis is one which is sure to determine the whole moral development of our policy in a good or a bad way for an indefinite future time. (p.429)

PERRY, Bliss. Praise of Folly and Other Essays. 1923.
There was Shaler's friend, William James. His books are read by scholars and pupils all over the world. But who will record the vibration of his rich baritone voice, his shyness, his whimsicality, his kindness, the strain of the irresponsible Irishman in him? (p. 209)

PERRY, Ralph Barton. Approach to Philosophy. 1910.
Religious reactions are 'total reactions.'
'To get at them,' says William James, 'you must go behind the foreground of existence and reach down to that curious sense of the whole residual cosmos as an everlasting presence, intimate or alien, terrible or amusing, lovable or odious, which in some degree everyone possesses. This sense of the world's presence, appealing as it does to our peculiar individual temperament, makes us either strenuous or careless, devout or blasphemous, gloomy or exultant about life at large; and our reaction, involuntary and inarticulate and often half unconscious as it is, is the completest of all our answers to the question, 'What is the character of this universe in which we dwell?' (Varieties of Religious Experience) (p. 65)
'General Booth, the founder of the Salvation Army, considers that the first vital step in saving outcasts consists in making them feel that some decent human being cares enough for them to take an interest in the question whether they are to rise or sink.' (Varieties of Religious Experience) (p. 71)
As William James has said:
'Even God's being is sacred from ours. To cooperate with his creation by the best and rightest response seems all he wants of us. In such cooperation with his purposes, not in any chimerical speculative conquest of him, not in any theoretical drinking of him up, must lie the real meaning of our destiny.' (The Will to Believe) (p. 305)

PERRY, Ralph Barton. The Citizen Decides. A Guide to Responsible Thinking in Time of Crisis. 1951.
In 1897 William James delivered an oration at the unveiling of a monument to Robert Gould Shaw, who had been killed at the head of a colored regiment in the Civil War. There are, said the orator, two kinds of courage, for both of which Colonel Shaw was to be honored: the fighting courage of a soldier, and the moral courage of the

good citizen. The former is more conspicuous, but the latter is more necessary:

'The deadliest enemies of nations are not their foreign foes; they always dwell within their borders. And from these internal enemies civilization is always in need of being saved. The nation blest above all nations is she in whom the civic genius of the people does the saving day by day, by acts without external picturesqueness; by speaking, writing, voting reasonably; by smiting corruption swiftly; by good temper between parties; by the people knowing true men when they see them, and preferring them as leaders to rabid partisans or empty quacks.' (Memories and Studies) (p. 126)

PERRY, Ralph Barton. Defense of Philosophy. 1931.

Let me take as my first illustration a passage from an early letter of William James, in which consolation is offered in the form of an invitation to look beyond the surrounding darkness, or to use memory and imagination to offset the narrowing effect of the present perspective:

'Remember when old December's darkness is everywhere about you, that the world is really in every minutest point as full of life as in the most joyous morning you ever lived through; that the sun is whanging down, and the waves dancing, and the gulls skimming at the mouth of the Amazon, as freshly as in the first morning of creation; and the hour is just as fit as any hour for a new gospel of cheer to be preached. I am sure that one can, by merely thinking of these matters of fact, limit the power of one's evil moods over one's way of looking at the Kosmos.' (Letters) (p. 47-8)

William James, who divided philosopies into the 'tender-minded' and the 'tough-minded,' and betrayed his strong temperamental preference for the tough, gloried in this innovating, individualistic spirit of philosophy.

'Philosophy,' he said, 'is able to fancy everything different from what it is. It sees the familiar as if it were strange, and the strange as if it were familiar. It can take things up and lay them down again. Its mind is full air that plays round every subject. It rouses us from our native dogmatic slumber and breaks up our caked prejudices.' (Some Problems of Philosophy) (p. 52-3)

PERRY, Ralph Barton. General Theory of Value. 1950.

James has also emphasized the fact that it is characteristic of mind to solve problems, or try until some end-result is attained. Cover the poles of a magnet with a card, he tells us, and the iron-filings, 'will press forever against its surface,' as bubbles will remain lodged beneath the bottom of an inverted jar of water. The movement of the iron-filings towards the magnet, or of the bubbles towards the outer air, is a mere simulation of that love or attraction that moves living things:

'Romeo wants Juliet as the filings want the magnet; and if no obstacles intervene he moves towards her by as straight a line as they. But Romeo and Juliet, if a wall be built between them, do not remain idiotically pressing their faces against its opposite sides like the magnet and the filings with the card. Romeo soon finds a circuitous way, by scaling the wall or otherwise, of touching Juliet's lips directly. With the filings the path is fixed; whether it reaches the end depends on accidents. With the lover it is the end which is fixed, the path may be modified indefinitely.' (Principles of Psychology) (p. 210)

While James explicitly affirmed this correlation of emotion with instinct, his name is more particularly associated with the so-called 'James-Lange Theory.' According to this theory the 'feel' of the emotion, the aspect presented in introspection, consists of organic sensations. Certain bodily changes, proprioceptive and interoceptive, 'follow directly the perception of the exciting fact,' and 'our feeling of the same changes as they occur is the emotion.'

'What kind of an emotion of fear would be left,' says this writer, 'if the feeling neither of quickened heart-beats nor of shallow breathing, neither of trembling lips nor of weakened limbs, neither of goose-flesh nor of visceral stirrings, were present, it is quite impossible for me to think. Can one fancy the state of rage and picture no ebullition in the chest, no flushing of the face, no dilation of the nostrils, no clenching of the teeth, no impulse to vigorous action, but in their stead limp muscles, calm breathing and a placid face? The present writer, for one, certainly cannot.' (Principles of Psychology) (p. 295)

According to James, the specification of an interest tends to diminish the strength of the general interest from which it was derived.

'The original impulse which got us homes, wives, dietaries, and friends at all, seems to exhaust itself in its first achievements and to leave no surplus energy for reacting on new cases....It existed miscellaneously, or as an instinct pure and simple, only before habit was formed. A habit, once grafted on an instinctive tendency, restricts the range of the tendency itself, and keeps us from reacting on any but the habitual object, although other objects might just as well have been chosen had they been the first-comers.' (p. 543)

The explicit acceptance of this standard by recent philosophers, is best illustrated by the following passage from William James:

'That act must be the best act, accordingly, which makes for the best whole, in the sense of awakening the least sum of dissatisfactions. In the casuistic scale, therefore, those ideals must be written highest which prevail at the least cost, or by whose realization the least possible number of other ideals are destroyed. Since victory and defeat there must be, the victory to be philosophically prayed for is that of the more inclusive side, --of the side which even in the hour of triumph will to some degree do justice to the ideals in which the vanquished party's interests lay. The course of history is nothing but the story of men's struggles from generation to generation to find the more and more inclusive order. Invent some manner of realizing your own ideals which also satisfy the alien demands,--that and that only is the path of peace.' (The Will to Believe) (p. 645-6)

Having defined the sense in which a harmonious personality is superior to a state of inner conflict, we have now to consider the more notable case of the superiority of a harmonious society to a state of conflict between persons. The problem is vividly presented by a striking passage in James's essay on 'The Moral Philosopher and the Moral Life.':

'If the hypothesis were offered us of a world in which Messers. Fourier's and Bellamy's and Morris's utopias should be all outdone and millions kept permanently happy on the one simple condition that a certain lost soul on the far-off edge of things should lead a life of lonely torture, what except a specifical and independent sort of emotion can it be which would make us immediately feel, even though an impulse arose within us to clutch at the happiness so offered, how hideous a thing would be its enjoyment when deliberately accepted as the fruit of such a bargain?' (The Will to Believe) (p. 669-70)

In concluding the essay in which he adopts the principle of inclusiveness, William James says:

'It would seem, too,....that the stable and systematic moral universe for which the ethical philosopher asks is fully possible only in a world where there is a divine thinker with all-enveloping demands. If such a thinker existed, his way of subordinating the demands to one another would be the finally valid casuistic scale; his claims would be the most appealing; his ideal universe would be the most inclusive realizable whole. If he now exist, then actualized in his thought already must be that ethical philosophy which we seek as the pattern which our own must evermore approach. In the interest of our own ideal of systematically unified moral truth, therefore, we, as would-be philosophers, must postulate a divine thinker, and pray for the victory of the religious cause.' (Principles of Psychology) (p. 688)

It is not to be supposed, on the other hand, that the highest good would lose its supremacy if it were realized. James appears to affirm this when he says:

'The solid meaning of life is always the same eternal thing,--the marriage, namely, of some unhabitual ideal, however special, with some fidelity, courage, and endurance; with some man's or woman's pains.--And whatever or wherever life may be there will always be the chance of that marriage to take place.' (Talks to Teachers) (p. 690)

PERRY, Ralph Barton. Moral Economy. 1909.

William James, in a passage that is frequently quoted, calls attention also to the danger of acquiring a chronic emotionality.

'The weeping of a Russian lady over the fictitious personages in the play, while her coachman is freezing to death on his seat outside, is the sort of thing that everywhere happens on a less glaring scale. Even the habit of excessive indulgence in music, for those who are neither performers themselves nor musically gifted enough to take it in a purely intellectual way, has probably a relaxing effect upon the character. One becomes filled with emotions which habitually pass without prompting to any deed, and so the inertly sentimental condition is kept up. The remedy would be, never to suffer one's self to have an emotion at a concert, without expressing it afterwards in some active way. Let the expression be the least thing in the world--speaking genially to one's aunt, or giving up one's seat in a horse-car, if nothing more heroic offers--but let it not fail to take place.' (Principles of Psychology) (p. 199)

PERRY, Ralph Barton. On All Fronts. 1941.

William James once wrote an essay entitled 'The Energies of Men.' He was primarily concerned to describe the reservoirs of power which lie below the level of habit, and which may be opened by some powerful stimulus of process of self-discipline. But he also noted the fluctuations which occur in the course of our daily lives.

'Every one is familiar (he said) with the phenomenon of feeling more or less alive on different days. Every one knows on any given day that there are energies slumbering in him which the incitements of that day do not call forth, but which he might display if these were greater. Most of us feel as if a sort of cloud weighed upon us, keeping us below our highest notch of clearness in discernment, sureness in reasoning, or firmness in deciding. Compared with what we ought to be, we are only half awake. Our fires are damped, our drafts are checked. We are making use of only a small part of our possible mental and physical resources.' (Memories and Studies) (p. 39-40)

PERRY, Ralph Barton. Present Conflict of Ideals. A Study of the Philosophical Background of the World War. 1922.

'In a general way then, and on the whole,' says William James, 'our abandonment of theological criteria and our testing of religion by practical common sense and the empirical method leave it in possession of its towering place in history. Economically the saintly group of qualities is indispensable to the world's welfare.' (Varieties of Religious Experience) (p. 299)

'Theism always stands ready with the most practically rational solution it is possible to conceive. Not an energy of our active nature to which it does not authoritatively appeal, not an emotion of which it does not normally and naturally release the springs. At a single stroke, it changes the dead blank it of the world into a living thou, with whom the whole man may have dealings.' (Will to Believe) (p. 300)

The originality of James lies in his accepting the manyness and differences of the world as final and irreducible; and his welcoming this manyness and diversity as the great redeeming feature of the world. To borrow the language of Shelley, James preferred the 'dome of many colored glass' to 'the white radiance of eternity.' (p. 316)

The fine quality of a pluralistic individualism expresses itself in that generosity of spirit which rejoices that there are more things in heaven and earth than one's personal philosophy had dreamed of. Such an individualism, as James writes in concluding the essay, 'absolutely forbids us to be forward in pronouncing on the meaninglessness of forms of existence other than our own; and it commands us to tolerate, respect and indulge those whom we see harmlessly interested and happy in their own ways, however unintelligible these may be to us. Hands off: neither the whole of truth nor the whole of good is revealed to any single observer, although each observer gains a partial superiority of insight from the peculiar position in which he stands. Even prisons and sickrooms have their special revelations. It is enough to ask of each of us that he should be faithful to his own opportunities and make the most of his own blessings, without presuming to regulate the rest of the vast field.' (Talks on Psychology and Life's Ideals) (p. 319-20)

In another essay James points to the moral and social implications of this individualism.

'There lies more than a mere interest of curious speculation in understanding this. It has the most tremendous practical importance....It is the basis of all our tolerance, social, religious and political. The forgetting of it lies at the root of every stupid and sanguinary mistake that rulers over subject-peoples make. The first thing to learn in intercourse with others is non-interference with their own peculiar ways of being happy, provided these ways do not assume to interfere by violence with ours. No one has insight into all ideals. No one should presume to judge them off-hand. The pretension to dogmatize about them in each other is the root of most human injustices and cruelties, and the trait in human character most likely to make the angels weep.' (Talks on Psychology and Life's Ideals) (p. 320)

In one of the most brilliant of his essays, entitled 'The Dilemma of Determinism,' James summarizes the sort of determinism against which he protests.

'It professes,' he says, 'that those parts of the universe already laid down absolutely appoint and decree what the other parts shall be. The future has no ambiguous possibilities hidden in its womb: the part we call the present is compatible with only one totality. Any other future complement than the one fixed from eternity is impossible. The whole is in each and every part, and welds it with the rest into an absolute unity, an iron block, in which there can be no equivocation or shadow of turning.

'With earth's first clay they did the last man knead,
And there of the last harvest sowed the seed.
And the first morning of creation wrote
What the last dawn of reckoning shall read!'

(The Will to Believe) (p. 322)

Even in those passages in which James inclines to the mystical view of a union with God, religion is made to spring from an irreconcilable moral dualism. The worshipper identifies himself with God, but it is the better part of himself and not the whole which is thus deified. He feels his moral will to be part of a greater will to goodness, a general force of righteousness at large. This appears, for example, in the following description of conversion:

'The individual, so far as he suffers from his wrongness and criticises it, is to that extent consciously beyond it, and in at least possible touch with something higher, if anything higher exist....When stage two (the stage of solution or salvation) arrives, the man identifies his real being with the germinal higher part of himself; and does so in the following way. He becomes conscious that this higher part is conterminous and continuous with a MORE of the same quality, which is operative in the universe outside of him, and which he can keep in working touch with, and in a fashion get on board of and save himself when all his lower being has gone to pieces in the wreck.' (Varieties of Religious Experience) (p. 328)

PERRY, Ralph Barton. Present Philosophical Tendencies. A Critical Survey of Naturalism, Idealism, Pragmatism and Realism together with a Synopsis of the Philosophy of William James. 1929.

'Sensations,' says James, 'are the mother-earth, the anchorage, the stable rock, the first and last limits, the terminus a quo, and the terminus ad quem of the mind.' Or, as he puts it more emphatically, 'these percepts, these termini, these sensible things, these mere matters-of-acquaintance, are the only realities we ever directly know, and the whole history of our thought is the history of our substitution of one of them for another, and the reduction of the substitute to the status of a conceptual sign.' (Meaning of Truth) (p. 226)

It is this misunderstanding which underlies the anti-intellectualist's contention that continuity cannot be described. 'For,' says James, 'you cannot make continuous being out of discontinuities, and your concepts are discontinuous. The stages into which you analyze a change are states, the change itself goes on between them. It lies along their intervals, inhabits what your definition fails to gather up, and thus eludes conceptual explanation altogether.' (A Pluralistic Universe) (p. 233)

'Everything you can think of,' says James, 'however

vast or inclusive, has on the pluralistic view a genuinely 'external' environment of some sort or amount. Things are 'with' one another in many ways, but nothing includes everything, or dominates over everything. The word 'and' trails along after every sentence.' (A Pluralistic Universe) (p. 244)

James's view is expounded in his essay 'The Will to Believe,' and in the more recent 'Faith and the Right to Believe.' He contends that in the case of religion we are warranted in adopting that believe which is most in accord with our hopes, and which gives most firmness and courage to the moral will, even though the belief is not decisively proved. James does not advance this view on the general ground that we may believe what we wish, but on the ground of the special circumstances peculiar to religious belief. (p. 265)

PERRY, Ralph Barton. Puritanism and Democracy. 1944.

'That act must be the best act, accordingly, which makes for the best whole, in the sense of awakening the least sum of dissatisfactions....The course of history is nothing but the story of men's struggles from generation to generation to find the more and more inclusive order.' (The Will to Believe) (p. 50)

The moral sentiment which insists that the individual is a moral finality, whose claims are not to be outweighed by any more counting of heads, is vividly expressed by William James:

'If the hypothesis were offered us of a world in which Messrs. Fourier's and Bellamy's and Morris's utopias should all be outdone, and millions kept permanently happy on the one simple condition that a certain lost soul on the far-off edge of things should lead a life of lonely torture, what except a specifical and independent sort of e-motion can it be which would make us immediately feel even though an impulse arose within us to clutch at the happiness so offered, how hideous a thing would be its enjoyment when deliberately accepted as the fruit of such a bargain?' (The Will to Believe) (p. 451-2)

'Thoughts are the precious seeds of which our universities should be the botanical gardens. Beware when God lets loose a thinker on the world...for all things then have to rearrange themselves. But the thinkers in their youth are almost always very lonely creatures. 'Alone the great sun rises and alone spring the great streams.' The university most worthy of rational admiration is that one in which your lonely thinker can feel himself least lonely, most positively furthered, and most richly fed.' (Memories and Studies) (p. 453)

It was this social quality that William James admired in the student body of Harvard:

'They come from the remotest outskirts of our country, without introductions, without school affilitations; special students, scientific students, graduate students, poor students of the College, who make their living as they go.... They hover in the background on days when the crimson color is most in evidence, but they nevertheless are intoxicated and exultant with the nourishment they find here ....When they come to Harvard, it is not primarily because she is a club. It is because they have heard of her persistently atomistic constitution, of her tolerance of exceptionality and eccentricity, of her devotion to the principles of individual vocation and choice.'

James generalized this norm of individualism, and applies it to all institutions. Speaking of a friend whose colorful idiosyncrasies he greatly admired, he said:

'The memory of Davidson will always strengthen my faith in personal freedom and its spontaneities, and make me less unqualifiedly respectful than ever of 'Civilization,' with its herding and branding, licensing and degree-giving, authorizing and appointing, and in general regulating and administering by system the lives of human beings. Surely the individual, the person in the singular number, is the more fundamental phenomenon, and the social institution, of whatever grade, is but secondary and ministerial. Many as are the interests which social systems satisfy, always unsatisfied interests remain over, and among them are interests to which system, as such, does violence whenever it lays its hand upon us. The best Commonwealth will always be the one that leaves the largest scope to their peculiarities.' (Letters) (p. 462)

A more modern version of the same idea is set forth in the following passage from William James. That which 'makes life significant' is to be found widely on every social level:

'Wishing for heroism and the spectacle of human nature on the rack, I had never noticed the great fields of heroism lying round about me, I had failed to see it present and alive. I could only think of it as dead and embalmed, labelled and costumed, as it is in the pages of romance. And yet there it was before me in the daily lives of the laboring classes. Not in clanging fights and desparate marches only is heroism to be looked for, but on every railway bridge and fire-proof building that is going up today. On freight trains, on the decks of vessels, in cattle-yards and mines, on lumber-rafts, among the firemen and the policemen, the demand for courage is incessant; and the supply never fails. There, every day of the year somewhere, is human nature in extremis for you, and wherever a scythe, and axe, a pick, or a shovel is wielded, you have it sweating and aching and with its powers of patient endurance racked to the utmost under the length of hours of the strain.

'As I awoke to all this unidealized heroic life around me, the scales seemed to fall from my eyes; and a wave of sympathy greater than anything I had ever before felt with the common life of common men began to fill my soul....There are compensations: and no outward changes of condition in life can keep the nightingale of its eternal meaning from singing in all sorts of different men's hearts....If the poor and the rich could look at each other in this way....how gentle would grow their disputes! What tolerance and good humor, what willingness to live and let live, would come into the world!' (Talks to Teachers) (p. 562-3)

PERRY, Ralph Barton. Shall Not Perish from the Earth. 1940.

William James was flagrantly individualistic--the paragon or the horrible example of individualism--according to your taste. He was individualistic on every count. He attributed ideas to the inventive reason of individuals and was an inveterate enemy of abstractionism. He attributed historical events to the causal influence of great men. He believed that every individual and every cause had its inalienable rights, with no selective or restraining principle save that of including as many as possible. He idealized on the lonely thinker and the social misfit. He dwelt upon the unique inwardness of each human life, however lonely. He preferred small powers to great, the members to the body, the parts to the whole. 'Surely,' he said, 'the individual, the person in the singular number, is the more fundamental phenomenon, and the social institution, of whatever grade, is but secondary and ministerial.' (p. 58-9)

POTTER, Charles Francis. The Faiths Men Live By. 1954.

Fear of the mighty powers of nature is deeply rooted in every one, even the most sophisticated. The great American philosopher and psychologist, Dr. William James, in a letter written in 1906, shortly after a California earthquake, confessed:

'....the room was shaken like a rat by a terrier, with the most vicious expression you can possibly imagine, it was to my mind absolutely an entity....and it was impossible not to conceive it as animated by a will, so vicious was the temper displayed--everything down, in the room, that could go down, bureaus, etc., etc., and the shaking so rapid and vehement.'

If the scholarly professor found it 'impossible not to conceive' the earthquake 'as animated by a will,' it is hardly surprising to find that primitive men personified, or at least attributed partial or occasional intention to, the powers of nature, and tried to counteract or placate them as best they could; hence animism, the earliest form or stage of religion, apparently originated. (p. 1-2)

POWYS, John Cowper. Enjoyment of Literature. 1938.

Alas! There are few modern philosophers as liberated from both rationalistic and religious prejudice as the late incomparable William James. (p. 36)

RADHAKRISHNAN, Sarvepalli and Others. History of Philosophy, Eastern and Western. Two volumes. 1952.

As a humanist, James realized the vital implications of philosophical problems for mankind, and at the same time saw the futility of a purely intellectual and logical approach to these problems, which often with its unintelligent hair-splittings and unmeaning verbal subtleties, leads us into a blind alley. He therefore suggested that in order to determine whether a given philosophical question has vital meaning or is merely verbel, we should consider what interests were at stake if one or other of the these in dispute were accepted and affirmed. There is 'no difference in the abstract truth that does not express itself in a difference in concrete fact, and in conduct consequent upon that fact,' and 'the whole function of philosophy ought to be to find out what difference it will make to you and me, at definite instants of our life, if this world formula or that world formula be the true one.' (Pragmatism) (v. 2. p. 340)

In his theory of the will to believe, James pleaded for the right of man to choose his beliefs even in the absence of definitive evidence. By this, however, he did not mean that we should believe according to our whims. He limited the sphere of such beliefs to religion and morals, where formal reasonings cannot settle the matter, and the issues being momentous and forced on us, our decision can be withheld only at the risk of losing the advantages that would follow if the belief were true. Where the issues of life are at stake, we should not be overscrupulous about errors; it is often better to incur the risk of being mistaken than give up the chance of guessing the truth. Thus James seeks a justification for our moral and religious beliefs and the actions based thereon, although the truth of such beliefs may not be logically certified in advance. (v. 2. p. 340)

RIESMAN, David. Thorstein Veblen. A Critical Interpretation. 1953.

Veblen responded to the ideas of his colleagues, but not to their reform activities. From Dewey, as well as earlier from William James, he gained a renewed sense of man as an active being, one who selects his environment as well as is shaped by it. (p. 19)

When in his writings he made sarcastic remarks about Dewey, James, Peirce and the pragmatist movement, he could hardly have believed he was being extra rough on thinkers who were, in many respects, his intellectual allies--the notion of an alliance would have meant taking seriously the weight he himself could throw. (p. 25)

But Veblen does not fully share James' muscular, unruly sense of human freedom (nor the excesses of James' moral athleticism); to the extent that he does, he is afraid of what men do with their arbitrary power. And so his apparently whole-hearted acceptance of the Jamesian psychology is always qualified and finally overborne by the desire to bind men to a minimal, near-biological routine, in which, if nothing spectacular is accomplished (except in the harmless, out-of-the-way paths of idle learning), no great destruction is wrought either. (p. 58)

NEVINS, Allan. John D. Rockefeller. Industrialist and Philanthropist. Two volumes. 1953.

William James had occasion in 1909 to write Rockefeller about a proposed gift for mental hygiene. He added: 'I have had much pleasure in reading your charming and interesting autobiographical papers, and I trust that you and a certain portion of the public are now feeling much more affectionate toward each other than was ever before the case. This is what I proposed to you many years ago! Expansiveness wins a way where reserve fails.' (v. 2. p. 353)

ROOSEVELT, Theodore. History as Literature and Other Essays. 1913.

Not only every truly religious, but every truly scientific, man must turn with relief from the narrowness of a shut-in materialism to the profound and lofty thought contained in the writings of William James, of his biographer, M. Emile Boutroux, and of another philosopher of the same school, M. Bergson. M. Boutroux's study of William James gives in brief form--and with a charm of style and expression possible only for those who work with that delicate instrument of precision, French prose--the views which men of this stamp hold; and be it remembered that, like James, they are thoroughly scientific men, steeped in the teachings of material science, who acknowledge no outside limitation upon them in their search for truth. (p. 268-9)

To men such as William James and these two French philosophers physical science, if properly studied, shows conclusively its own limitations, shows conclusively that beyond the material world lies a vast series of phenomena which all material knowledge is powerless to explain, so that science itself teaches that outside of materialism lie the forces of a wholly different world, a world ordered by religion--religion which, says M. Boutroux, must, if loyal to itself, work according to its own nature as a spiritual activity, striving to transform men from within and not from without, by persuasion, by example, by love, by prayer, by the communion of souls, not by restraint or policy; and such a religion has nothing to fear from the progress of science, for the spirit to which it is loyal is the faith in duty, the search for what is for the universal good and for the universal love, the secret springs of all high and beneficent activity. (p. 271-2)

ROOSEVELT, Theodore. Letters Selected and Edited by Elting E. Morison. Volume One and Volume Six. 1951.

One of my studies (French) is extremely difficult, but I get along pretty fairly in the others while my anatomical course is extremely interesting. (The instructor in Roosevelt's anatomical course was William James.) (v. 1. p. 29)

Letter to Theodore Roosevelt, Junior. February 14, 1908.

I just received your letter and I am extremely pleased with your success in the midyear's. You have admirable marks. Now, do not repeat a feat of your father's. I think it was in my senior year (but it may have been my junior year) when I got remarkable marks for the first half of the course under William James and was sure I was going to do wonderfully in it, so sure that I loafed and did not study and trusted to natural smartness to give a specious appearance of familiarity with the subject; and as a result got left and stood low in the course on account of shortcomings in my finals. (v. 6. p. 944)

ROYCE, Josiah. The Problem of Christianity. Two volumes. 1913.

Despite my frequent mention of differences, there is one respect in which I am in full agreement with the spirit of pragmatism, as James defined it. Any metaphysical thesis, if it has a meaning at all, is the expression of an attitude of the will of the one who asserts this thesis. (v. 2. p. 291)

'Why,' says Professor James, addressing a supposed fellow-man in one of his essays on Radical Empiricism, 'Why do I postulate your mind? Because I see your body acting in a certain way. Its gestures, facial movements, words, and conduct generally are 'expressive,' so I deem it actuated, as my own is, by an inner life like mine. This argument from analogy is my reason, whether an instinctive belief runs before it or not. But what is 'your body' here but a percept in my field? It is only in animating that object, my object, that I have any occasion to think of you at all.' (v. 2. p. 302-3)

ROYCE, Josiah. The Sources of Religious Insight. 1912.

My dear friend, the late William James, in his book called 'The Varieties of Religious Experience,' defined, for his own purposes, religious experience as the experience of individuals who regard themselves as 'alone with the divine.' In portraying what he meant by 'the divine,' James emphasized, although in a language different from what I am using, the very features about the objects of religious experience which I have just been trying to characterize in my own way. Those who have religious experience, according to James, get into touch with something which, as he says, gives 'a new dimension' to their life. As a result of their better and more exalted religious experience, they win a sense of unity with 'higher powers' whose presence seems to them to secure a needed but otherwise unattainable spiritual unity, peace, power in their lives. This 'divine' thus accomplished inwardly what the individual 'alone with the divine' feels to be saving, to be needed, to be his pearl of great price. This is James's way of defining the objects of religious experience. (p. 27)

James, as a psychologist, well knew this truth about

the value and the limitations of private experience; yet it was characteristic of his enterprising soul that he was always looking, in his 'pluralistic universe,' for the strange, new religious experiences of other and still other individuals, without being able thereby even to define what all these ardent souls were seeking, namely, some genuine home land of the spirit, some place or experience or insight in which is to be revealed that for the sake of which all the feelings, the caprices, the longings, the efforts of individuals are justified--and fulfilled. (p. 30)

And as to what these deeper sources of insight are, the teacher whom I have already repeatedly cited--William James--asserts a doctrine that, as you already know, I do not regard as adequate, but that I must again here emphasize, because its contrast with that social theory of religion which I just characterized is so instructive.

James, in his 'Varieties of Religious Experience,' shows the utmost liberality toward differences of faith, and insists in the opening chapters of his book that religious experience is a field where one must beware of defining sharp boundary lines or of showing a false exclusiveness. Yet one boundary line he himself defines with the greatest sharpness; and in respect of one matter he is rigidly exclusive. Religious experience, he insists, is, as you will remember from our first lecture, the experience of an individual who feels himself to be 'alone with the divine,' and the social types of religious experience James rigidly excludes from the 'varieties' whereof he takes account. (p. 61-2)

RUSSELL, Bertrand. History of Western Philosophy. 1945.

William James (1842-1910) was primarily a psychologist, but was important in philosophy on two accounts: he invented the doctrine which he called 'radical empiricism,' and he was one of the three protagonists of the theory called 'pragmatism' or 'instrumentalism.' In later life he was, as he deserved to be, the recognized leader of American philosophy. He was led by the study of medicine to the consideration of psychology; his great book on the subject, published in 1890, had the highest possible excellence. I shall not, however deal with it, since it was a contribution to science rather than to philosophy.

There were two sides to William James's philosophical interests, one scientific, the other religious. On the scientific side, the study of medicine had given his thoughts a tendency towards materialism, which, however, was held in check by his religious emotions. His religious feelings were very Protestant, very democratic, and very full of a warmth of human kindness. He refused altogether to follow his brother Henry into fastidious snobbishness. 'The prince of darkness,' he said, 'may be a gentleman, as we are told he is, but whatever the God of earth and heaven is, he can surely be no gentleman.' This is a very characteristic pronouncement.

His warm-heartedness and his delightful humour caused him to be almost universally beloved. The only man I know of who did not feel any affection for him was Santayana, whose doctor's thesis William James had described as 'the perfection of rottenness.' There was between these two men a temperamental opposition which nothing could have overcome. (p. 811)

RUSSELL, Bertrand. Mysticism and Logic and Other Essays. 1925.

As regards our present question, namely, the question of the unity of the world, the right method, as I think, has been indicated by William James. 'Let us now turn our backs upon ineffable or unintelligible ways of accounting for the world's oneness, and inquire whether, instead of being a principle, the 'oneness' affirmed may not merely be a name like 'substance' descriptive of the fact that certain specific and verifiable connections are found among the parts of the experiential flux.' (Some Problems of Philosophy) (p. 100)

RUSSELL, Bertrand. Philosophical Essays. 1910.

As an introduction to pragmatism, it is interesting to read William James's essay on 'The Will to Believe,' first published in 1896, and reprinted in book form in the following year. In this essay, though the word 'pragmatism' does not appear, we find much that is characteristic of James's later views. The thesis he is advocating is that, in certain cases, it is right to believe wholeheartedly in one of two alternatives, even when there is no evidence as to which of them is true. These cases arise, he says, when we are compelled to choose between two hypotheses, each of which seems to us possible, and when it makes a great difference which we choose. The instances he has in mind are chiefly questions of morals and religion. In a moral perplexity we are compelled to come to some decision, since inaction is as much a decision as action. In regard to religion, also, we must act as though it were true or as though it were false; we are therefore practically compelled to choose. His contention is that in such cases, it would be foolish to refuse to have faith merely on the ground that we do not find conclusive evidence on either side of the question. To quote his own words:--

'Our passional nature not only lawfully may, but must, decide an option between propositions. Whenever it is a genuine option that cannot by its nature be decided on intellectual grounds; for to say, under such circumstances, 'Do not decide, but leave the question open,' is itself a passional decision,--just like deciding yes or no,--and is attended with the same risk of losing the truth.' (p. 89-90)

William James proceeds to point out that, in the case of religion, the choice between believing and disbelieving possesses all the characteristics of the options which, according to him ought to be decided by the emotions. He tacitly assumes that there is no evidence for or against religions, and he points out that by refusing either to believe or to disbelieve we lose the benefits of religion just as much as by deciding to disbelieve.

'Scepticism, then, is not avoidance of option; it is option of a certain particular kind of risk. Better risk loss of truth than chance of error,--that is your faith-vetoer's exact position. He is actively playing his stake as much as the believer is; he is backing the field against the religious hypothesis, just as the believer is backing the religious hypothesis against the field....It is not intellect against all passions, then; it is only intellect with one passion laying down its law. And by what, forsooth, is the supreme wisdom of this passion warranted? Dupery for dupery, what proof is there that dupery through hope is so much worse than dupery through fear?' (Pragmatism) (p. 91-2)

A few quotations will serve to amplify and elucidate the above brief statement. After explaining recent changes in the methodology of science, James says:--

'Riding now on the front of this wave of scientific logic, Messrs. Schiller and Dewey appear with their pragmatistic account of what truth everywhere signifies. Everywhere, these teachers say, 'truth' in our ideas and beliefs means the same thing that it means in science. It means, they say, nothing but this, that ideas (which themselves are but parts of our experience) become true just in so far as they help us to get into satisfactory relations with other parts of our experience.'

Again:--

'I am well aware how odd it must seem to some of you to hear me say that an idea is 'true' so long as to believe it is profitable to our lives. That it is good, for as much as it profits, you will gladly admit....But is it not a strange misuse of the word 'truth,' you will say, to call ideas also 'true' for this reason?....You touch here upon the very central point of Messrs. Schiller's, Dewey's and my own doctrine of truth....Let me now say only this, that truth is one species of good, and not, as is usually supposed, a category distinct from good, and co-ordinate with it. The true is the name of whatever proves itself to be good in the way of belief, and good, too, for definite assignable reasons.' (Pragmatism) (p. 100)

He proceeds:--

'Pragmatism, on the other hand, asks its usual question. 'Grant an idea or belief to be true,' it says, what concrete difference will its being true make in any one's actual life? How will the truth be realized? What experiences will be different from those which would obtain if the belief were false? What, in short, is the truth's cash-value in experiental terms?'

'The moment pragmatism asks this question it sees the answer: True ideas are those that we can assimilate, validate, corroborate and verify. False ideas are those that we cannot....

'The truth of an idea is not a stagnant property inherent in it. Truth happens to an idea. It becomes true, is made true by events. Its verity is in fact an event, a process: the process namely of its verifying itself, its veri-fication. Its validity is the process of its valid-action.' (Pragmatism) (p. 101-2)

In regard to metaphysics, pragmatism professes to be a kind of universal provider, willing and able to suit all tastes. As William James puts it:--

'Against rationalism as a pretension and a method pragmatism is fully armed and militant. But, at the outset, at least, it stands for no particular results. It has no dogmas, and no doctrines save its method. As the young Italian pragmatist Papini has well said, it lies in the midst of our theories, like a corridor in a hotel. Innumerable chambers open out of it. In one you may find a man writing an atheistic volume; in the next some one on his knees praying for faith and strength; in a third a chemist investigating a body's properties. In a fourth a system of idealistic metaphysics is being excogitated; in a fifth the impossibility of metaphysics is being shown. But they all own the corridor, and all must pass through it if they want a practical way of getting into or out of their respective rooms.' (Pragmatism) (p. 114)

RUSSELL, Bertrand. Principles of Social Reconstruction. 1916.

This problem was considered by William James in an admirable address on 'The Moral Equivalent of War,' delivered to a congress of pacifists during the Spanish-American War of 1898. His statement of the problem could not be bettered; and so far as I know, he is the only writer who has faced the problem adequately. But his solution is not adequate; perhaps no adequate solution is possible. (p. 95)

RUSSELL, Bertrand. Sceptical Essays. 1928.

In the English-speaking world, the greatest influence in the overthrow of German idealism was William James --not as he appears in his Psychology, but as he came to be known through the series of small books which were published in the last years of his life and after his death. In an article published in Mind so long ago as 1884, reprinted in the posthumous volume Essays in Radical Empiricism, he sets out his temperamental bias with extraordinary charm:--

'Since we are in the main not sceptics, we might go on and frankly confess to each other the motives for our several faiths. I frankly confess mine--I cannot but think that at bottom they are of an aesthetic and not of a logical sort. The 'through-and-through' universe seems to suffocate me with its infallible impeccable all-pervasiveness. Its necessity, with no possibilities; its relations, with no subjects, make me feel as if I had entered into a contract with no reserved rights, or rather as if I had to live in a large seaside boarding-house with no private bedroom in which I might take refuge from the society of the place. I am distinctly aware, moreover, that the old quarrel of sinner and pharisee has something to do with the matter. Certainly, to my personal knowledge, all Hegelians are not prigs, but I somehow feel as if all prigs ought to end, if developed, by becoming Hegelians. There is a story of two clergymen asked by mistake to conduct the same funeral. One came first and had got no further than 'I am the Resurrection and the Life' when the other entered 'I am the Resurrection and the Life,' cried the latter. The 'through-and-through' philosophy, as it actually exists, reminds many of us of that clergyman. It seems too button-up and white-chokered and clean-shaven a thing to speak for the vast slow-breathing unconscious Kosmos with its dread abysses and its unknown tides.'

I think it may be wagered that no one except William

James has ever lived who would have thought of comparing Hegelianism to a seaside boarding-house. (p. 58-9)

RUSSELL, Bertrand. Unpopular Essays. 1950.

Among eminent philosophers, excluding men still alive, the most personally impressive, to me, was William James. This was in spite of a complete naturalness and absence of all apparent consciousness of being a great man. No degree of democratic feeling and of desire to identify himself with the common herd could make him anything but a natural aristocrat, a man whose personal distinction commanded respect. (p. 214)

SANTAYANA, George. Persons and Places. The Middle Span. Volume Two. 1945.

Of the older Harvard worthies I was on good terms with two, Charles Eliot Norton and William James. They were perhaps the most distinguished, but not the most trusted; they too had had to be swallowed. They too, although in my time their position was established, had seemed at first questionalbe and irregular. (p. 163)

Concerning William James, I have made sundry scattered observations for the public without attempting a fair total portrayal of the man or of his philosophy; neither he nor his philosophy lent themselves to being summed up. But here, where I am portraying only my own impressions, I may add a word more about the feelings that he excited in me. I trusted his heart but I didn't respect his judgment. I admired his masculine directness, his impressionistic perceptions, and his picturesque words. I treasured his utterances on the medical side of things, such as that the best way to understanding the normal is to study the abnormal. All this belonged to his independent, radical, naturalistic temper, to his American sense of being just born into a world to be re-discovered. But he was really far from free, held back by old instincts, subject to old delusions, restless, spasmodic, self-interrupted: as if some impetuous bird kept flying aloft, but always stopped in mid-air, pulled back with a jerk by an invisible wire tethering him to a peg in the ground. The general agreement in America to praise him as a marvellous person, and to pass on, is justified by delight at the way he started, without caring where he went. In fact, he got nowhere; and for that reason his influence could be great and beneficent over those who knew him, but soon seemed to become untraceable in the confused currents of the world. I, for instance, was sure of his goodwill and kindness, of which I had many proofs; but I was also sure that he never understood me, and that when he talked to me there was a manikin in his head, called G.S. and entirely fantastic, which he was addressing. No doubt I profited materially by this illusion, because he would have liked me less if he had understood me better; but the sense of that illusion made spontaneous friendship impossible. I was uncomfortable in his presence. He was so extremely natural that there was no knowing what his nature was, or what to expect next; so that one was driven to behave and talk conventionally, as in the most artificial society. I found no foothold, I was soon fatigued, and it was a relief to be out again in the open, and alone. (p. 166-7)

SANTAYANA, George. Persons and Places. The Background of My Life. Volume One. 1944.

James and Royce were then the 'young' professors of philosophy, they represented the dangers and scandals of free thought, all the more disquieting in that their free thought enveloped religion. (p. 245)

SANTAYANA, George. Soliloquies in England. 1922.

For instance, when more than twenty years ago, I wrote some interpretations of Poetry and Religion, this is what William James said of them: 'What a perfection of rottenness....how fantastic a philosophy!--as if the 'world of values' were independent of existence. It is only as being that one thing is better than another. The idea of darkness is as good as that of light, as ideas. There is more value in light's being.' (p. 247)

SANTAYANA, George. Winds of Doctrine. Studies in Contemporary Opinion. 1913.

'The prince of darkness,' James says, 'may be a gentleman, as we are told he is, but whatever the God of earth and heaven is, he can surely be no gentleman.' (Pragmatism) (p. 125)

I remember once putting a question on this subject to Professor James; and his answer was one which I am glad to be able to record. In relation to his having said that 'as far as the past facts go, there is no difference....be the atoms or be the God their cause,' I asked whether, if God had been the cause, apart from the value of the idea of him in our calculations, his existence would not have made a difference to him, as he would be presumably self-conscious. 'Of course,' said Professor James, 'but

I wasn't considering that side of the matter; I was thinking of our idea.' (p. 129)

But there is another distinguished man, lately lost to this country, who has given some rude shocks to this tradition and who, as much as Whitman, may be regarded as representing the genuine, the long silent American mind-I mean William James. He and his brother Henry were as tightly swaddled in the genteel tradition as any infant geniuses could be, for they were born before 1850, and in a Swedenborgian household. Yet they burst those bands almost entirely. The ways in which the two brothers freed themselves, however, are interestingly different. Mr. Henry James has done it by adopting the point of view of the outer world, and by turning the genteel American tradition as he turns everything else, into a subject-matter for analysis. For him it is a curious habit of mind, intimately comprehended, to be compared with other habits of mind, also well known to him. Thus he has overcome the genteel tradition in the classic way, by understanding it. With William James too this infusion of worldly insight and European sympathies was a potent influence, especially in his earlier days; but the chief source of his liberty was another. It was his personal spontaneity, similar to that of Emerson and his personal vitality, similar to that of nobody else. Convictions and ideas came to him, so to speak, from the subsoil. He had a prophetic sympathy with the dawning sentiments of the age, with the moods of the dumb majority. His scattered words caught fire in many parts of the world. His way of thinking and feeling represented the true America, and represented in a measure the whole ultra-modern, radical world. (p. 203-4)

For one thing, William James kept his mind and heart wide open to all that might seem, to polite minds, odd, personal, or visionary in religion and philosophy. He gave a sincerely respectful hearing to sentimentalists, mystics, spiritualists, wizards, cranks, quacks, and imposters--for it is hard to draw the line, and James was not willing to draw it prematurely. He thought, with his usual modesty, that any of these might have something to teach him. The lame, the halt, the blind, and those speaking with tongues could come to him with the certainty of finding sympathy; and if they were not healed, at least they were comforted, that a famous professor should take them so seriously; and they began to feel that after all to have only one leg, or one hand, or one eye, or to have three, might be in itself no less beauteous than to have just two, like the stolid majority. Thus William James became the friend and helper of those groping, nervous, half-educated, spiritually disinherited, passionately hungry individuals of which America is full. He became, at the same time, their spokesman and representative before the learned world; and he made it a chief part of his vocation to recast what the learned world has to offer, so that as far as possible it might serve the needs and interests of these people. (p. 205)

HOWGATE, George W. George Santayana. 1938.

In Professor Palmer's words, there was therefore no 'Harvard 'school' of philosophy....We wished....our students....to study....under the guidance of an expert believer and then to have the difficulties....presented by an expert opponent.' The department thus became a group of original philosophers expounding their respective systems, and refuting each other's arguments in the classroom and out. For many students this melee of free philosophical inquiry was valuable instruction, but Santayana's convictions were already formed, and they were remarkably solid, so that the practice of the department neither perplexed him, as it would have done a weaker mind, nor won his admiration. He says,

'As an undergraduate at Harvard, I was already alive to the fundamental questions, and even had a certain dialectical nimbleness, due to familiarity with the fine points of theology: the arguments for and against free will and the proofs of the existence of God were warm and clear in my mind. I accordingly heard James and Royce with more wonder than serious agreement: my scholastic logic would have wished to reduce James at once to a materialist and Royce to a solipsist, and it seemed strangely irrational in them to resist such simplification.' (p. 20-1)

As time passed, William James, representing his department, began to wonder whether Santayana was spending his time profitably, as became the incumbent of the Walker Fellowship. And with his usual frankness James wrote:

'Our fellowships are for helping men to do some definite intellectual thing, and you must expect to have to show next May (if the fellowship is to be continued) that you are on a line of investigation of some sort which is likely to result in something more than a 'culture' which to the ordinary committee-man would look vague. I know your ability; and also your way of talking small about yourself. But your ability imposes arduous duties....What you write ought to contain (in addition to the merits of expression and fresh thinking which it certainly will contain) evidence either of considerable research....or of original experiment or observation. I can hardly defend your cause in the committee, if on the whole you do not seem pretty definitely working on the lines which lead to philosophical professorships.'

'But, (wrote Santayana)....it is very doubtful that I should ever get a professorship of philosophy anyway, and I hardly care to sacrifice my tastes to that bare possibility....what I shall write will certainly not smack so much of a professorship of philosophy as if it were on the normal jerk of the kneepan.'

Nevertheless, Santayana claimed to be 'quite at ease' about his 'duties,' stated his intention of asking again for the fellowship, and 'by no means' gave himself up as a 'bad job.' Accordingly, he submitted James a paper, which the latter found 'a little too much like a poem,' and later offered sufficient evidence of scholarship to win from the committee a renewal of his fellowship. (p. 32)

One might dismiss The Sense of Beauty as a philosophical treatise or a textbook on aesthetics. But there was no mistaking the plain prose of Interpretations of Poetry and Religion, with its informality and its human interest. Even those who were repelled by the theory were often constrained to acknowledge the strength of argument, to admire the independent judgment throughout, and to delight in the beauty of style. Upon reading the book, William James wrote immediately to George Herbert Palmer, 'Although I absolutely reject the Platonism of it, I have literally squealed with delight at the imperturbable perfection with which the position is laid down on page after page. It is refreshing to see a representative of moribund Latinity rise up and administer such reproof to us barbarians in the hour of our triumph.' (p. 107)

I think Santayana in many respects understood neither James nor Royce. A certain troubled earnestness and moral restlessness, frequently the possession of the Protestant mind, seemed to the Catholic Santayana confused and wayward. It seemed to him that James and 'the people about him' and 'modern philosophers anywhere' had no knowledge of the 'good life.' 'They had standards of character and right conduct; but as to what might render human existence good, excellent, beautiful, happy and worth having as a whole, their notions were utterly thin and barbarous. They had forgotten the Greeks, or never known them.' They were bound, being Puritans, to 'smell of brimstone.' But to cry shrilly that whatever displeases one is barbarism is neither to understand it nor to do it justice. And Professor Perry rightly reminds Santayana that

'James and Royce and others of the lingering brimstone age in American philosophy, did not regard duty as a stage of angelic perfection, but as being a relatively tolerable state of mind in a world in which evil abounds. Moralism is, it is true, unbeautiful; it is strained, harsh, distraught. But what, the state of the world being such as it is, shall we say of the philosophers whom Mr. Santayana describes as concentrating their lives as much as possible in pure intelligence in order that they may be led by it into the way of peace? There is a point of view from which a peace so purchased is hard, complacent, inhumane, and frivolous.' (p. 192)

And there is in Santayana's essays just as much kindliness for the persons of both James and Royce as there is unfriendliness toward their philosophies. Speaking of James, Santayana says,

'In person he was short rather than tall, erect, brisk, bearded, intensely masculine. While he shone in expression and would have wished his style to be noble if it could also be strong, he preferred in the end to be spontaneous, and leave it at that....The rough, homely, picturesque phrase, whatever was graphic and racy, recommended itself to him....Everybody liked him, and delighted in him for his generous, gullible nature and brilliant sallies. He was a sort of Irishman among the Brahmins, and seemed hardly imposing enough for a great man....I think he was glad when the bell rang, and he could be himself again until the next day. But in the midst of this routine of the class-room the spirit would sometimes come upon him, and leaning his head on his hand, he would let fall golden words, picturesque, fresh from the heart, full of the knowledge of good and evil. Incidentally there would crop up some humorous characterization, some candid confession of doubt or of instinctive preference, some pungent scrap of learning; radicalisms plunging sometimes into the sub-soil of all human philosophies; and, on occasion, thoughts of simple wisdom and wistful piety, the most unfeigned and manly that anybody ever had.' (p. 193)

I am afraid Santayana never quite penetrated the reserve of Beacon Street, was never quite taken into its heart. For the most part he accepted Boston with amused tolerance; only once do we learn of the impatient scorn which festered long in his bosom. Replying to William James's caustic remarks on Interpretations of Poetry and Religion, Santayana with unprecedented bitterness exclaims,

'You tax me several times with impertinence and superior airs. I wonder if you realize the years of suppressed irritation which I have passed in the midst of an unintelligible, sanctimonious and often disingenuous Protestantism, which is thoroughly alien and repulsive to me, and the need I have of joining hands with something far away from it and far above it.' (p. 273-4)

SAPPENFIELD, Bert R. Personality Dynamics. An Integrative Psychology of Adjustment. 1954.

'In many respects man is the most ruthlessly ferocious of beasts....And killing off a neighboring tribe from whom no good thing comes, but only competition, may materially better the lot of the whole tribe. Hence the gory cradle....in which our race was reared; hence the fickleness of human ties, the ease with which the foe of yesterday become the ally of to-day, the friend of to-day the enemy of to-morrow....' (Principles of Psychology) (p. 143)

SCHOEN, Max, SCHRIKEL, H. G. and AMES, Van Meter. Understanding the World, An Introduction to Philosophy. 1947.

As William James puts it, 'The obstinate insistence that tweedledum is not tweedledee is the bone and marrow of life.' (Principles of Psychology) (p. 257)

SCHWARTZ, Herman S. The Art of Relaxation. 1954.

'If you should individually achieve calmness and harmony in your own person, you may depend upon it that a wave of imitation will spread from you as surely as the circles spread outward when a stone is dropped into a lake.'

William James. (p. 1)

ZEITLIN, Jacob and WOODBRIDGE, Homer. Life and Letters of Stuart P. Sherman. Two volumes. 1929.

The process of making a choice out of the many diverse possibilities of character that are open to any man is thus described by William James:

'Such different characters may conceivably at the outset of life be alike possible to a man. But to make any one of them actual, the rest must more or less be suppressed.

So the seeker of his truest, strongest, deepest self must review the list carefully, and pick out the one on which to stake his salvation. All other selves thereupon become unreal, but the fortunes of this self are real. Its failures are real failures, its triumphs real triumphs, carrying shame and gladness with them....Our thought, incessantly deciding, among many things of a kind, which ones for it shall be realities, here chooses one of many possible selves or characters, and forthwith reckons it no shame to fail in any one of those not adopted expressly as its own.' (v. 1. p. 297)

SIMPSON, George Eaton and YINGER, J. Milton. Racial and Cultural Minorities. An Analysis of Prejudice and Discrimination. 1953.

William James, in discussing the way in which the 'social self' of man exists in society says,'....a man has as many social selves as there are individuals who recognize him and carry an image of him in their minds.' Then, in speculation upon what a man would feel if he were completely socially excluded, he says, 'No more fiendish punishment could be divised, were such a thing physically possible, than that one should be turned loose in society and remain absolutely unnoticed by all the members thereof. If no one turned round when we entered, answered when we spoke, or minded what we did, but if every person we met 'cut us dead,' and acted as if we were non-existent things, a kind of rage and impotent despair would ere long well up in us, from which the cruelest bodily tortures would be a relief, for these would make us feel that, however bad might be our plight, we had not sunk to such a depth as to be unworthy of attention at all.' (p. 165-6)

SMITH, John E. Royce's Social Infinite. 1950.

Royce quoted at some length from James to make this point clear.

'True ideas lead us, namely, through the acts and other ideas which they investigate, into or up to or towards other parts of experience with which we feel all the while that the original ideas remain in agreement. The convictions and transitions come to us, from point to point, as being progressive, harmonious, satisfactory. This function of agreeable leading is what we mean by an idea's verification.' (p. 47-8)

SMITH, Logan Pearsall. Unforgotten Years. 1939.

To soar, however, into so exalted a region it would be necessary, she felt, for her to expand her intellectual wings; she must, in fact, study philosophy with more attention; and for that study Harvard, with its famous philosophers, Royce and William James and Professor Palmer, was obviously the place. So from Smith College my sister transferred herself to Cambridge, and, as I have said, I followed in her train. This migration was the more easily effected owing to William James's friendship with my parents. He was an admirer of my mother's religious writings; he had enlisted my father's assistance in the formation of an American Society for Psychical Research, and had more than once stayed with us in Germantown when he came to Philadelphia in connection with this work. (p. 113-4)

I actually sat beside my present brother-in-law, Berenson, at a course of William James's lectures, but no communication passed between us, and it was not till long afterwards, when he had married my elder sister, that we began that series of confabulations to which I owe so much. For my parents' sake William James did, however, befriend their callow off-spring, and I was often invited to his hospitable house. I need not try to describe the charm of the most charming man I ever met; Ralph Perry has performed that task in his admirable biography, but I may perhaps add a touch to his account of that free and spontaneous spirit by repeating an anecdote he related to me one night, telling me that I might repeat it anywhere but in Cambridge.

He had gone, he told me, by tram that afternoon to Boston; and as he sat and meditated in the Cambridge horsecar two strains of thought had occupied his mind. One of these was the notion, which Mrs. James had recently derived from the perusal of Kipling's writings, that our civil order, that all the graces and amenities of our social life, had for their ultimate sanction nothing but force, however much we might disguise it--the naked fist, in fact, the blow of the sword, the crack of the pistol, or the smoke and roar of guns. Superimposed upon this meditation began to recur, with greater and greater persistence, the memory of certain remarks of his brother Henry, who, on a recent visit to America, had indignantly protested against the outrageous pertness of the American child and the meek pusillanimity with which the older generation suffered the behavior of their children without protest.

It was not long, William James said, before he became aware of what had aroused this second line of thought; it was the droning sound which filled the horsecar--the voice, in fact, of an American child, who was squeaking over and over again an endless, shrill, monotonous sing-song. Growing more and more irritated by this squeaking, William James resolved that he at least would not suffer it without protest; so, addressing the mother of the vocal infant, he said politely, 'I think, madam, you can hardly be aware that your child's song is a cause of annoyance to the rest of us in this car.' The lady thus addressed paid no attention; but a gallant American, who had heard it, turned on him and said with great indignation, 'How dare you, sir, address a lady in this ungentlemanly fashion!' At this insult William James, recalling the doctrine of naked force which his wife had impressed upon him, replied with manly promptness, 'Sir, if you repeat that remark, I shall slap your face.' The remark, to his consternation, was repeated, and the professor was compelled to make good his word. The slap was conscientiously administered; the occupants of the horsecar arose in indignation, pressing their cards upon the victim of the assault, and protesting their willingness to be witnesses at any legal proceedings which might ensue. Then they all sat down; and as the car clattered along through the dust towards Boston, with the child still shrilly singing, the grave burden of the public disapproval which William James had encountered became almost more, he said, than he could bear.

He looked from hostile face to hostile face, longing for some sign of sympathy and comprehension, and fixed at last all his hopes on a lady who had taken no part in the uproar, and whose appearance suggested foreign travel perhaps, or at any rate a wider point of view. He felt that she at least understood the motive of his action; and so great was his longing for sympathy that when at last the car reached Boston and they all got out he committed the error of trying to make sure of her appreciation. 'You, madam,' he said, addressing her, 'you, I feel sure, will understand....' Thereupon the lady drew back from him and exclaimed, 'You brute!' (p. 116-20)

Now since the death of William James (who may be regarded as the last blossom on the old New England tree), what books of this enduring quality has America produced? (p. 282)

SMITH, T. V. The American Philosophy of Equality. 1927.

The relentlessness with which the ghostly soul pursues man is seen in James's brilliant and almost poignant account of the history of the soul-conception. Though as a psychologist he himself had reached the 'stream of consciousness' stage, yet as a man and a philosopher, writing at the very close of the nineteenth century and representing the most forward-looking thought in America, James confessed that 'to posit a soul influenced in some mysterious way by the brain-states and responding to them by conscious affections of its own, seems to me the line of least logical resistance, so far as we have attained.' (Principles of Psychology) (p. 174-5)

SMITH, T. V. Beyond Conscience. 1934.

And finally a word from William James, who was an artist both before and after he was a scientist and philosopher:

'In spite of the appeal which this impersonality of the scientific attitude makes to a certain magnanimity of temper, I believe it to be shallow, and I can now state my reason in comparatively few words. That reason is that, so long as we deal with the cosmic and the general, we deal only with the symbols of reality, but as soon as we deal with private and personal phenomena as such, we deal with realities in the completest sense of the term.' (Varieties of Religious Experience) (p. 249)

SMITH, T. V. Constructive Ethics. With Contemporary Readings. 1948.

'There is an inevitable tendency,' writes William James, in The Moral Philosopher and the Moral Life, 'to slip into an assumption which ordinary men follow when they are disputing with one another about questions of good and bad. They imagine an abstract moral order in which the objective truth resides; and each tries to prove that this pre-existing order is more accurately reflected in his own ideas than in those of his adversary. It is because one disputant is backed by this over-arching abstract order that we think the other should submit.' (p. 49)

'There is no such thing possible,' racily claims William James, 'as an ethical philosophy dogmatically made up in advance. We all help to determine the content of ethical philosophy so far as we contribute to the race's moral life. In other words, there can be no final truth in ethics any more than in physics, until the last man has had his experience and his say. In the one case as in the other, however, the hypotheses which we now make while waiting and the acts to which they prompt us, are among the indispensable conditions which determine what that 'say' shall be.' (p.165)

William James (1842-1910) is probably America's most widely known philosopher, both at home and abroad. Early sensitized to art, trained for medicine, apprenticed to psychology, James graduated into philosophy as a climactic vocation. He came with all the strength of variegated experience, and with the hidden weakness of a scar upon his soul.

James' perilous experience in early manhood with melancholia, or worse, left him sensitive to all who suffer anxiety in this anxious age. The moralist in him worried over the science of him, and could not rest until he had settled into a conviction that freedom was his only fate. Coming to mental health through philosophers who taught him to believe in freedom and through poets, notably Wordsworth, who made that freedom feel lustrous and fine, James here shares in his own racy style and with the touch of a gracious bedside manner reflections that are bound to leave the reader wiser or better or both. (p. 313)

SMITH, T. V. Democratic Tradition in America. 1941.

What indeed save danger, the breath of defeat, the scent of death?--only these as crucible could refine gold from the cultural tinsel and the personal conceit of the youthful Holmes. 'Some teacher of the kind,' Holmes has judged, 'we all need....in order that we may remember all that buffoons forget.' The American environment has been such a teacher for many. For William James, this stern teacher was a psychic fault that, opening as a fissure, disclosed stark unreason as nigh neighbor to his pride. Drawing slowly back from the sight of insanity, through the prolonged pain of hypochondria, James shed his trappings and in spite of learning became a man. Nature had provided in Holmes no such defective temperament as painful means to save him from softness. Hardier than James, solider, bolder, Holmes required medicine worse than any psychic unease to make nursling into man. War was to be his medicine--war where both poverty and pride prevented the hireing of a substitute. (p. 80.1)

He was reticent about his inmost convictions even when as youths he and James discussed high things. James once tried to interest him in psychical research. Holmes retorted: 'Why don't you study Mohammedism? Hundreds of millions of men and women think you will be eternally damned without it.' And then followed a conclusion which recurs often in Holmes's later life, being written crucially into one great court decision: 'We go through life staking our salvation on incomplete and imperfect knowledge. Life is like an artichoke; you pull out a leaf, but only the tip is edible.' (p. 104-5)

SMITH, T. V. The Philosophic Way of Life. 1929.

'There was no sense of security,' as Santayana with clearest discernment says of him, 'no joy in James' apology for personal religion. He did not really believe; he merely believed in the right of believing that you might be right if you believed.' When he saw the crowd of orthodox salvation-seekers he was drawing around him from men of little humor, he could but seek to puff them away with the sincere but stinging judgment that 'what most religious men most need is that their faiths should be broken up and ventilated, that the northwest wind of science should get into them and blow their sickliness and barbarism away.' Saved thus from religious morbidity, he was free to follow his speculative interests in discovering new vistas and blazing new paths for science, paths even into territory hitherto preserved as sacred. (p. 77-8)

This subservience of thought to action and feeling led James to his best known, though perhaps most equivocal formulation, 'The Will to Believe.'

James's apparent betrayal of science in this famous essay grows out of one and only one consideration. He is as clear there as elsewhere that ideas and beliefs are by nature hypotheses, and so subject to the scientific demand for verification before they can be finally and fully trusted. He who can verify a belief and does not is flabby in his tender-mindedness. (p. 92-3)

Through all his changes James himself lived adventurously with none too much worry over consistency. He could not accept a rigid naturalism, such as his realistic disciples were developing at the time of his death; for he never gave up the hypothesis that immortality might be a fact. He never believed in it 'keenly,' as he said, 'but more strongly as I grow older; because I am just getting fit to live.' He could not accept a rigid theism, on the other side. He wrote to a friend that his system was 'theistic, but not essentially so.' He accepted, more or less opportunistically, what seemed necessary to him at given stages, and hoped that if his various beliefs were too inconsistent, it was because the universe itself was discontinuous and pluralistic. But it must not, in turn, grow so pluralistic as to invalidate optimism of a fruitful outcome of our human venture. (p. 107-8)

SOCKMAN, Ralph W. How to Believe. 1953.

The effect of this description is heightened when we hear William James, himself not a mystic, trying to express in a similar figure his religious experience. He admitted that his belief in God rested on the logic of his own sense of need. But James also confessed to a feeling which outran logic. 'It is,' he said, 'very vague and impossible to describe or put into words. In this it is somewhat like another experience that I have constantly, a tune that is always singing in the back of my mind but which I can never identify or whistle or get rid of. Something like that is my feeling for God, or a beyond. Especially at times of moral crises it comes to me, as the sense of an unknown something backing me up. It is most indefinite, to be sure, and rather faint. And yet I know that if it should cease, there would be a great hush, a great void in my life.' (Hibbert Journal, October 1911, p. 232) (p. 42)

SPILLER, Robert E., and others. Literary History of the United States. Revised Edition. 1953.

What were the larger implications of James' thought for the conflict between the traditional emphasis on the autonomy of the individual and the demands of the new interdependent society for cooperative living? Hating all forms of tyranny, powers, bigness, loving the infinite variability he detected in the universe, convinced that human nature could mold a better future, James celebrated the energies of men, actual and potential. In his scheme men are morally free agents determining their own destiny. He emphasized the 'instincts' of competition, acquisitiveness, and freedom of action; and his social attitudes were largely those of the traditional laissez faire school of his political mentor, E. L. Godkin. 'Religiously and Philosophically,' James wrote, 'our ancient doctrine of live and let live may prove to have a far deeper meaning than our people now seem to imagine it to possess.' (p. 983-4)

The idea of an open universe was unquestionably deeply related to American experience and faith, and time has shown that it was not to be lightly laid aside. In James it found its most brilliant and engaging champion. In demanding a world that left plenty of room for effort and that made effort the most valued of man's activities, and in relating this demand to the confident faith that the individual need not be defeated by nature or by his fellows or by himself, James was epitomizing the dominant theme in the literature of ideas that made his generation a pivotal one in American intellectual development. (p. 985)

From his Boston moorings Holmes drifted far in two important directions. For one thing he became a skeptic. In his youth he and James had tried their hands together at stripping some of the obscuring garments from 'our dilapidated old friend the Kosmos,' but he came to think that 'certainty generally is an illusion,' and that we must be content with working hypotheses. 'The best of truth,' he said, echoing James, 'is the power of thought to get itself accepted in the competition of the market.' The implications of such a view for religious belief are disintegrative. (p. 1282)

GALLUP, Donald. Editor. The Flowers of Friendship. Letters written to Gertrude Stein. 1953.

Leon Solomons died in 1900 as the result of an infection contracted in the laboratory. William James had been appointed Gifford lecturer on natural religion at the University of Edinburgh, and held this appointment, on leave from Harvard, for two years, 1899-1901.

From William James, Geneva (Switzerland), October 17, 1900.

Dear Miss Stein,

Ever since Solomons's untimely and never too much to be regretted death, I have had an impulse to write to you, to express my sorrow to a sympathetic friend...I never was more startled by anything, and never was anything outwardly at least more irrational and ascribable to mere chance than such an event. Exactly what he would have done had he lived, it is impossible to say, but it would have been absolutely original and remarkable, absolutely clear, and it might have been very important. Such a mixture of a rather wild independence, with amiability; of a rather contemptuous intellectuality with breadth of sympathy; made of him a very peculiar and extraordinary character. His eagerness, daring, honesty, good spirits, and scorn of all that was nonsensical and mendacious in life were glorious. We shall never look upon his like, and seldom on his equal.... (p. 19-20)

William James had of course received from Gertrude Stein a copy of Three Lives, followed by a letter and a volume of Charles Peguy. James had become emeritus from Harvard in 1907, and in 1908 had lectured on philosophy at Oxford. He died just three months after the following letter was written.

Bad-Nauheim, May 25, 1910 (Extract from letter from James to Gertrude Stein).

I have had a bad conscience about 'Three Lives.' You know (?) how hard it is for me to read novels. Well, I read 30 or 40 pages, and said 'this is a fine new kind of realism--Gertrude Stein is great! I will go at it carefully when just the right mood comes.' But apparently the right mood never came. I thought I had put the book in my trunk, to finish overhere, but I don't find it on unpacking. I promise you that it shall be read some time! You see what a swine I am to have pearls cast before him! As a rule reading fiction is as hard for me as trying to hit a target by hurling feathers at it. I need resistance, to cerebrate! (p. 50)

STEVENSON, Adlai E. Major Campaign Speeches. 1952.

'Reason is one of the very feeblest of Nature's forces, if you take it at any one spot and moment. It is only in the very long run that its effects become perceptible. Reason assumes to settle things by weighing them against one another without prejudice, partiality, or excitement; but what affairs in the concrete are settled by it and always will be just prejudices, partialities, cupidities, and excitements. Appealing to reason as we do, we are in a sort of forlorn hope situation, like a small sandbank in the midst of a hungry sea ready to wash it out of existence. But sandbanks grow when the conditions favor; and weak as reason is, it has the unique advantage over its antagonists that its activity never lets up and that it presses always in one direction, while men's prejudices vary, their passions ebb and flow, and their excitements are intermittent. Our sandbank, I absolutely believe, is bound to grow--bit by bit it will get dyked and breakwatered.'

William James. (p. x)

For, as William James truly said, 'When we touch our own upper limit and live in our own highest center of energy, we may call ourselves saved.' (p. 188)

FURNAS, J. C. Voyage to Windward. The Life of Robert Louis Stevenson. 1951.

But more experienced students of such matters might have advised Joad to read William James's 'On a Certain Blindness in Human Beings' for the effect of the contrast between James's excellent lean style (of which, I assume, the Dutchess would approve) and the full flavor of Stevenson in the long passages from 'The Lantern-Bearers' here used to illustrate James's psychological point. In fact, the founder of pragmatism here publicly hopes that this essay of Stevenson's will be immortal, 'both for the truth of its matter and the excellence of its form,' which is notable from a man who managed both to write well and to think hard. In winnowing literature for further illustration, he harnesses Stevenson with Josiah Royce, Wordsworth, Walt Whitman, and Tolstoi....fast company for a mere phrase-juggler. (p. 444-5)

TAYLOR, Harold. On Education and Freedom. 1954.

Whatever else his philosophy contains, James' messages to educators and to philosophers states that each of them ignores the real world of empirical fact at his own peril, and that an education or a philosophy which separates the realm of thought from the realm of feeling, or the sphere of theory from that of action, will be incapable of achieving depth or breadth. If the philosophers and educators do not talk to men and women who want to hear them in ways which they can relate to their own experience, they will not be heard, and those in search of education and of philosophical insight will receive it elsewhere under less desirable auspices. William James expressed this view in the following passage:

'The world to which your philosophy-professor introduces you is simple, clean and noble. The contradictions of real life are absent from it. Its architecture is classic. Principles of reason trace its outline, logical necessities cement its parts. Purity and dignity are what it most expresses. It is a kind of marble temple shining on a hill.

'In point of fact it is far less an account of this actual world than a clear addition built upon it, a classic sanctuary in which the rationalist fancy may take refuge from the intolerably confused and gothic character which mere facts present. It is no explanation of our concrete universe, it is another thing altogether, a substitute for it, a remedy, a way of escape....(It) will never satisfy the empiricist temper of mind. It will seem rather a monument of artificiality. So we find men of science preferring to turn their backs on metaphysics as on something altogether cloistered and spectral, and practical men shaking philosophy's dust off their feet and following the call of the wild.' (Pragmatism) (p. 137-8)

TRUEBLOOD, Elton. Alternative to Futility. 1948.

George Fox proposed to cut straight through all the religious red tape. If anything seemed artificial and unnecessary, the young shoemaker's apprentice determined to dispense with it, no matter how precious it might have been at other times or how glorified by tradition. Naked reality was what he sought. It is to this that William James was referring when he said, 'The Quaker religion is something which it is impossible to overpraise. In a day of shams, it was a religion of veracity rooted in spiritual inwardness and a return to something more like the original gospel truth than men had ever known in England.' (p. 54-5)

TRUEBLOOD, Elton. Common Ventures of Life. 1949.

The great use of life is to spend it for something that will outlast it.

William James. (p. 80)

TRUEBLOOD, Elton. The Knowledge of God. 1939.

The estimation in which the traditional 'proofs' are held in the modern world was accurately judged by William James who knew they could not be despised and yet were 'not solid enough to serve as religion's all sufficient foundation.'

'The arguments for God's existence have stood for hundreds of years with the waves of unbelieving criticism breaking against them, never totally discrediting them in the ears of the faithful, but on the whole slowly and surely washing out the mortar from between their joints.' (Varieties of Religious Experience) (p. 4)

'We may lay it down as certain,' wrote James, 'that in the distinctively religious sphere of experience, many persons (how many we cannot tell) possess the objects of their belief, not in the form of mere conceptions which their intellect accepts as true, but rather in the form of quasi-sensible realities directly apprehended.' (Varieties of Religious Experience) (p. 69)

The sober judgment of Professor William James was, 'There is a certain composite photograph of universal saintliness, the same in all religions, of which the features can easily be traced.' (Varieties of Religious Experience) (p. 106)

In his Gifford Lectures, William James, after making some flattering remarks about the religion which Fox founded, went on to say:

'No one can pretend for a moment that in point of spiritual sagacity and capacity, Fox's mind was unsound. Everyone who confronted him personally, from Oliver Cromwell down to county magistrates and jailers, seems to have acknowledge his superior power. Yet from the point of view of his nervous consitution, Fox was a psychopath or detraque of the deepest dye. His Journal abounds in entries of this sort.' (Varieties of Religious Experience)

James then quotes at length Fox's own account of his approach to the city of Lichfield, when he left his shoes with the shepherds on the outskirts of the city and walked barefoot through the streets, shouting to the market day crowd, 'Woe to the bloody city of Lichfield.'

Readers of James' book who know nothing of George Fox, except what James tells them, are bound to have a most misguided impression of the man. (p. 128)

TRUEBLOOD, Elton. Life We Prize. 1951.

The man who really lives always has vastly more to do that he can accomplish and for such a man retirement is almost without significance. How can a man retire from the effort which he believes is sorely needed and which is directed to a really grand cause? It was characteristic of that wonderfully fortunate man, Rufus Jones, the Quaker philosopher, that, though he was eighty-five when he died, he corrected the proof of his last book on the day of his death. It is hardly surprising that he lived in this way if we listen to his teacher, William James:

'Whenever a process of life communicates an eagerness to him who lives it, there the life becomes truly significant....But, whenever it is found, there is the zest, the tingle, the excitement of reality; and there is importance in the only real and positive sense in which importance ever anywhere can be.'

But how does the zest, which gives the sense of importance, come? How did William James find it? (p. 50)

'The great use of life,' said William James, 'is to spend it for something that will outlast it.' (p. 123)

WALLAS, Graham. Art of Thought. 1926.

William James, in one of the best known of his 'Talks to Teachers' (The Gospel of Relaxation) insists on the special importance of this advice for America. Some Americans he says, on returning from Europe, observe the 'desperate eagerness and anxiety' in their compatriots' faces, and say: 'What intelligence it shows! How different from the stolid cheeks, the codfish eyes, the slow inanimate behaviour we have been seeing in the British Isles.' 'But,' says James, 'that eagerness, breathlessness, and anxiety are not signs of strength: they are signs of weakness and of bad co-ordination. The even forehead, the slab-like cheek, codfish eye, may be less interesting for the moment, but they are more promising signs than intense expression is of what we may expect of their possessor in the long run.' (p. 161-2)

Would any man of learning who was not a modern American have been likely to write, as James wrote after opening (in 1885) the first psychological laboratory at Harvard, 'I try to spend two hours a day in a laboratory for psycho-physics which I started last year, but of which I fear the fruits will be slow in ripening, as my experimental aptitude is but small. But I am convinced that one must guard in some such way against the growing tendency to subjectivism in one's thinking as life goes on.' (Letters) (p. 186)

Eighteen years ago William James complained that 'We all know persons who are models of excellence, but who belong to the extreme philistine type of mind. So deadly is their intellectual respectability that we can't converse about certain subjects at all, can't let our minds play over them, can't even mention them in their presence. I have numbered amongst my dearest friends persons thus inhibited intellectually, with whom I would gladly have been able to talk freely about certain interests of mine, certain authors, say, as Bernard Shaw, Chesterton, Edward Carpenter, H. G. Wells, but it wouldn't do, it made them too uncomfortable, they wouldn't play. I had to be silent. An intellect thus tied down by literality and decorum makes on one the same sort of an impression that an able-bodied man would who should habituate himself to do his work with only one of his fingers, locking up the rest of his organism and leaving it unused.' (Selected Papers on Philosophy) (p. 201-2)

WALLAS, Graham. The Great Society. 1920.

Professor James said:

'From the guessing of newspaper enigmas to the plotting of the policy of an empire there is no other process than this. We trust to the laws of cerebral nature to present us spontaneously with the appropriate idea.' (Principles of Psychology) (p. 178)

WALLAS, Graham. Human Nature in Politics. 1910.

'The moral tragedy of human life comes almost wholly from the fact that the link is ruptured which normally should hold between vision of the truth and action, and that this pungent sense of effective reality will not attach to certain ideas.' (Principles of Psychology) (p. 42)

WALLAS, Graham. Social Judgment. 1935.

Otto himself gives an instance from William James's Varieties of Religious Experience, where the numinous feeling and the simultaneous rationalization of that feeling by inferring from it the presence of a divine personality were equally natural, and equally convincing aspects of one experience. The witness, a clergyman, says: 'The perfect stillness of the night was thrilled by a more solemn silence. The darkness held a presence that was all the more felt because it was not seen. I could not any more have doubted that He was there, than that I was. Indeed, I felt myself to be, if possible, the less real of the two.' (Varieties of Religious Experience) (p. 154-5)

WELLS, H. G. Anticipations of the Reaction of Mechanical and Scientific Progress upon Human Life and Thought. 1902.

One has only to see a Parisian book-shop, and to recall an English one, to realize the as yet unattainable standing of French. The serried ranks of lemon-colored volumes in the former have the whole range of human thought and interest; there are no taboos and no limits; you have everything up and down the scale, from frank indecency to stark wisdom. It is a shop for men. I remember my amazement to discover three copies of a translation of that most wonderful book, the Text-book of Psychology of Professor William James, in a shop in l'-Avenue de l'Opera - three copies of a book that I have never seen anywhere in England outside my own house - and I am an attentive student of book-shop windows! (p. 258)

WELLS, H. G. Experiment in Autobiography. 1934.

I once saw James quarrelling with his brother William James, the psychologist. He had lost his calm; he was terribly unnerved. He appealed to me, to me of all people, to adjudicate on what was and what was not permissible behaviour in England. William was arguing about it in an indisputably American accent, with an indecently naked reasonableness. I had come to Rye with a car to fetch William James and his daughter to my home at Sandgate. William had none of Henry's passionate regard for the polish upon the surfaces of life and he was immensely excited by the fact that in the little Rye inn, which had its garden just over the high brick wall of the garden of Lamb House, G. K. Chesterton was staying. William James had corresponded with our vast contemporary and he sorely wanted to see him. So with a scandalous directness he had put the gardener's ladder against that ripe red wall and clambered up and peeped over!

Henry had caught him at it.

It was the sort of thing that isn't done. It was most emphatically the sort of thing that isn't done....Henry had instructed the gardener to put away that ladder and William was looking thoroughly naughty about it.

To Henry's manifest relief, I carried William off and in the road just outside the town we ran against the Chestertons who had been for a drive in Romney Marsh; Chesterton was heated and I think rather swollen by the sunshine; he seemed to overhand his one-horse fly; he descened slowly but firmly; he was moist and steamy but cordial; we chatted in the road for a time and William got his coveted impression. (p. 453-4)

WELLS, H. G. The Rights of Man. Or What Are We Fighting For. 1940.

The valid criticism that still remains is to be found very competently set out by William James in a small but very important book, The Moral Equivalent of War. He finds, and one must remember he was a very great and subtle psychologist, something very unsatisfactory and impracticable in the prospect of a world of peace and security in which everyone is to move about freely without any sense of ownership in the community, participation in the community or obligation to the community. The more collectivist we become--and continually we become more collectivist--the more the sense of proprietorship has to be transferred to the community as a whole. The community is something to which we look for the protection of our rights indeed, but it is also something we have to take care of and serve. And this is not to be attained by mere preachment and sentiment.

And so he suggests a universal conscription for one or two years of the formative period of life, somewhen between sixteen, let us say, and twenty-five, during which the young citizen, man or woman, will have to undertake some of that residue of unpleasing, irksome, dangerous or subordinate work that must still be done, whatever feats of mechanism or organization the future may have in store for us. (p. 40-1)

BROME, Vincent. H. G. Wells: A Biography. 1951.

William James, brother of Henry, and a man Wells considered as deep an influence in his middle age as Huxley was in his youth, wrote:

'My dear Wells,

I have just read your Utopia (given me by F.C.S. Schiller on the one day that I spent in Oxford on my way back to Cambridge Mass. after a few weeks on the Continent) and Anticipations and Mankind in the Making having duly proceeded together with numerous other lighter volumes of yours, the 'summation of the stimuli' reaches the threshold of discharge and I can't help overflowing in a note of gratitude. You 'have your faults, as who has not?' but your virtues are unparalleled and transcendent, and I believe that you will prove to have given a shove to the practical thought of the next generation that will be amongst the greatest of its influences for good. All in the line of English genius too, no wire-drawn French doctrines, and no German shop technicalities inflicted in an unerbittlich consequent manner, but everywhere the sense of the full, concrete, and the air of freedom playing through all the joints of your argument.' (p. 90)

WHITEHEAD, Alfred North. Aims of Education and Other Essays. 1929.

The modern scientific age then gradually supervenes, and again in William James we find the typical imaginative scholar. (p. 152)

WHITEHEAD, Alfred North. Dialogues as Recorded by Lucien Price. 1954.

During a discussion of William James's 'Varieties of Religious Experience,' he said:

'The difficulty of communication in words is but little realized. If I had to write something about your personality, of course I could--but how much would remain that couldn't be put into words. So, when the rare balance of knowledge and perception appears, as in William James--one who could communicate so much more than most--it is perhaps an advantage that his system of philosophy remained incomplete. To fill it out would necessarily have made it smaller. In Plato's 'Dialogues' there is a richness of thought, suggestion, and implication which reaches far. Later, when he came to be more explicit concerning some of those implications, we have a shrinkage.

'Something similar can happen in scholarship. There is, of course, great importance in scholarship--exact knowledge, rationalization--but a great many scholars are engaged in reducing men of genius to the commonplace.

'Consider John Dewey. In carrying on the philosophy of William James I think he enormously narrowed it. With James the consciousness of the ever-present complexity and possibility in human experience is always implicit in his writing. Dewey is without it. William James's awareness of the wide scope and the interrelations of all questions made him one of the great philosophic minds in history.' (p. 337-8)

WHITEHEAD, Alfred North. Philosophy of Alfred North Whitehead. Edited by Paul A. Schlipp. 1941.

Professor Whitehead once remarked in conversation that the real greatness of William James lay in the fact that, instead of offering a stereotyped definition of truth, he had left with his readers a sense of the need for a receptive mind and heart, and a readiness to find significance in new experiences from whatever direction they might come. One feels that the remark might be applied to Professor Whitehead himself. Like James he has taught not so much by offering formal definitions, which might too easily become instances of 'misplaced concreteness,' but rather by helping his students to be responsive to the rich variety of the changing pattern of events. (p. 489)

WHITEHEAD, Alfred North. Science and the Modern World. 1925.

James denies that consciousness is an entity, but admits that it is a function. The discrimination between an entity and a function is therefore vital to the understanding of the challenge which James is advancing against the older modes of thought. In the essay in question, the character which James assigns to consciousness is fully discussed. But he does not unambiguously explain what he means by the notion of an entity, which he refuses to apply to consciousness. In the sentence which immediately follows the one which I have already quoted, he says:

'There is, I mean, no aboriginal stuff or quality of being, contrasted with that of which material objects are made, out of which our thoughts of them are made; but there is a function in experience which thoughts perform, and for the performance of which this quality of being is invoked. That function is knowing. 'Consciousness' is supposed necessary to explain the fact that things not only are, but get reported, are known.'

Thus James, is denying that consciousness is a 'stuff.'

(p. 199-200)

WINSTON, Robert Watson. Horace Williams, The Gadfly of Chapel Hill. 1942.

At this time, in his extensive correspondence, he continued to lambast the bread-and-butter philosophy of William James and the pretensions of the Ph.D.'s. James he called a joke. (p. 222)

YOUNG, Ella Flagg. Isolation in the School. 1906. (University of Chicago Contributions to Education No. 1)

James has expressed the theory of teleological functioning so well that I quote his remarks at some length:

'The reflex theory of the mind commits physiologists to regarding the mind as an essentially teleological mechanism. I mean by this that the conceiving or theorizing faculty--the mind's middle department--functions exclusively for the sake of ends that do not exist at all in the world of impressions we receive by way of our senses but are set by our emotional and practical subjectivity altogether. It is a transformation of the world of our impressions into a totally different world, the world of our conception and the transformation is affected in the interests of our volitional nature, and for no other purpose whatever....We easily delude ourselves about this middle stage. Sometimes we think it final, and sometimes we fail to see amid the monstrous diversity in the length and complication of the cogitations which may fill it that it can have but one essential function--the function of defining the direction which our activity, immediate or remote, shall take.

'Receiving impressions' to all eternity would never result in developing what we call 'mind.' The active response, the forthputting of the mind's own powers according to its own constitution, is the prominent and the really impressive thing for the psychologist.' (p. 61-2)

REFERENCES

Abbott, Lyman
Henry Ward Beecher. 1903. (p. 124)
Adams, Henry
Education of Henry Adams. 1918. (p. 307)
-- Letters, 1858-1891. Edited by W. C. Ford. 1930. (p. 264, 286)
-- Letters, 1892-1918. Edited by W. C. Ford. 1938 (p. 485, 490, 524, 539, 544-5, 546, 555, 558, 646)
Addams, Jane
Excellent becomes the permanent. 1932. (p. 6)
-- The long road of woman's memory 1916 (p. XI)
-- My friend, Julia Lathrop. 1935 (p. 163)
-- Newer Ideals of peace. 1915 (p. 24)
-- Twenty years at Hull House. 1930. (p. 308)
Adler, Mortimer
What man has made of man. 1937. (p. 131, 199)
Alexander, Hartley Burr
Liberty and democracy, and other essays in war time. 1918. (p. 42)
-- The world's rim. Great mysteries of the North American Indians. 1953. (p. 49-50)
Allport, Gordon W.
Becoming basic considerations for a psychology of personality 1955 (p. 36, 41, 51-4, 86, 91, 93)
-- Nature of prejudice. 1954. (p. 42, 178, 402, 447, 456, 485)
Ames, Van Meter
Proust and Santayana. 1937. (p. 52, 76, 77)
Anderson, Thornton
Brooks Adams. Constructive conservative. 1951. (p. 37-8, 96)

Babbitt, Irving
Democracy and leadership. 1924. (p. 328, 329)
-- Literature and the American college. 1908. (p. 27)
-- Masters of modern French criticism. 1912. (p. IX, 53, 253, 254)
-- The new Laokoon. An essay on the confusion of the arts. 1910. (p. 212)

Babbitt, Irving
On being creative; and other essays. 1932. (p. XIX)
-- Rousseau and romanticism. 1919. (p. XIII, 78, 181, 183, 384)
-- Spanish character and other essays. 1940. (p. 74, 231)
Baker, Rachel
Sigmund Freud. 1952. (p. 129-30, 170-1)
Baker, Ray Stannard
Spiritual unrest. 1910. (p. 189, 201, 204, 205, 206)
-- Woodrow Wilson. Life and Letters. Eight volumes. 1939. (v. 7 p. 275)
Baldwin, Leland D.
Recent American history. 1954. (p. 19)
Balsan, Consuelo Vanderbilt
The glitter and the gold. 1952. (p. 132)
Barrus, Clara.
Life and letters of John Burroughs. Two volumes. 1925. (v. 1 p. 371; v. 2 p. 36, 166, 338)
-- Whitman and Burroughs, comrades. 1931. (p. 346)
Barzun, Jacques
Darwin, Marx, Wagner. Critique of a heritage. 1941. (12 references in index)
-- God's country and mine. 1954. (p. 129)
-- Of human freedom. 1939. (12 references in index)
-- Race. A study in modern superstition. 1937. (p. 273)
-- Romanticism and the Modern ego. 1943. (17 references in index)
-- Teacher in America. 1945. (p. 38, 131, 156, 195, 196, 208, 260, 276-7, 292-3, 306)
Beck, Robert H., Cook, Walter W., and Kearney, Nolan C.
Curriculum in the modern elementary school. 1953. (p. 14)
Becker, Carl L.
Modern history. The rise of a democratic, scientific, and industrialized civilization. 1931. (p. 728)
Belden, Albert D.
George Whitefield, the awakener. 1930. (p. 264, 268)
Bell, Eric Temple
The search for truth. 1934. (p. 59-66)
Bennett, Charles A.
Dilemma of religious knowledge. 1931. (p. 84)
Berenson, Bernard
Rumor and reflection. 1952. (p. 19, 126)
Berger, Morral, Abel, Theodore and Poge, Charles H., editors.
Freedom and control in modern society. 1954. (p. 178, 191)

Berkhof, L.
Systematic theology. 1949. (p. 24-5, 54, 488)
Bernard, Harold W.
Psychology of learning and teaching. 1954. (24 references in index)
Bernhardt, Karl S.
Practical psychology. Second edition. 1953. (p. 27)
Bewley, Marius. The complex fate. Hawthorne, Henry James and some other American writers. 1954. (p. 55, 146-8)
Bianchi, Martha Dickinson
Life and letters of Emily Dickinson. 1924. (p. 95)
Blackwood, Andrew Watterson
Biographical preaching for today. 1954. (p. 158)
Blanshard, Brand and others
Preface to philosophy. 1946. (p. 193)
Boas, George and others
Studies in intellectual history. 1953. (Wiener, Philip A. Lovejoy's role in American philosophy.) (p. 166)
Bodley, R. V. C.
In search of serenity. 1955. (p. 110-1, 154)
Bond, F. Fraser.
Give yourself background. 1937. (p. 103)
Bosselman, Beulah C.
The troubled mind. A psychiatric study of success and failure in human adaptation. 1953. (p. 3)
Bourne, Randolph
Education and living. 1917. (p. 66, 68, 69, 72)
-- History of a literary radical. 1920. (p. 41, 42)
-- Untimely papers. 1919. (p. 114, 115, 119)
Bowen, Catherine Brinker
Yankee from Olympus. Justice Holmes and his family. 1944. (11 references in index)
Braddy, Nella
Anne Sullivan Macy. The story behind Helen Keller. 1933. (p. 313)
Brennan, Joseph G.
Meaning of philosophy. 1953. (p. 85-8, 90-1, 168, 181, 220, 246, 257, 290-1, 298-300)
Brightman, Edgar S.
Autonomy and theonomy (in Bryson, Lyman and others. Editors. Freedom and authority in our time. 1953.) (p. 473)
-- Philosophy of religion. 1940. (27 references in index)
Brinton, Crane, Christopher, John B. and Wolff, Robert Lee
A history of civilization. Two volumes. 1955. (v. 2. p. 357, 358, 359, 525)

Brinton, Crane
Ideas and Men. 1950. (p. 42, 462, 495, 496)
Broad, C. D.
Religion, philosophy and psychical research. 1953. (p. 102)
Brogan, D. W.
American themes. 1947. (p. 171, 262, 265, 267)
-- The free state. Some considerations on its practical value. 1945. (p. 13)
-- The price of freedom. 1951. (p. 273)
-- Price of revolution. 1951. (p. 273)
Bromberg, Walter
Man above humanity. A history of psychotherapy. 1954. (p. 121, 128, 140-1, 188)
Brome, Vincent
H. G. Wells. A biography. 1951. (p. 90, 237)
Brooks, Van Wyck.
The confident years, 1885-1915. 1952. (21 references in index)
-- Emerson and others. 1927. (p. 127, 244)
-- Flowering of New England, 1815-1865. 1937. (p. 207, 231, 383)
-- Letters and leadership. 1918. (p. 99)
-- On literature today. 1941. (p. 26, 28)
-- Opinions of Oliver Allston. 1941. (9 references in index)
-- Sketches in criticism. 1932. (p. 37-45, 48, 77, 146-7, 150, 177)
-- Times of Melville and Whitman. 1947. (7 references in index)
-- Writer in America. 1953. (p. 64, 75, 95-6, 116, 136, 185, 188, 191)
-- World of H. G. Wells. 1915. (p. 94-5, 112)
-- World of Washington Irving. 1945. (p. 181)
Broun, Heywood
Collected edition compiled by Heywood Hale Broun. 1941. (p. 303)
Brownell, W. C.
Democratic distinction in America. 1927. (p. 237)
Buchan, John
Pilgrim's way. 1940. (p. 204)
Burke, Kenneth
A grammar of motives. 1945. (p. 64-6, 69, 72-4, 77, 275, 277, 286-8, 298, 300)
Burns, Edward M.
Western civilizations. Their history and culture. Fourth edition. 1954. (p. 696)

Burroughs, John
Breath of life. 1915. (p. 254)
Burroughs, John
Heart of Burrough's journals. Edited by Clara Barrus. 1928. (p. 222, 240, 250, 272)
-- Last harvest. 1922. (p. 234)
-- Summit of the years. 1913. (p. 187)
-- Under the apple trees. 1916. (p. 201, 205)
-- Under the maples. 1921. (p. 22)
Butler, Nicholas Murray
Meaning of education. 1915. (p. 113-4)
Butts, R. Freeman and Remin, Lawrence C.
History of education in American culture. 1953. (p. 334-5, 342-3, 405)

Cailliet, Emile
Christian approach to culture. 1953. (p. 92)
Canby, Henry Seidel
Alma Mater. The Gothic age of the American college. 1936. (p. 88, 121)
-- American memoir. 1947. (p. 182)
-- Education by violence. Essays on the war and the future. 1919. (p. 140)
-- Everyday Americans. 1920. (p. 125)
-- Turn west, turn east. Mark Twain and Henry James. 1951. (31 references in index)
Cardozo, Benjamin N.
Law and literature. And other essays and addresses. 1931. (p. 172)
-- Nature of the judicial process. 1922. (p. 12)
-- Paradoxes of legal science. 1928. (p. 61)
-- Selected writings, edited by Margaret E. Hall. 1947. (p. 109, 212, 287, 419-20)
Carman, Harry J. and Syrett, Harold C.
History of the American people. Two volumes. 1953. (v. 2 p. 216-7)
Carter, Everett
Howells and the age of realism. 1954. (p. 26, 153-6, 232, 253, 254)
Catlin, George
In the path of Mahatma Gandhi. 1950. (p. 248)
-- Story of the political philosophers. 1939. (p. 191, 282, 621, 663, 770)
Chalmers, Gordon Keith
The republic and the person. 1952. (p. 125, 139, 189)
Chamberlin, William Henry
The confessions of an individualist. 1940. (p. 6)

Chapman, John Jay
Memories and Milestones. 1915. (p. 19-28, 160)
Chase, John
Editor. Years of the modern. An American appraisal. 1949. (Portrait of the American by Henry Steele Commager p. 3-31) (p. 11, 16, 39) (Adventure in ideals by Norman Cousins p. 311-35) (p. 329)
Chase, Stuart
Power of words. 1953. (p. 34, 66, 75, 100, 130, 140)
-- The proper study of mankind. An inquiry into the science of human relations. 1948. (p. 40, 48, 62)
Chase, Stuart and Chase, Marian Tyler
Roads to agreement. Successful methods in the science of human relations. 1951. (p. 23, 210)
Chase, Stuart
The tyranny of words. 1938. (p. 5, 45, 53, 208, 214, 218)
Chesterton, G. K.
The common man. 1950. (p. 31-2)
Chiaroscuro, Augustus John
Fragments of autobiography. First series. 1952. (p. 172)
Chisholm, Leslie L.
Work of the modern high school. 1953. (p. 60-1)
Coffin, Henry Sloane.
A half century of Union Theological Seminary, 1896-1945. 1954. (p. 150, 184)
Cohen, Felix.
Editor. Holmes-Cohen correspondence. (p. 20, 44) in (Journal of the History of Ideas. January 1948)
Cohen, Morris R.
Faith of a liberal. Selected essays. 1946. (p. 8, 70, 95, 299, 310, 335-6, 358-61, 369, 379, 391-2, 396, 446, 448)
-- Meaning of human history. 1947. (p. 20, 35, 79, 216, 219-20, 250, 268, 289)
-- Law and the social order. 1933. (p. 222, 266)
-- Reason and nature. An essay on the meaning of the scientific method. 1931. (19 references in index)
-- Studies in philosophy and science 1949. (p. 30, 31, 39, 115, 137, 162, 172)
Cole Stewart G. and Cole, Mildred Wiese
Minorities and the American promise. The conflict of principle and practice. 1954. (p. 102, 147, 285)
Collins, James.
History of modern European philosophy. 1954. (p. 315, 376, 436, 634, 746, 770, 817)
-- The mind of Kierkegard. 1953. (p. 147, 153)

Commager, Henry Steele
The American mind. An interpretation of American thought and character since the 1880's. 1950. (p. 90-107, 117, 165, 167, 385, 387-8)
-- Editor. Living ideas in America. 1951. (p. 642-7)
Commins, W. D. and Fagin, Barry
Principles of educational psychology. Second edition. 1954. (15 references in index)
Compton, Charles H.
Who reads William James? (in Who Reads What? 1934. p. 91-100) (p. 95-9)
Cook, Lloyd and Cook, Elaine
Inter-group education. 1954. (p. 121, 122, 205)
Corbin, John
Return of the middle class. 1922. (p. 186)
Cotton, Edward H.
Life of Charles W. Eliot. 1926. (p. 194)
Cotton, James Harry
Royce on the human self. 1954. (24 references in index)
Cowley, Malcolm
The literary situation. 1954. (p. 142)
Crothers, Samuel McChord.
Among friends. 1910. (p. 107)
-- Dame school of experience. And other essays. 1920. (p. 154-5)
-- Humanly speaking. 1912. (p. 80-4)
Curti, Merle.
Editor. American Scholarship in the twentieth century. 1953. (p. 5, 40, 60, 175, 178-181)
Curti, Merle & others.
History of American civilization. 1953. (p. 502-3)
Cutts, Norman E. and Moseley, Nicholas
The only child. A guide for parents and only children of all ages. 1954. (p. 236)

Dark, Sidney
Outline of Wells. The superman in the street. 1922. (p. 19)
Davidson, Robert F.
Philosophies men live by. 1952. (31 references in index)
Davie, Emily
Editor. Profile of America; an autobiography of the U.S.A. 1954. (p. 258, 344, 346)
Day, Donald
Franklin D. Roosevelt's own story. Told in his own words from his private and public papers as selected by

Donald Day. 1951. (p. 267)
Day, Dorothy
The long loneliness. Autobiography. 1952. (p. 118-9, 140)
DeVoto, Bernard
Mark Twain's America. 1932. (p. 112, 187)
Dewey, John
Art as experience. 1934. (p. 56, 72, 91, 119, 123, 168, 206-7, 210, 217)
-- Characters and events. Popular essays in social and political philosophy. Two volumes. 1929. (v. 1 p. 107-22, v. 2. 10 references in index)
-- Common faith. 1934. (p. 19)
-- Education today. 1940. (p. 151)
-- Experience and nature. 1929. (p. 130-1, 312, 400)
-- How we think. 1910. (p. 119, 121)
-- Human nature and conduct. 1922. (p. 112, 179, 195)
-- Influence of Darwin on philosophy; and other essays on contemporary thought. 1910. (p. 104, 194, 202, 222, 246)
Dewey, John and Bentley, Arthur F.
Knowing and the known. 1949. (p. 52, 75, 98, 101, 204, 210, 259)
Dewey, John
Philosophy and civilization. 1931. (p. 13, 16-22, 24-29, 99, 107, 162, 234, 261)
-- Philosophy of John Dewey selected and edited by Joseph Ratner. 1928. (p. 8, 91, 92, 211, 217-8, 290, 292, 525, 526)
-- Problems of men. 1946. (p. 188-9, 260, 379-95, 396-409)
-- Public and its problems. 1927. (p. 159-60)
-- Quest for certainty. A study of the relation of knowledge and action. 1929. (p. 209, 238, 284-5)
-- School and society. 1900. (p. 93)
-- Wit and wisdom, edited with an introduction by A. H. Johnson. 1949. (p. 36)
DeWolf, L. Harold
Theology of the living church. 1953. (p. 162, 190, 218, 289)
Dimnet, Ernest
What we live by. 1932. (p. 166, 204)
Dorfman, Joseph
Thorstein Veblen and his America. 1934. (p. 39, 46, 76, 91, 139, 152-3, 209, 450)
DuBois, W. E. Burghardt
Dusk of dawn. An essay toward an autobiography of a

race concept. 1940. (p. 33, 37, 38, 39, 259, 296, 322)

Drake, William E.
The American school in transition. 1955. (p. 22, 416, 417, 421, 518, 532, 573)

Ducasse, C. J.
Philosophical scrutiny of religion. 1953. (p. 160-1, 165, 203, 247, 291-4, 297, 315, 320-1, 350, 410)

Dunham, Burrows
Giant in Chains. 1953. (p. 41, 50, 83-101, 106, 111, 115, 122)

Durant, Will
Story of philosophy. 1926. (9 references in index)

Earnest, Ernest
Academic procession. His informal history of the American college. 1953. (p. 155, 157)

Eastburg, Frederick E.
General principles of psychology. 1953. (p. 7, 47, 78)

Edel, Leon.
Henry James. The untried years. 1953. (58 references in index)
-- The psychological novel, 1900-1950. 1955. (p. 26-8, 40-1, 79, 83, 159)

Edman, Irwin
The contemporary and his soul. 1931. (p. 85, 91)
-- Four ways of philosophy. 1937. (p. 203, 288)
-- Human traits and their social significance. 1920. (34 references in index)

Edman, Irwin and Schneider, Herbert W.
Editors. Landmarks in philosophy. 1941. (p. 872-5)

Edman, Irwin
Philosopher's holiday. 1938. (p. 154)
-- Under whatever sky. 1951. (p. 173)

Emery, Edwin and Smith, Henry Ladd
The press and America. 1954. (p. 327, 350)

Erskine, John
American character and other essays. 1915. (p. 46)
-- The complete life. 1943. (p. 51)
-- Democracy and ideals. 1920. (p. 61)
-- My life as a teacher. 1948. (p. 186)

Fecher, Charles A.
The philosophy of Jacques Maritain. 1953. (p. 29, 67, 92, 342)

Filler, Louis
Randolph Bourne. 1943. (p. 37, 49, 50, 63, 76, 91, 102)

Finkelstein, Louis
American Spiritual autobiographies. Fifteen self portraits. 1948. (p. 13-4)
Fisher, Dorothy Canfield
Mothers and children. 1914. (p. 25)
-- Why stop learning. 1927. (p. 134)
Forest, Ilse
Child development. 1954. (p. 10, 133)
Fosdick, Harry Emerson
Adventurous religion. 1926. (p. 77)
-- As I see religion. 1932. (p. 19, 148)
-- Assurance of immortality. 1926. (p. 53, 135)
-- Faith for tough times. 1952. (p. 34, 50-1)
-- A great time to be alive. 1944. (p. 224)
-- On being a real person. 1943. (10 references in index)
-- On being fit to live with. 1946. (p. 212)
-- Secret of victorious living. 1934. (p. 5, 242)
-- Successful Christian living. Sermons on Christianity today. 1937. (p. 247-8)
-- The three meanings, Prayer, Faith, Service. 1949. (Prayer, p. 9; Faith, p. 9)
Frank, Jerome
Law and the modern mind. 1930. (p. 17, 60, 135, 136, 326-7)
Frank, Waldo
Chart for rough waters. Our role in a new world. 1940. (p. 78)
-- In the American jungle. 1937. (p. 174)
-- Our America. 1919. (p. 27)
-- The re-discovery of America. An introduction to a philosophy of American life. 1929. (p. 23, 24)
-- Time exposures. Being portraits of twenty men and women. 1926. (p. 123)
Freemantle, Anne
The age of belief. The medieval philosophers, selected, with introduction and interpretive commentary. 1955. (p. 149-50)
Furnas, J. C.
Voyage to windward. The life of Robert Louis Stevenson. 1951. (p. 444-5)

Gallup, Donald
Editor. The flowers of friendship. Letters written to Gertrude Stein. 1953. (p. 7, 9, 13, 18, 19-20, 50-1)
Garland, Hamlin
Roadside meetings. 1940. (p. 461)

Geldard, Frank A.
The human senses. 1953. (p. 6, 250)
Gerhart, Eugene C.
American liberty and natural law. 1953. (p. 3)
Gifford, William Alva.
The seekers. Why Christian orthodoxy is obsolete. 1954. (p. 285, 293)
Gillin, John
Editor. For a science of social man. 1954. (p. 46, 51, 166, 235)
Gladden, Washington
Live and learn. 1914. (p. 129, 130-1)
Godkin, Edwin Lawrence
Life and letters, edited by Rollo Ogden. Two volumes. 1907. (v. 1 p. 221; v. 2 p. 6)
Good, Carter V. and Scates, Douglas E.
Methods of research. Educational, psychological, socia-logical. 1954. (13 references in index)
Gosse, Edmund
Aspects and impressions. 1922. (p. 19, 20, 48, 49)
Gottlober, A. B.
Understanding stuttering. 1953. (p. 31)
Gould, George and Yoakam, Gerald A.
The teacher and his work. Second edition. 1954. (p.225)
Grimes, Alan Pendleton
American political thought. 1955. (p. 437-40, 441, 442, 448, 452)
Guttmacher, Manfred S. and Weihofen, Henry
Psychiatry and the law. 1952. (p. 64)

Hackett, Francis
Horizons. A book of criticisms. 1919. (p. 101)
-- The invisible censor. 1921. (p. 44, 75)
-- On judging books. 1947. (p. 93, 215)
-- What Mein Kampf means to America. 1941. (p. 59)
Hadley, Arthur Twining
Some influences in modern philosophic thought. 1913. (p. 69, 73, 118-9)
Hall, James Norman
My island home. An autobiography. 1952. (p. 147)
Halsey, George D.
Supervising people. Revised edition. 1953. (p. 41)
Hand, Learned
The spirit of liberty. Papers and addresses. Collected and with an introduction and notes by Irving Dilliard. 1952. (p. 82, 213, 258)

Handlin, Oscar
Adventure in freedom. Three hundred years of Jewish life in America. 1954. (p. 159)
Harris, Errol E.
Nature, mind and modern science. 1954. (p. 272)
Hapgood, Norman
Changing years. 1930. (p. 41, 55, 57-8, 60-73, 86, 130, 177, 210, 313, 316)
Hartz, Louis
The liberal tradition in America. 1955. (p. 219)
Hawton, Hector
Feast of unreason. 1952. (p. 213)
Hayakawa, S. I.
Language, meaning and maturity. 1954. (p. 22, 49, 202, 204, 205, 209, 210, 258)
Heim, Karl
Christian faith and natural science. 1953. (p. 286)
Hellman, George S.
Benjamin N. Cardozo. American judge. 1940. (p. 122-3)
Hibben, John Grier
Defense of prejudice. And other essays. 1912. (p. 146)
-- Problems of philosophy. 1898. (p. 83-4)
Hilgard, Ernest R.
Introduction to psychology. 1953. (p. 290, 317, 419, 562-4)
Hiltner, Seward
The new concern of recent years. 1953. (p. 63, 67) (in Mapes, Paul B. editor. The Church and mental health.)
Hocking, William E.
Experiment in education. What we can learn from teaching Germany. 1954. (p. VII)
-- Human nature and its remaking. Revised edition. 1923. (p. 27, 64, 75-6, 269-70, 365, 450, 458)
-- Lasting elements of individualism. 1937. (p. 153)
-- Lectures on recent trends in American philosophy. 1941. (p. 10-3, 29)
-- Man and the state. 1926. (p. 352-3, 382)
-- The meaning of God in human experience. 1922. (11 references in index)
Hocking, William E. and others
Preface to philosophy. 1946. (p. 193)
Hocking, William E.
Self and freedom. 1928. (p. 7, 60)
-- Types of philosophy. Revised edition. 1939. (17 references in index)
Holmes, Justice Oliver Wendell and Laski, Harold J.

Holmes - Laski Letters. The correspondence, 1916-1935, edited by Mark DeWolfe Howe. Two volumes. 1953. (42 references in index)

Holmes - Pollock letters

The correspondence of Mr. Justice (Oliver Wendell) Holmes and Sir Frederick Pollock, edited by Mark DeWolfe Howe and John G. Palfrey. Two volumes. 1941. (28 references in index)

Holmes, Justice Oliver Wendell

His book notices and uncollected letters, edited by Harry C. Shriver. 1936. (p. 173)

Hook, Sidney

Education for modern man. 1946. (p. 81, 103)

-- Hero in history. 1943. (p. 15-7, 70, 81-2)

-- John Dewey. An intellectual portrait. 1939. (p. 8, 17, 227, 334)

-- Reason, social myths and democracy. 1940. (p. 135, 249)

-- Towards the understanding of Karl Marx. 1933. (p. 99)

Hopkins, L. Thomas

The emerging self in school and leisure. 1954. (p. 105, 276)

Horn, Gunnar

Public school publicity. 1948. (p. 4)

Hospers, John

An introduction to philosophical analysis. 1953. (p. 32)

Howe, M. A. DeWolfe.

John Jay Chapman and his letters. 1937. (48 references in index)

Hough, Lynn Harold

Evangelical humanism. 1925. (p. 20, 35, 92)

-- Great humanists. 1953. (p. 181)

-- The meaning of human experience. 1945. (p. 244)

Howe, Quincy

World between wars. 1953. (p. 23, 137-8, 701)

Howgate, George W.

George Santayana. 1938. (31 references in index)

Howells, William Dean

Life in letters of William Dean Howells, edited by Mildred Howells. Two volumes. 1928. (v. 2 p. 284, 293)

-- Literary Friends and acquaintance. 1902. (p. 287)

-- Literature and life. Studies. 1902. (p. 180)

Hudson, Winthrop S.

Great tradition of the American churches. 1953. (p. 202)

Hughes, H. Stuart

The United States and Italy. 1953. (p. 78)

Hullfish, H. Gordon
Educational freedom in an age of anxiety. 1953. (p. 50)
Hutchison, John A. and Martin, James Alfred
Ways of faith. An introduction to religion. 1953. (p. 5, 39-41, 437, 466)

Inge, William Ralph
Christian ethics and modern poblems. 1930. (p. 21-2, 138, 306, 361)
-- Church in the world. Collected essays. 1927. (p. 257)
-- End of an age. 1948. (p. 77)
-- Eternal values. 1933. (p. 29)
-- Lay thoughts of a Dean. 1926. (p. 336)
-- More lay thoughts of a Dean. 1931. (p. 20, 54)
-- Mysticism in religion. (p. 27, 128)
-- New twilight of the Gods. 1932. (p. 16)
-- Our present discontents. 1938. (p. 52, 183, 325)
-- Outspoken essays. First series. 1927. (p. 260)
-- Pacifist in trouble. 1939. (p. 221)
-- Philosophy of Plotinus. Two volumes. 1918. (v. 2. p. 152)
-- Wit and wisdom of Dean Inge, selected and arranged by Sir James Marchant. 1927. (p. 87)
Innis, Harold I.
Changing concepts of time. 1952. (p. 125)
Ivey, Paul W.
Successful salesmanship. 1937. (p. 4. 96)

Jacks, L. P.
The alchemy of thought. 1910. (p. 85, 113-4, 124)
-- The confessions of an octogenerian. 1942. (p. 108, 118, 195, 238, 239, 241, 249)
-- The inner sentinel. A study of ourselves and something more. 1930. (p. 4, 47, 175)
-- Life and letters of Stopford Brooke. Two volumes. 1917. (v. 2 p. 603)
-- My American friends. 1933. (p. 13, 14)
James, Henry
Charles W. Eliot. Two volumes. 1930. (v. 1 p. 107, 209, 255, 256, 275, v. 2 p. 14, 25, 86-7, 122)
Johnson, A. H.
Whitehead's theory of reality. 1952. (p. 145-9)
Johnson, Alvin
Pioneer's progress. An autobiography. 1952. (p. 95, 144, 161, 171, 210)
Johnson, Donald M.
The psychology of thought and action. 1955. (p. 8, 9, 51)

Johnson, Paul E.
Psychology of pastoral care. 1953. (p. 306, 322-3)
Johnson, Raynor C.
The imprisoned splendour. 1953. (10 references in index)
Jones, Ernest
Life and work of Sigmund Freud. Volume 1. 1953. (v. 1 p. 373)
Jones, Howard Mumford
Books and the independent mind. 1954. (p. 10)
-- The bright Medusa. 1952. (p. 47)
-- Ideas in America. 1944. (p. 7, 155, 208)
-- The pursuit of happiness. 1953. (p. 121-30, 146)
Jones, Rufus M.
The eternal gospel. 1938. (p. 167)
-- Finding the trail in life. 1926. (p. 9)
-- Fundamental ends of life. 1924. (p. 104-5, 112)
-- The inner life. 1916. (p. 158-61)
-- The luminous trail. 1947. (p. 136)
-- New eyes for invisibles. 1943. (p. 13)
-- The new quest. 1928. (p. 141, 171)
-- Pathways to the reality of God. 1931. (p. 12-3, 17-8, 37-8)
-- Some exponents of mystical religion. 1930. (p. 14, 219-20)
-- The trail of life in college. 1929. (p. 180, 188)
-- The trail of life in the middle years. 1934. (p. 7-9, 52, 221, 223, 237)
Jones, W. T.
History of Western philosophy. 1952. (p. 731, 949, 959)
Jordy, William H.
Henry Adams. Scientific historian. 1952. (p. 46, 82, 214-6, 219, 235, 250, 253)
Josephson, Matthew
Portrait of the artist as American. 1930. (p. 59, 72, 73, 101-2, 107-11, 253-4, 267, 268, 269, 281-3)
Jung, C. G.
The spirit of psychology (in Eranos-Jahrbuch. Spirit and nature. Papers. 1954. p. 371-444) (p. 379, 385, 396, 421)
-- Two essays on analytical psychology. (p. 53, 173)

Kallen, Horace
Of truth (in Burkhardt Frederick. Editor. Cleavage in our culture. 1952.) (p. 31, 41)
Kaltenborn, H. V.
Fifty fabulous years. 1950. (p. 47-50)

Keller, Helen
Midstream. My later life. 1929. (p. 316-8)
Kennedy, William Sloane
Real John Burroughs. Personal recollections and friendly estimate. 1924. (p. 50, 54)
King, Marion.
Books and people. Five decades of New York's oldest library. 1954. (p. 70, 75, 102, 238, 278)
Kirk, Russell
A program for conservatives. 1954. (p. 46, 88)
Kirkpatrick, Edwin A.
Fundamentals of child study. 1926. (p. 233)
Klausmeier, Herbert J.
Principles and practices of secondary school teaching. 1953. (p. 18)
Klineberg, Otto
Social psychology. Revised edition. 1954. (p. 94, 107-8, 125, 126, 439)
Knight, Frederic B.
General psychology. 1953. (p. 251, 308-9)
Knight, Grant C.
The strenuous age in American literature. 1954. (p. 26, 95, 107, 112, 144-5, 214)
Koch, Hal
Grundtvig. 1952. (p. XI, XII)
Konvitz, Milton R.
Civil rights in immigration. 1953. (p. 63, 157)
-- Life and mind of Morris R. Cohen. (p. 11, 31) (in Baron, Salo W. editor. Freedom and reason. 1951.)
Kreyche, Robert J.
Logic for undergraduates. 1954. (p. 15)
Krutch, Joseph Wood
The measure of man. 1953. (p. 115-6, 182)

LaFarge, Oliver
The manner is ordinary. 1954. (p. 17, 19, 21, 23, 68, 70-1)
LaFollette, Belle Case and LaFollette, Fola.
Robert M. La Follette. Two volumes. 1953. (v. 1 p. 112, 426)
Lamont, Corliss
Illusion of immortality. 1950. (10 references in index)
-- Soviet civilization. 1955. (p. 113, 226)
Landis, Paul H.
So this is college. 1954. (p. 113)
Laski, Harold
The American democracy. A commentary and interpretation.

1948. (18 references in index)

Laski, Harold J.

Danger of being a gentleman. 1939. (p. 81, 240)

-- Dangers of obedience, and other essays. 1930. (p. 110, 114, 126, 155)

-- Foundations of sovereignty, and other essays. 1921. (p. 169)

-- Grammar of politics. 1925. (p. 23, 261, 400, 544)

-- Liberty in the modern state. 1930. (p. 97)

-- Parliamentary government in England. 1938. (p. 277)

-- Reflections on the constitution. 1951. (p. 150-1)

-- Studies in the problems of sovereignty. 1917. (p. 1)

-- Where do we go from here. 1940. (p. 115)

Lerner, Max

Actions and passions. 1949. (p. 53)

-- It is later than you think. 1938. (p. 103)

-- Ideas are weapons. 1939. (p. 43, 55, 204, 353, 515-6)

--Mind and faith of Justice Holmes. His speeches, essays, letters and judicial opinions. Selected and edited by Max Lerner. 1951. (p. 129, 369, 403-5, 409-18, 423, 454)

Levinson, Ronald B.

In defense of Plato. 1953. (p. 583)

Lewisohn, Ludwig.

Expression in America. 1932. (p. 260, 312, 331-6)

-- Story of American literature. 1939. (p. 260, 312)

Lindeman, Eduard C.

Meaning of adult education. 1926. (p. 52)

-- Social discovery. An approach to the study of functional groups. 1924. (p. 301)

-- Social education. 1933. (p. 7-9, 17, 19, 190)

Link, Arthur S.

American epoch. A history of the United States since the 1890's. 1955. (p. 42)

Lippmann, Walter

American inquisitors. A commentary on Dayton and Chicago. 1928. (p. 117-8)

--Drift and mastery. An attempt to diagnose the current unrest. 1914. (p. 297)

-- Essays in the public philosophy. 1955. (p. 144, 145)

-- Inquiry into the principles of the good society. 1937. (p. 198)

-- Liberty and the news. 1920. (p. 94)

-- Men of destiny. 1928. (p. 65)

-- Preface to morals. 1929. (p. 18, 24-6)

-- Preface to politics. 1913. (p. 11, 47-9, 83, 113-4, 119, 233, 236)

Lippman, Walter
Public opinion. 1922. (p. 16, 80, 118, 138, 139-40, 152-3, 187, 230, 418)
Lovett, Sidney
A boy's recollections of William James. (Yale Review, v. 63 p. 524-33, Summer, 1954)
Lucas, Henry S.
Short history of civilization. 1953. (p. 903-4)
Luccock, Robert E.
If God be for us. Sermons on the gifts of the gospel. 1954. (p. 133)
Lynd, Albert
Quackery in the public schools. 1953. (p. 182)

MacIver, R. M.
Editor. The hour of insight. 1954. (p. 115, 121)
Manchester, Frederick A. and Shepard, Odell
Editors. Irving Babbitt, man and teacher. 1941. (p. 21, 67)
Mannheim, Karl.
Essays on sociology and psychology. 1953. (p. 264)
Martin, Everett Dean
Behavior of crowds. A psychological study. 1920. (p. 22, 37, 57-8, 127-8, 142, 298-301)
-- Civilizing ourselves. Intellectual maturity in the modern world. 1932. (p. 78, 220)
-- Conflict of the individual and the mass in the modern world. 1932. (p. 49, 79, 80, 86)
-- Farewell to revolution. 1935. (p. 47)
-- Liberty. 1930. (p. 81)
-- A liberal education. 1929. (p. 15-6)
-- Meaning of a liberal education. (p. 66, 107, 201, 211, 264, 267, 284)
-- The mystery of religion. A study in social psychology. 1924. (16 references in index)
-- Psychology. What it has to teach you, yourself and your world. 1924. (37 references in index)
Martin, Kingsley
Harold Laski, 1893-1950. A biographical memoir. 1953. (p. 71)
Maugham, W. Somerset
Vagrant mood. Six essays. 1953. (p. 207, 210)
Maurer, Herrymon
What can I know. The prophetic answer. 1953. (p. 41, 98-9, 139, 224)
Mason, S. F.
Main currents of scientific thought. 1953. (p. 480)

Mayer, Charles
In quest of new ethics. 1954. (p. 63-4)
Mead, Hunter
Types and problems of philosophy. An introduction. Revised edition. 1953. (p. 66, 101, 105, 177, 179, 236, 247, 248, 396, 407, 431-6)
Meiklejohn, Alexander
Education between two worlds. 1941. (p. 93)
Meyer, Agnes E.
Out of these roots. The autobiography of an American woman. 1953. (p. 111)
Miller, Perry
The New England mind, from colony to province. 1953. (p. 69)
Miller, Randolph Crump
A symphony of the Christian year. 1954. (p. 110)
Mitchell, Wesley C.
Mitchell on Veblen. 1952. (p. 389, 393, 394)
Montague, C. E.
Disenchantment. 1922. (p. 95)
Montague, M. F. Ashley
Man's most dangerous myth. The fallacy of race. 1952. (p. 196)
Montague, William P.
Belief unbound. A promethean religion for the modern world. 1930. (p. 53-4)
-- Great visions of philosophy. 1950. (p. 159, 204, 277, 293, 314)
Moore, Harry T.
The intelligent heart. The story of D. H. Laurence. 1954. (p. 69)
Moore, Virginia
The Unicorn. William Butler Yeats' search for reality. 1954. (p. 126-7, 310-1, 331, 457, 461)
Morain, Lloyd and Morain, Mary
Humanism as the next step. 1954. (p. 83)
Moore, Cecil A. Backgrounds of English literature 1700-1760. 1953. (p. 192)
More, Paul Elmer
Drift of romanticism. 1913. (p. 217)
-- Hellenistic philosophies. 1923. (p. 157-8)
-- A New England group and others. 1921. (p. 159, 165)
-- Shelburne essays. Seventh series. 1910. (p. 195-212, 252)
Most, Paul R. and Vincent, William S.
Introduction to American education. 1954. (p. 230, 276)

Mueller, Gustav E.
Dialectic. A way into and within philosophy. (p. 110)
Mumford, Lewis
Condition of man. 1944. (p. 302, 327)
-- Conduct of life. 1951. (p. 72, 88, 193, 229, 278)
-- Culture of cities. (p. 32, 257)
-- Faith for living. (p. 67, 75)
-- The golden day. A study in American experience and culture. 1926. (p. 134, 183-93, 226, 227, 228, 255)
-- Story of Utopias. 1922. (p. 122)
Münsterberg, Hugo
American problems from the point of view of a psychologist. 1910. (p. 53)
-- Tomorrow. Letters to a friend in Germany. 1916. (p. 75)
Mursell, James L.
How to make and break habits. 1953. (p. 186-7)
Myers, Alonzo F. and Williams, Clarence O.
Education in a democracy. Fourth edition. 1954. (p. 98-9)
Myerson, Abraham
Speaking of man. 1950. (p. 36, 205, 259)

Nagel, Ernest
Soverign reason and other studies in the philosophy of science. 1954. (p. 46, 53, 89, 93)
Nevins, Allan
Study in power. John D. Rockefeller, Industrialist and philanthropist. Two volumes. 1953. (v. 2 p. 353)
Niebuhr, H. Richard
Christ and culture. 1951. (p. 84)
Niebuhr, Reinhold
The contribution of religion to social work. 1932. (p. 59)
-- Does civilization need religion? 1928. (p. 213-4)
-- The nature and destiny of man. A Christian interpretation. Volume 1. Human Nature. 1941. (p. 73)
-- Reflections on the end of an era. 1934. (p. 130)
Nisbet, Robert A.
Quest for community. A study in the ethics of order and freedom. 1953. (p. 40)
Northrop, F. S. C.
Idealogical differences and world order. Studies in the philosophy and science of the world cultures. 1949. (p. 198, 222, 327)
-- The logic of the sciences and the humanities. 1948. (p. 58, 97, 100, 369, 386, 387)
-- The meeting of East and West. An inquiry concerning world understanding. 1946. (10 references in index)

Northrop, F. S. C.
Science and first principles. 1931. (p. 282)
Norton, Charles Eliot
Letters with biographical comment by his daughter and M. A. DeWolfe Howe. Two volumes. 1913. (v. 1 p. 264; v. 2 p. 281, 348, 379, 411, 412)
Notcutt, Bernard
Psychology of personality. 1953. (p. 27, 34, 35, 55, 100, 110, 115)

Oberndorf, C. P.
History of psychoanalysis in America. 1953. (p. 41, 56, 231, 253, 258)
Oldham, J. H.
Life is commitment. 1953. (p. 76, 77, 120)
Osborn, Alex F.
Applied imagination. Principles and procedures of creative thinking. 1953. (p. 201, 215)
Osgood, Robert Endicott
Ideals and self-interest in America's foreign relations. 1953. (p. 54, 94)
Ostrow, Albert A.
How to enjoy yourself. 1954. (p. 27, 51-2, 102)
Outler, Albert C.
Psychotherapy and the Christian message. 1954. (p. 90)
Overstreet, Bonaro W.
Brave enough for life. 1941. (p. 84, 90-5, 119-20, 142)
-- Freedom's people. How we qualify for a democratic society. 1945. (p. 51)
-- How to think about ourselves. 1948. (p. 110)
-- Understanding fear in ourselves and others. 1951. (p. 124-5)
Overstreet, Harry A.
About ourselves. Psychology for normal people. 1927. (p. 222, 242)
-- Brave enough for life. A search for a philosophy of life. 1941. (p. 84, 90, 119, 142)
-- Great enterprise. Relating ourselves to our world. 1952. (p. 117-22)
-- A guide to civilized loafing. 1934. (p. 181)
-- Influencing human behavior. 1925. (p. 21-2, 126-7)
Overstreet, Harry A. and Overstreet, Bonaro W.
Leaders for adult education. 1941. (p. 28)
Overstreet, Harry A.
The mature mind. 1949. (p. 68)
-- We move in new directions. 1933. (p. 64)

Overstreet, Harry A. and Overstreet, Bonaro W.
Where children come first. A study of the P.T.A. idea. 1949. (p. 98)
Parkes, Henry Bamford.
The United States of America. 1954. (p. 481, 497-9)
Paul, Leslie
The English philosophers. 1953. (p. 266, 320, 338)
Parrington, Vernon Louis
Beginnings of critical realism in America. (Main currents in American thought. Volume 3. 1930) (p. 402)
Patrick, Catherine
What is creative thinking. 1955. (p. 102, 114, 116, 121, 198)
Peale, Norman Vincent
A guide to confident living. 1948. (p. 187-8)
-- The power of positive thinking. 1952. (p. 137, 201, 251)
-- You can win. 1950 (p. 134)
-- and Blanton, Smiley
Faith is the answer. 1950. (p. 43)
Peattie, Donald C.
An almanac for moderns. 1935. (p. 346)
Perry, Bliss
And gladly teach. Reminiscences. 1935. (p. 150, 177, 180, 223, 225, 267, 288)
-- American mind. 1912. (p. 15)
-- Emerson today. 1931. (p. 7, 60, 103)
-- Life and letters of Henry Lee Higginson. 1921. (22 References in index)
-- Praise of folly and other essays. 1923. (p. 71, 110, 111, 209)
Perry, Ralph Barton
Approach to philosophy. 1910. (p. 65, 71, 305)
-- Characteristically American. 1949. (p. 34, 49-52, 54, 57, 65, 70-92)
-- The citizen decides. A guide to responsible thinking in time of crisis. 1951. (p. 126)
-- Defense of philosophy. 1931. (p. 4-5, 47-8, 52-3)
-- General theory of value. 1950. (41 references in index)
-- Hope for immortality. 1945. (p. 5)
-- Moral economy. 1909. (p. 116-7, 199, 249)
-- On all fronts. 1941. (p. 39-40)
-- Philosophy of the recent past. 1926. (p. 57, 83, 186-94, 206, 214, 217)
-- Present conflict of ideals. A study of the philosophical background of the World War. 1922. (11 references in index)
-- Present philosophical tendencies. A critical survey of naturalism, idealism, pragmatism and realism, together with a synopsis of the philosophy of William James. 1929. (27 references in index)

Perry, Ralph Barton
Puritanism and democracy. 1944. (p. 50, 451-3, 462, 562-3)
-- Realms of value. A critique of human civilization. 1954. (p. 30, 126, 445, 489)
-- Shall not perish from the earth. 1940. (p. 55, 58-60)
Pfuetze, Paul E.
The social self. 1954. (17 references in index)
Phelps, William Lyon
Autobiography with letters. 1939. (p. 248, 332)
Potter, Charles Francis
The faiths men live by. 1954. (p. 1-2, 4)
Pound, Reginald
Arnold Bennett. 1953. (p. 192)
Powys, John Cowper
Art of happiness. 1935. (p. 43)
-- The complex vision. 1920. (p. XXIII, 293-6, 303-6)
-- Confessions of two brothers. 1916. (p. 53)
-- Enjoyment of literature. 1938. (p. 36, 343)
-- Mortal strife. 1942. (p. 42, 43, 188, 210)
-- Obstinate Cymric. Essays. 1935-1947. 1947. (p. 7, 130, 139-40, 159, 167)

Quarles, Benjamin
Negro in the Civil War. 1953. (p. 9)

Radhakrishnan, Sarvepalli and others.
History of philosophy, eastern and western. Two volumes. 1952. 1953. (v. 2, 10 references in index)
Raeymaker, Louis de.
Philosophy of being. A synthesis of metaphysics. 1954. (p. 191)
Raju, P. T.
Idealistic thought of India. 1953. (p. 39, 50)
Rall, Harris F.
Religion as salvation. 1953. (p. 45, 135, 142)
Randall, John H. Jr. and others
Preface to philosophy. 1946. (p. 483)
Raven, Charles E.
Natural religion and Christian theology. 1953. (p. 193)
Riesman, David.
Individualism reconsidered, and other essays. 1954. (p. 23, 131, 280, 303, 308, 391-2, 394)
-- Thorstein Veblen. A critical interpretation. 1953. (p. 19, 25, 40-1, 58, 79, 120)
Rhine, Joseph B.
New world of the mind. 1953. (p. 275, 303)

Roosevelt, Theodore
History as literature, and other essays. 1913. (p. 268-9, 271)
-- Letters selected and edited by Elting E. Morison. Eight volumes. 1951-1954. (v. 1 p. 29, v. 6 p. 944)
Rossiter, Clinton. Seed time of the Republic. The origin of the American tradition of political liberty. 1953. (p. 294)
Royce, Josiah
Lectures on modern idealism. 1919. (p. 139, 181, 239)
-- Outlines of psychology. 1903. (p. 35, 96, 250, 289)
-- Philosophy of loyalty. 1924. (p. 189, 315-40)
-- The problem of Christianity. Two volumes. 1913. V. 1 The Christian doctrine of life. V. 2 The Real world and the Christian ideas. (17 references in index)
-- Race questions. Provincialism and other American problems. 1908. (p. 149-50)
-- Sources of religious insight. 1912. (p. 27-31, 46-8, 61-4, 82, 91, 92, 104, 139, 177-8)
-- William James and other essays on the philosophy of life. 1911. (p. 3-45, 210, 217, 224)
Rubin, Louis D. and Jacobs, Robert
Southern renascence. The literature of the modern South. 1953. (p. 98, 431)
Russell, Bertrand
Analysis of the mind. 1921. (p. 22-5, 44-6, 82, 111, 174, 248, 252, 280-5)
-- Free thought and official propaganda. 1922. (p. 14, 19)
-- Freedom and organization, 1814-1914. 1934. (p. 158)
-- History of western philosophy. 1945. (p. 328, 759, 791, 801, 811-8, 819, 833, 834)
-- Human knowledge. Its scope and limits. 1948. (p. 205)
-- Mysticism and logic, and other essays. 1925. (p. 100)
-- On education, especially in early childhood. 1926. (p. 193)
-- Our knowledge of the external world. 1914. (p. 4, 10, 13)
-- Outline of philosophy. 1927. (p. 218, 231)
-- Philosophical essays. 1910. (p. 88-126, 127-49)
-- Philosophy. 1927. (p. 210, 223)
-- Principles of social reconstruction. 1916. (p. 95)
-- Religion and science. 1949. (p. 188)
-- Selected essays. 1927. (p. 313, 324)
-- Sceptical essays. 1928. (p. 56, 58-64, 70, 71, 146, 154)
-- Unpopular essays. 1950. (p. 214)
Russell, James E.
Editor. National policies for education, health and social services. 1955. (p. 235)

Russell, William F.
How to judge a school. 1954. (p. 75)

Sabine, Paul E.
Atoms, men and God. 1953. (p. 176-7)
Sangster, W. E.
The pure in heart. A study in Christian sanctity. 1954. (p. 218)
Santayana, George
Persons and places. My host the world. Volume 3. 1953. (p. 60, 113)
-- Persons and places. The background of my life. Volume 1. 1944. (p. 241-3, 245, 248)
-- Persons and places. The middle span. Volume 2. 1945. (p. 7, 39, 45, 127-8, 152, 163, 166-70)
-- Philosophical opinion in America. 1918. (p. 8, 10, 12)
-- Philosophy of, edited by Paul A. Schlipp. 1951. (21 references in index)
-- Some turns of thought in modern philosophy. 1933. (p. 25)
-- Soliliques in England. 1922. (p. 247-9)
-- Winds of doctrine. Studies in contemporary opinion. 1913. (p. 12, 124-5, 129, 203-11)
Sappenfield, Bert R.
Personality dynamics. An integrative psychology of adjustment. 1954. (p. 143)
Sarte, Jean Paul
Existential psychoanalysis. 1953. (p. 25, 184)
Saveth, Edward N.
Understanding the American past. 1954. (p. 557)
Schifferes, Justus J.
Healthier living. A text in personal and community health. 1954. (p. 287, 290, 473, 564)
Schindler, John A.
How to live 365 days in the year. 1954. (p. 9)
Schnittkind, Henry Thomas and Schnittkind, Dana Arnold.
Living adventures in philosophy. 1954. (p. 268-77, 305)
Schoen, Max; Schrickel, H. G. and Ames, Van Meter.
Understanding the world. An introduction to philosophy. 1947. (p. 177-80, 182, 190, 256-7, 342, 412-3)
Schwartz, Herman S.
The art of relaxation. 1954. (p. 1, 159)
Sellery, G. C.
Max Otto. A biographical note (in Burkhardt, Frederick. Editor. Cleavage in our culture. 1952) (p. 181)
Seely, Charles S.
Philosophy and the ideological conflict. 1953. (p. 85)

Seton, Marie
Sergei Eisenstein. A biography. 1952. (p. 143, 483)
Sherman, Helen and Coe, Marjorie
The challenge of being a woman. 1955. (p. 36)
Sherman, Stuart P.
Critical woodcuts. 1926. (p. 21, 112, 253)
-- Emotional discovery of America. 1932. (p. 36, 41, 42)
-- On contemporary literature. 1917. (p. 46)
-- Points of view. 1924. (p. 176, 195, 237-8)
-- Shaping men and women. 1928. (p. 104)
Shinn, Roger Lincoln
Christianity and the problem of history. 1953. (p. 266)
Shoemaker, Samuel M.
How to become a Christian. 1953. (p. 137)
Sievers, W. David
Freud on Broadway. A history of psychoanalysis and the American Drama. 1955. (p. 28, 31, 36, 42, 43, 69, 119, 426)
Simpson, George E. and Yinger, J. Milton
Racial and cultural minorities. 1953. (p. 164, 165-6)
Smith, Alson J.
Immortality. The scientific evidence. 1954. (p. 9, 27-8, 136, 137, 156)
Smith, John E.
Royce's social infinite. 1950. (p. 47-8, 64, 78, 110)
Smith, Mortimer
The diminished mind. A study of planned mediocrity in our public schools. 1954. (p. 78)
Smith, Logan Pearsall
Unforgotten years. 1939. (p. 113-4, 116-21, 128, 282)
Smith, T. V.
The American philosophy of equality. 1927. (p. 174-80, 206, 259-60)
-- Beyond conscience. 1934. (p. 36, 53, 249)
-- Constructive ethics. With contemporary readings. 1948. (p. 49, 152, 165, 231-2, 240, 313-36)
-- Democratic tradition in America. 1941. (p. 75, 79, 80, 91, 94, 104-5)
-- Democratic way of life. 1926. (p. 172)
-- Philosophic way of life. 1929. (p. VIII, 66, 69-110, 113, 177, 186, 220-1, 223)
-- Promise of American politics. 1936. (p. 86, 199-200)
Sockman, Ralph W.
How to believe. 1953. (p. 42, 121)
Somerville, John
The enjoyment of study in school or on your own. 1954. (p. 42, 138)

Sorokin, Petirim A.
The ways and power of love. 1954. (10 references in index)
Spencer, Samuel R. Jr.
Booker T. Washington and the Negro's place in American life. Edited by Oscar Handlin. 1955. (p. 118, 145)
Spiller, Robert E. and others.
Literary history of the United States. Revised edition. 1953. (p. 371, 799, 951, 982-5, 1044, 1282, 1425)
Stevens, David H.
Changing humanities. 1953. (p. 119, 140)
Stevens, William Oliver
Psychics and common sense. 1953. (p. 42, 44-5, 52, 72, 185, 186-7)
Stevenson, Adlai E.
Major campaign speeches. 1952. (p. X, 188)
Stolurow, Lawrence M.
Readings in learning. 1953. (p. 184-5, 410)
Stratton, George Malcolm
Man, creator or destroyer. 1952. (p. 51-2, 83, 84)
Swain, James Edgar
History of world civilization. 1947. (p. 597)

Taylor, Harold
On education and freedom. 1954. (p. 132, 136-8, 140, 148, 158-60, 218)
Thompson, Manley.
Pragmatic philosophy of C. S. Pierce. 1953. (p. 35, 122, 186, 187, 275, 297)
Thouless, Robert H.
Authority and freedom. Some psychological problems of religious belief. 1954. (p. 114)
Tillich, Paul
Courage to be. 1952. (p. 136)
Trueblood, Elton
Alternative to futility. 1948. (p. 54-5)
-- Common ventures of life. 1949. (p. 80)
-- Knowledge of God. 1939. (17 references in index)
-- Life we prize. 1951. (p. 50-1, 123)
-- Logic of belief. An introduction to the philosophy of religion. 1942. (p. 117, 199, 210, 311, 317-8)
Tsanoff, Rodoslav
Great philosophies. 1953. (p. 553, 573, 591, 603-7, 609-11, 614, 616, 638)
Turner, F. J.
Significance of sections in American history. 1932. (p. 225)

Ulich, Robert
The human career. A philosophy of self-transcendence. 1955. (p. 18, 39, 95, 108, 151, 182-4)
U.N.E.S.C.O.
The teaching of philosophy. An international enquiry. 1953. (p. 166)

Voss, Carl H.
Editor. The universal God. The eternal quest in which all men are brothers. An interfaith anthology of man's search for God. 1953. (p. 94-5, 258)

Wallas, Graham
Art of thought. 1926. (p. 77, 161-2, 186-7, 201, 202, 214, 228, 285)
-- The great society. 1920. (p. 66, 73, 79, 121, 127, 178)
-- Human nature in politics. 1910. (p. 17, 42, 64, 189)
-- Men and ideas. 1940. (p. 177)
-- Our social heritage. 1921. (p. 30)
-- Social judgment. 1935. (p. 154-5)
Walter, W. Grey
The living brain. 1953. (p. 41)
Webb, Walter P.
Great frontier. 1952. (p. 54, 130)
Weber, Carl J.
Hardy in America. 1946. (p. 161)
Weingast, David Elliott
Walter Lippmann. A study in personal journalism. 1949. (p. 6, 11)
Wells, George Ross
The art of being a person. 1939. (p. 38)
Wells, H. G.
Anticipations of the reaction of mechanical and scientific progress upon human life and thought. 1902. (p. 258, 296)
-- The art of being a person. 1939. (p. 28)
-- Experiment in autobiography. 1934. (p. 415, 453-4)
-- First and last things. A confession of faith and a rule of life. 1908. (p. 71)
-- Future in America. A search after realities. 1906. (p. 213-4)
-- God, the invisible King. 1917. (p. 21)
-- Mankind in the making. 1904. (p. 210)
-- Outline of man's work and wealth. 1936. (p. 570)
-- The rights of man. Or what are we fighting for. 1940. (p. 40-1)

Wells, H. G.
Shape of things to come. 1933. (p. 5)
-- Year of prophesying. 1924. (p. 205)
West, Herbert Faulkner
Rebel thought. 1953. (p. 6, 29, 119, 175, 237-42, 269-70, 273)
Werner, M. R.
Bryan. 1929. (p.133-4, 219-20)
Whicher, Stephen E.
Freedom and fate. An inner life of Ralph Waldo Emerson. 1953. (p. 172)
White, Eugene E. and Henderlider, Clair R.
Practical public speaking. 1954. (p. 151, 204)
White, Victor
God and the unconscious. 1953. (p. 23)
Whitehead, Alfred North
Aims of education and other essays. 1929. (p. 152)
-- Dialogues as recorded by Lucien Price. 1954. (p. 10, 81, 113, 186, 318-9, 321, 323, 337-8)
--Philosophy of Alfred North Whitehead edited by Paul A. Schlipp. 1941. (18 references in index)
-- Science and the modern world. 1925. (p. 3, 199-200, 205)
Whitehead, Arthur North
Essays in science and philosophy. 1947. (p. 210)
Wickham, Harvey
The unrealists. 1930. (p. 29-67)
Wiener, Philip P.
Cohen's philosophical interpretations of the history of science. (in Baron, Salo W. editor. Freedom and reason. 1951.) (p. 77)
Wild, John
Editor. Return to reason. 1953. (p. 88, 217)
Wiley, Paul L.
Conrad's measure of man. 1954. (p. 14)
Williams, Henry Horace
Logic for living. Lectures of 1921-22. 1951. (p. 132)
Williams, Stanley T.
The Spanish background of American literature. Two volumes. 1955. (v. 1 p. 241, 243, 244, 399, 401)
Winston, Robert Watson
Horace Williams. The gadfly of Chapel Hill. 1942. (p. 222)
Wish, Harvey.
Contemporary America. The national scene since 1900. Revised edition. 1955. (p. 35, 36-7, 94, 326, 335, 643)

Young, Ella Flagg
Ethics in the school. 1906. (University of Chicago. Contributions to Education, Number 4) (p. 19-20)
-- Isolation in the school. 1906. (University of Chicago. Contributions to Education, Number 1) (p. 52, 53, 61, 62)

Zeitlin, Jacob and Woodbridge, Homer
Life and letters of Stuart P. Sherman. Two volumes. 1929. (v. 1 p. 297)

Zenkovsky, V. V.
History of Russian philosophy. Translated by George L. Kline. Two volumes. 1953. (p. 5, 688)

Index to Titles
of
Works by William James